DEBTER
DEB-THER • DEBTELIN
Materials for Central Asiatic and Altaic Studies

2

DEBTER
DEB-THER • DEBTELIN
Materials for Central Asiatic and Altaic Studies

2

MANDJURICA
I
SPECIMENS
OF THE SOLON
AND THE DAGUR LANGUAGES

by

A. O. Ivanovskiy

The Russian edition of St. Petersburg (1894)
reprinted by the Research Group for Altaic
Studies of the Hungarian Academy of Sciences
with a foreword in English by G. Kara

Additional Note

For Solon we have now Hiu Lie's large paper in Tungusica, vol. I (Wiesbaden 1978), pp. 126–178 (Solonisches Material aus dem Huin-gol. Nach R. Kamimakis Sprachmaterial ...). From Prof. J. Ikegami (Sapporo) I learned that the Japanese author's name is to be read Kamimakise Saburo. – The newest work on Dagur is Zhong Suchun's short sketch, Dawor yu jianzhi, in Zhongguo shaoshu minzu yuyan jianzhi congshu 1, Beijing 1982, 106 p.

A project of the Research Group for Altaic Studies
of the Hungarian Academy of Sciences

ISBN 963 05 3261 1 (series)
ISBN 963 05 3262 X (vol.)

Printed in Hungary

Aleksey Osipovich Ivanovskiy (1863–1903), Russian orientalist, studied Chinese and Manchu philology at the St.Petersburg University (graduated in 1885), travelled in China in 1889–1891. Well-versed also in Mongolian, Tibetan and Buddhist studies, he taught at the St.Petersburg University from 1891, published papers and books, among them materials for the history of minorities of South-Western China (1887–1889), a Manchu reader (Man'čžurskaja chrestomatija 1–2, 1893–1895), a study on Spatharius' mission (Zapiski Vost. Otd. Russk. Archeol. Obšč., vol. 2, 1888), Chinese songs of Northern Manchuria (ZVORAO, vol. 8, 1895) and the Mandjurica, the first and only issue of a planned series (1894).

As its sub-title shows, it presents materials for the study of two small but interesting Altaic languages spoken in Northern Manchuria and some other parts of China. Both Solon and Dagur (Dahur or Daur) represent isolated idioms of their group. The first which belongs to the Tungus branch of the Manchu-Tungus group is now the southernmost Tungus dialect. Dagur, a Mongol island in the Sino-Manchu world, conserves some archaic pecularities and peculiar innovations, important for the Mongolian as well as Altaic language history. In some degree Dagur may also be considered a surviving variety of the language of the Kitan.

Despite the great advance of Altaic studies in this century, materials concerning Solon and Dagur remain insufficient. Nicholas Poppe's important monographs (Dagurskoe narečie, Leningrad 1930, Materialy po solonskomu jazyku, Leningrad 1931) and his edition of a Hailar Dagur-Manchu glossary (Asia Major X, 1934) describe the Hailar dialect of these languages, of which Hailar Dagur is less archaic than the Nonni dialects (see also his Introduction to Mongolian Comparative Studies, Helsinki 1955, and his Introduction to Altaic Linguistics, Wiesbaden 1965). Samuel E.Martin's Dagur Mongolian Grammar, Texts and Lexicon (Bloomington 1961) is based on the speech of one informant, Peter Urgunge Onon, a Naun Dagur (from the same informant we have W.M. Austin's Brief Outline and Hattori Shirô's notes, see Martin, p.1). Louis Ligeti published only some data from his rich materials collected in the Nonni (Naun) Valley and in Hailar (see e.g. his Rapport préliminaire, Budapest–Leipzig 1933, Les mots solons dans un ouvrage chinois des Ts'ing, in Acta Orient. Hung. IX, 1959, Les anciens éléments mongols dans le mandchou, in Acta Orient. Hung. X, 1960 etc., AOH IX with further bibliographical data including Kamikami Raisaburô's Soron zoku no shakai, Tokyo 1940).

Some Dagur booklets were printed in China in an experimental and ephemeral Dagur Cyrillic orthography (1957); these booklets representing the archaic Qiqihar (Tsitsihar) dialect give further important instruction for the student of Dagur. Dagur is also discussed in B.Kh.Todaeva's works dealing with Mongol languages and dialects of China (*Mongol'skie jazyki i dialekty Kitaja*, Moskva 1960, etc.) and some Inner Mongolian papers (*e.g.* by Činggeltei in *Mongγol kele bičig*, 1957–1958).

Earlier records like those of Fedor V. Muromskiy who worked in the first decade of this century in the Ili Region of East Turkestan are also of great value. Most of his posthumous papers are now accessible in Stanisław Kałużyński's exemplary publications (*Rocznik Orientalistyczny* XXXII:2, XXXIII:1–2; *Die Sprache des mandschurischen Stammes Sibe aus der Gegend von Kuldscha*, Warszawa 1977).

„In the multi-national population of Northern Manchuria, undoubtedly the Solons and the Dahurs are the most interesting for ethnography and linguistics. Not long ago the Solons' name thundered wherever the troops of the proper (so-called Eight Bannered) army of the ruling Manchu dynasty of China entered, while the Dahur language is now so much accepted, that Chinese merchants, not learning, for its uselessness, the Manchu language, do not fail to speak Dahur, as the majority of the customers speak this language" – wrote Ivanovskiy in his introduction (p.I). He visited Mergen and Qiqihar in 1890 (from the end of August till the beginning of November) and had an earlier knowledge of Dagur in Donchifa, a village near Aigun. In his record he uses the Russian linguistic alphabet. His Solon materials are from 11 informants (S 1–5 of Butkha, S 6 from a Dagur opium-smoker, Nongibu, of Mergen, S 7 from a Manchu clerk in Mergen; S 1–7 = „Oronchon-Solon"; S 8–11 = „Manegir Solon"), Dagur words and sentences were recorded from 8 informants including Dagurs of Mergen (D 2 from Nongibu; D 3–4), of Donchifa (D 6–7 on the Russian side of the Amur near Aigun), from a village near Aigun (D 9), from Aigun itself (D 8) and from a Mongol-Chinese of Mukden who lived then in Mergen.

Ivanovskiy gives 25 Solon and 28 Dagur sentences as well as 6 Sino-Dagur proverbs and some Manchu-Dagur parallel text fragments in Manchu characters (pp. 1–15), a list of Solon words (pp. 15–35), a list of Dagur words (pp. 36–73), and an appendix which is a short glossary of words said to be Bargu-Mongolian (pp. 74–76). Pp. 77–79 bear corrections and additions.

G. Kara

А. О. Ивановскій.

MANDJURICA.

I.

ОБРАЗЦЫ

СОЛОНСКАГО И ДАХУРСКАГО ЯЗЫКОВЪ.

САНКТПЕТЕРБУРГЪ, 1894.

ПРОДАЕТСЯ У КОМИСІОНЕРОВЪ ИМПЕРАТОРСКОЙ АКАДЕМІИ НАУКЪ:

И. Глазунова, въ С. П. Б.   Эггерсъ и Комп., въ С. П. Б.

Н. Киммеля, въ Ригѣ.

Цѣна 80 к.

Напечатано по распоряженію Императорской Академіи Наукъ.

Октябрь 1894 г.　　　　　　　Непремѣнный секретарь, Академикъ *Н. Дубровинъ*.

ТИПОГРАФІЯ ИМПЕРАТОРСКОЙ АКАДЕМІИ НАУКЪ.

Вас. Остр., 9 линія, № 12.

ВВЕДЕНІЕ.

Среди разноплеменнаго населенія сѣверной Маньчжуріи несомнѣнно наибольшій интересъ, какъ этнографическій, такъ и лингвистическій представляютъ Солоны и Дахуры. Имя Солоновъ еще недавно гремѣло вездѣ, куда ни проникали отряды собственнаго (такъ называемаго восьмизнаменнаго) войска нынѣшней маньчжурской династіи въ Китаѣ, а дахурскій языкъ получилъ теперь въ Мэргэнѣ и Цицикарѣ такое право гражданства, что торговцы изъ китайцевъ, не изучающіе по безполезности маньчжурскаго языка, обязательно всѣ говорятъ по дахурски, такъ какъ главный контингентъ покупателей говоритъ на этомъ языкѣ.

Живутъ эти Дахуры, а также и Солоны [1]), можно сказать, по всей странѣ. Такъ, хотя главнымъ райономъ обитанія Дахуръ считаются бассейны рр. Нонь-и-ула и Нэмэръ, однако кромѣ того [2]) около Айгуна они живутъ въ девяти деревняхъ на нашемъ лѣвомъ берегу Амура (Сяо-Доньчифа, Бордо 薄爾多, Манга, Норъ-токсо и др.), также въ нѣкоторыхъ деревняхъ по правому, китайскому берегу выше Айгуна и ниже его (Харшань, Хормольцзинъ и др.); затѣмъ въ западномъ поселкѣ (Си-тунь 西屯) первой станціи (Тоу-чжань 頭站), въ деревняхъ Тормо-тунь и Кунъ-бира [3]). Далѣе, около Мэргэна (правда, уже въ бассейнѣ р. Нонь) они живутъ повсемѣстно (напр. въ деревняхъ Сы-цзя-цза 四家子, Эрлъ-ши-ли-тунь 二十里屯, Да-Ши-ла-цза 大石臘子, Сяо-Ши-ла-цза 小石臘子 и Боркэ), равно какъ и около Цицикара, гдѣ попадаются

---

1) Если понимать это слово (подобно китайцамъ) въ обширномъ, собирательномъ смыслѣ, какъ сказано ниже (на страницѣ 3-ьей).

2) Всѣ дальнѣйшія указанія основаны на данныхъ, добытыхъ мною во время путешествія по Маньчжуріи. Точно также я пишу вездѣ Дахуры, а не Дауры потому, что такъ произносится это слово вездѣ въ Маньчжуріи.

3) По пекински 昆 Гунь-бира, на рѣкѣ того же имени. Эта рѣка у всѣхъ, проѣзжавшихъ раньше меня, названа Ганъ, но это ошибочно: р. 甘 Ганъ-бира дальше, а на р. Кунъ-бира есть только деревня Ганъ-цза 崗子, близь Тоу-чжань.

ихъ деревни и на главномъ почтовомъ трактѣ (напр. Дэнъ-цзы-кэ 登 子 科, по дахурски Хотóн-Дындэкэ́, передъ станціей Тахаръ-чжань 塔 哈 爾 站); нѣсколько ихъ семействъ живутъ и въ Хайларѣ. Солоны же, главнымъ образомъ, живутъ въ мѣстностяхъ, подвѣдомственныхъ двумъ главноуправляющимъ (цзунъ-гуань, ухэри-да): Хайларскому и Бутхаскому, гдѣ населеніе почти сплошь солонское, причемъ районъ власти послѣдняго (бутхаскаго) главноуправляющаго (какъ завѣдующаго всѣми Бутханами, т. е., ясачнымъ, охотничьимъ населеніемъ, какъ солонскимъ, такъ и дахурскимъ) очень обширенъ и, такъ сказать, отличается черезполосностью, входя въ районы Мэргэньскаго и Цицикарскаго фудутуновъ; поэтому подвластные ему Бутханы живутъ и по р. Нэмэрѣ и по тракту между Мэргэнемъ и Цицикаромъ (напр. въ деревняхъ Да-Кабха, Байлу-Кабха и др. около станціи Лаха-чжань). Затѣмъ по Хингану и При-Амурью бродятъ Ороньчоны, о которыхъ говорится ниже [1].

Что же такое эти Дахуры 達 呼 爾。打 虎 兒 и Солоны, что они представляютъ изъ себя въ смыслѣ административно-политическихъ и этнографическихъ группъ? Прежде всего, конечно, обратимся къ китайскимъ свѣдѣніямъ. По послѣднимъ, Солоны и Дахуры и были тѣми обитателями, которыхъ нашла [2] въ сѣверной Маньчжуріи нынѣшняя династія, когда, побуждаемая появленіемъ русскихъ на Амурѣ, задумала занять эту сѣверную Маньчжурію [3]. Относительно Солоновъ и Дахуръ китайскіе источники указываютъ [4] еще, что они жили по Аргуни и Зеѣ, откуда ихъ китайское правительство вслѣдствіе грабежей русскихъ перевело въ 1639 году въ бассейнъ рѣки Нонь-и-цзяна; однако, по оставленіи русскими Амура, часть ихъ опять вернулась туда [5]. Конечно, китайское правительство позаботилось о привлеченіи ихъ на свою службу. Благодаря постояннымъ заботамъ этого правительства, часть Солоновъ и Дахуръ болѣе или менѣе окитаилась, стала жить въ домахъ китайскаго образца, носить одежду знаменныхъ Маньчжуръ. Вотъ такіе Солоны и Дахуры, подобно поддавшимся въ первое время возникновенія нынѣшней Дайцинской династіи Китайцамъ и Монголамъ, были одинаково [6] включены въ составъ военнообязаннаго сословія

---

1) Нѣкоторые изъ нихъ зимою живутъ и въ китайскихъ деревняхъ.

2) Прочіе: — Маньчжуры, Китайцы и Барху — переселились впослѣдствіи.

3) Или страну Солоновъ, какъ она нерѣдко называется въ китайскихъ сочиненіяхъ, напр. Хэй-лунъ-цзянъ-цзи-ши (Х. л. цз.-вай-цзи 外 記) 黑 龍 江 紀 事, цз. 3, л. 1.

4) Это подтверждается еще и свѣдѣніями первыхъ русскихъ на Амурѣ.

5) Дай-цинъ-и-тунъ-чжи, цз. 36, л. 1. Дахуры и теперь живутъ на лѣвомъ берегу Амура, о Солонахъ же (помимо Ороньчонъ) память сохранилась въ названіи нѣкоторыхъ деревень, напр. Тугуни (на лѣвомъ берегу, выше Айгуна) — солонская фамилія, представители которой живутъ и теперь въ вышеупомянутой деревнѣ Да-Кабха (Байлу-Кабха).

6) Отсюда, надо думать, возникло показаніе, что Солоновъ существуетъ двѣ группы, говорящія различными языками: Онкоръ-Солоны и Дахуръ (Дабуръ)-Солоны. Такого дѣленія мнѣ уже нигдѣ въ Маньчжуріи не приходилось слышать, только слово Онкоръ сохранилось въ формѣ Хонкору или Хонкоръ, какъ называютъ Солоновъ Дахуры. Вообще же, всѣ обитатели Маньчжуріи называютъ ихъ просто «Солонъ» (Со-лунь) и «Дахуръ» (отчего я вездѣ такъ ихъ и называю), прибавляя только иногда въ видѣ собирательнаго Бутха — «Бутха-Солонъ» и «Бутха-Дахуръ».

сподвижниковъ этой династіи, раздѣленнаго на одни и тѣ же 8 знаменъ (корпусовъ), но только различающагося по народностямъ, то есть, существуетъ 8 знаменъ маньчжурскихъ, 8 монгольскихъ и 8 китайскихъ (хань-цзюнь).

Точно также, и Солоны, и Дахуры, по образованіи изъ нихъ извѣстнаго числа ротъ, были распредѣлены по 8 знаменамъ, только Солоны по маньчжурскимъ, а Дахуры [1]) по монгольскимъ. Эти Солоны и Дахуры въ качествѣ знаменныхъ (па-ци́-ды 八 旗 的 или ци́-жень 旗 人) получаютъ отъ правительства опредѣленное жалованье (обыкновенно рядовой — 24 ланы въ годъ), несутъ дѣйствительную службу и разсылаются наравнѣ съ прочими знаменными въ гарнизоны по городамъ.

Другая часть того и другого племени оставлена въ запасѣ, не получаетъ жалованья, но и не несетъ дѣйствительной службы [2]). Это и есть, такъ называемые, «Бутха» (бутхай-нялма) или Бутханы т. е. звѣропромышленники, охотники. Вся' ихъ обязанность состоитъ въ представленіи ежегодно императору извѣстнаго количества соболей, кабановъ, фазановъ и т. п. Для этого они въ извѣстное время собираются на облавы подъ предводительствомъ «главноуправляющихъ» (цзунъ-гуань, ухэри-да). Эти Бутханы, хотя и живутъ отчасти въ домахъ китайскаго образца, но сохранили еще свои прежніе обычаи, свою одежду и живутъ исключительно охотою.

Къ Солонамъ китайскіе источники, равно какъ и всѣ обитатели сѣверной Маньчжуріи причисляютъ (судя по языку — вполнѣ основательно) бродячихъ (за немногими исключеніями) обитателей сѣверной части Хинганскаго хребта и прибрежій Амура — Ороньчоновъ [3]) («оленеводовъ» — маньчжурское названіе), иначе Цилиней (китайское названіе, по имени урочища, гдѣ происходилъ торгъ съ ними) или Манегировъ. Послѣднее слово (Манéгиръ), употребляемое теперь русскими, безъ сомнѣнія, есть названіе одного изъ родовъ этого племени. Сами представители послѣдняго называютъ себя безразлично: Ороньчо, Цилинь 旗 林。麒 麟。齊 凌, Манегиръ или Солонъ, какъ, по ихъ мнѣнію, будетъ понятнѣе собесѣднику. Въ недавнее время для привлеченія ихъ къ службѣ и осѣдлости былъ выстроенъ городъ Синъ-ань-чэнъ 與 安 城 («Хинганскій городъ»), но развалился отъ дѣйствія подпочвенныхъ водъ, и «главноуправляющій» живетъ въ нѣсколькихъ верстахъ отсюда, на 4-ой отъ Айгуна станціи (Калтархи-чжань 喀 兒 塔 兒 奚).

Что касается до названій «Солонъ» и «Дахуръ», то ихъ значеніе и происхожденіе толкуются въ китайской и европейской литературѣ различнымъ обра-

---

[1]) Нѣкоторые изъ нихъ достигали высшаго званія — ду-туновъ (корпусныхъ командировъ).

[2]) Въ случаѣ надобности изъ нея можетъ быть призвано на дѣйствительную службу извѣстное количество людей; тогда они съ момента призыва получаютъ знаменное жалованье.

[3]) Они образуютъ какъ бы сѣверную вѣтвь Солоновъ, которой еще почти нисколько не коснулась китайская цивилизація и которая какъ бы связываетъ Солоновъ Маньчжуріи съ сибирскими Тунгусами.

зомъ. При настоящихъ нашихъ свѣдѣніяхъ по исторіи и древностямъ Маньчжуріи и прилегающихъ странъ, наиболѣе вѣроятными являются мнѣніе В. П. Васильева о связи имени Дахуръ съ названіемъ киданьскаго аймака Да-хо, и объясненіе слова Солонъ Л. И. Шренкомъ [1]) изъ тунгузскаго «соло-ней» (верхніе люди). Вопросъ о происхожденіи этихъ племенъ еще болѣе теменъ и еще болѣе различно трактуется. Китайскіе источники [2]) выводятъ Солоновъ изъ Камнихань (Забайкалья) и считаютъ потомками Киданей (Си-Ляо). Дахуры же по нимъ остатокъ китайскаго гарнизона, оставленнаго Танскимъ Тай-цзу (618 — 626) во время похода на Киданей (Ляо) для охоты на лисицъ (откуда и ихъ названіе Дахуˊ-ли 打 狐 狸 «охотящіеся за лисицами»). Палладій [3]) считаетъ Дахуръ потомками монголо-китайскихъ гарнизоновъ, оставленныхъ здѣсь династіей Юань (1280—1367). Солоны же по его мнѣнію происходятъ или отъ Урянха, или изъ Кореи (ц-во Синьло 新 羅). Шренкъ считаетъ Дахуръ и Солоновъ тунгузскими племенами съ сильною примѣсью монгольскаго элемента.

Всѣ эти предположенія и изысканія, будучи основаны отчасти на показаніяхъ китайской исторіи (Палладій, Васильевъ), отчасти на антропо-этнографическихъ данныхъ (Шренкъ) являются болѣе или менѣе остроумными, болѣе или менѣе вѣроятными, но всѣ они имѣютъ одинъ общій недостатокъ: ни одинъ изслѣдователь не руководствовался лингвистическими данными. Объясняется это очень просто: до сихъ поръ почти ничего не было извѣстно относительно этихъ языковъ, кромѣ нѣсколькихъ голословныхъ показаній китайскихъ источниковъ [4]). Все, что было извѣстно, это нѣсколько словъ, записанныхъ лицами, проѣзжавшими здѣсь (Крапоткинъ и др.), въ общей сложности—десятка два, три. Правда, въ «Сборникѣ главнѣйшихъ оффиціальныхъ документовъ по управленію Восточною Сибирью»[5]), въ томѣ IV-омъ («Инородческое населеніе Пріамурскаго края»), въ приложеніи къ статьѣ подполковника Назарова приведено 91 дахурское слово, но въ очень невѣрномъ и искаженномъ видѣ, напр. сагала — губы (вм. сахала, саhала — борода, усы); очоръ вм. кочоро, кучуръ; гилязу вм. шилазу, дчева вм. чживи, и т. д. [6]).

Поэтому то я въ началѣ своего пребыванія въ Маньчжуріи, именно во время двухъ поѣздокъ: въ Мэргэнь (20 авг. — 6 сент. 1890 г.) и въ Цицикаръ (11 октя-

---

1) «Объ инородцахъ Амурскаго края», т. I (СПБ. 1883), стр. 141 — 141.

2) Хэй-лунъ-цзянъ-цзи-ши, цз. 3; Чу-сай-лу 出 塞 錄, 2-ая часть, л. 5 и д.

3) «Дорожныя замѣтки на пути отъ Пекина до Благовѣщенска, черезъ Маньчжурію, въ 1870 г.» (Зап. И. Р. Г. Об., по общ. геогр., т. IV), стр. 443 — 444.

4) Между тѣмъ относительно сибирскихъ Тунгусовъ собранъ уже довольно значительный матеріалъ. Назову только: Маакъ «Путешествіе на Амуръ», Castrén «Grundzüge einer Tungusischen Sprachlehre» и Schiefner «A. Czekanowski's tungusisches Wörterverzeichniss» (Mél. As. t. VIII, 335 — 416).

5) Издавался въ Иркутскѣ въ очень ограниченномъ количествѣ экземпляровъ и въ продажу не поступалъ.

6) Такъ же исковерканы и китайскія слова, напр. кэнджи вмѣсто яˊнь-цзинъ глаза, губы хооза вм. хуˊ-цза борода.

бря — 16 ноября того же года) поставилъ себѣ цѣлью собрать, по возможности, большій матеріалъ по этимъ языкамъ. Къ этому меня побуждало еще и то, что съ дахурскимъ языкомъ я уже познакомился, живя въ теченіи нѣсколькихъ мѣсяцевъ ниже Айгуна около дахурской деревни Доньчифа.

Я надѣюсь, что, хотя по краткости времени и особенно по новизнѣ предмета, въ связи съ другими спеціальными задачами[1]), я могъ собирать только матеріалъ главнымъ образомъ лексическій, въ видѣ отдѣльныхъ словъ, но и этотъ матеріалъ по своей исключительной новизнѣ, давая первые образчики солонскаго и дахурскаго языковъ, даже въ сыромъ видѣ не будетъ безполезенъ. Лица, спеціально посвятившіе себя сравнительному изученію тунгузскихъ языковъ, могутъ воспользоваться имъ и онъ, будучи приведенъ ими въ надлежащій видъ, послужитъ для достиженія той цѣли, къ которой я стремился — выяснить лингвистическимъ путемъ вопросъ о происхожденіи Солоновъ и Дахуръ.

Записывалъ я собираемые матеріалы въ своемъ дневникѣ прямо русскими буквами, отмѣчая тутъ же всѣ особенности произношенія, которыя не передавались буквами русскаго алфавита. Уже здѣсь въ Петербургѣ эти матеріалы были мною переписаны на основаніи «Русской лингвистической азбуки», при чемъ для возстановленія оттѣнковъ произношенія, я, кромѣ своей памяти, пользовался еще вышеупомянутыми помѣтками. При этой перепискѣ я не позволялъ себѣ исправлять своихъ черновыхъ записей, хотя бы и являлись сомнѣнія, поэтому и оставилъ напр. ц, нг и нг.

Къ дахурскому языку я имѣлъ довольно времени прислушаться (какъ уже сказано выше) еще во время пребыванія на Амурѣ, въ окрестностяхъ Айгуна, звуки же солонскаго языка мнѣ стали, конечно, болѣе ясны и внятны во вторую поѣздку (въ Цицикаръ), но въ эту поѣздку и были собраны мною главные матеріалы, а въ первую поѣздку я только записалъ солонскія слова отъ Манéгировъ Нонохóна (S[10]) и Бэйѣ (S[11]).

Относительно метода спрашиванія скажу, что для избѣжанія вліянія маньчжурскаго языка (а для солонскаго — и дахурскаго) я спрашивалъ обыкновенно самъ по китайски[2]), указывая по возможности то, о чемъ спрашивалъ; къ маньчжурскому языку прибѣгалъ только для записыванія грамматическихъ формъ[3]), да еще при записываніи дахурскихъ отрывковъ. Въ послѣднемъ случаѣ и нельзя было по-

<hr>

1) Во время моего пребыванія въ этихъ мѣстахъ, главными предметами моего изученія служили мѣстныя нарѣчія китайскаго языка и въ особенности маньчжурскій языкъ, который нѣкоторые уже считали мертвымъ языкомъ, а между тѣмъ, оказалось, на немъ еще говорятъ и пишетъ значительная часть населенія Сѣверной Маньчжуріи.

2) Исключенія указаны ниже при перечисленіи лицъ, сообщившихъ матеріалы.

3) Поэтому то при грамматическихъ формахъ мною ниже и приведены соотвѣтствующія маньчжурскія, въ отвѣтъ на которыя мнѣ и были сказаны данныя солонскія или дахурскія формы. Замѣчу кстати, что, по незначительности объема, эти грамматическія формы не соединены мною въ одно цѣлое, а просто приведены въ спискахъ словъ.

ступить иначе: Дахуры всегда пишутъ по маньчжурски, я первый сдѣлалъ попытку писать fio дахурски маньчжурскими буквами и взявшійся за это дахуръ Доцинъ зналъ только по маньчжурски.

Перейду теперь къ лицамъ, сообщившимъ мнѣ предлагаемый лингвистическій матеріалъ. Относительно времени занятія съ перечисляемыми лицами, замѣчу, что, гдѣ не указано времени, значитъ, означенное лицо я имѣлъ подъ руками всего одинъ или два раза.

Солонскіе матеріалы собраны отъ слѣдующихъ 17 лицъ:

1. Бутханъ[1]) или Бутха-Солонъ (означенъ ниже посредствомъ S[1]) изъ деревни Архоцянь (какъ онъ назвалъ) или Аркачá (назвалъ Нонгибу S[6]) въ 35 ли къ СЗ. отъ станціи Бордо-чжань, чтò на трактѣ изъ Мэргэня въ Цицикаръ. Его (какъ и слѣдующаго) вслѣдствіе почти совершеннаго непониманія имъ по китайски, я спрашивалъ преимущественно при помощи Нонгибу по дахурски. Свой языкъ онъ, какъ и слѣдующій, назвалъ бутха-солонскимъ.

2. Бутха-Солонъ (обозначенъ S[2]) изъ деревни Ибчи[2]), въ 40 ли къ СЗ. отъ Бордо-чжань.

3. Бутха-Солоны (S[3]): женщина и мальчикъ въ деревнѣ Да-Кабха, чтò по тракту между станціями Лаха-чжань 拉哈 и Нинъ-нянь-чжань 甯年站. Говорилъ преимущественно мальчикъ, женщина помогала ему (если онъ не понималъ вопроса). Всѣ свободно говорили по дахурски, такъ и спрашивалъ (черезъ Нонгибу), но для точности я еще указывалъ пальцемъ на тотъ предметъ, который просилъ назвать по солонски. Слышалъ отчетливо. Они сказали, что говорятъ внѣ дома по дахурски, а между собою всегда говорятъ по солонски (сó-лунь-хуа 索倫話). Эти трактовые Солоны, надо замѣтить, даже не пускаютъ къ себѣ не говорящихъ по солонски.

4. Два Бутха-Солона (S[4]) изъ деревни Арунь-тунь къ С. отъ Цицикара. Немного говорятъ по китайски. Спрашивалъ я ихъ по дахурски (черезъ Нонгибу и заставляя перевести по солонски записанныя раньше дахурскія слова). Назвали себя они Бутха-Солонами.

5. Два брата изъ фамиліи Тугдунъ (S[5]) въ деревнѣ Байлý-Кабхá (родъ выселка изъ деревни Да-Кабха, близь послѣдней). Себя назвали звѣроловными Бутха-Солонами[3]). Переводилъ Нонгибу по дахурски, отчасти и я самъ спрашивалъ по китайски и показывалъ желаемую вещь. Такимъ образомъ они назвали мнѣ по солонски все, что я нашелъ въ ихъ крошечной фанзѣ (оба брата холостые).

6. Дахурскій бошко (урядникъ) Нонгибу (S[6]), родомъ изъ одной деревни около Мэргэня, служитъ въ послѣднемъ городѣ, старый записной курильщикъ опіума и

---

1) Такъ онъ назвалъ себя.
2) Гдѣ, по его словамъ, есть я́мынь (т. е. живетъ начальникъ) для управленія ими.
3) При чемъ пояснили, что Бутха-Солоны все равно что Ороньчоны, и что всѣ они не занимаются земледѣліемъ.

иногда ему какъ будто изменяла память. Въ Мэргэнѣ говорилъ солонскія (называя ихъ ороньчонскими) слова и его старшій (не родной) братъ. Нонгибу служилъ въ караулѣ Олóци (на Аргунѣ, близь Нерчинскаго завода), подъ начальствомъ слѣдующаго (S[7]), гдѣ и научился по солонски (ороньчонъ-солонски по нему). Говоритъ немного (но скверно) по русски. Съ нимъ имѣлъ дѣло въ общей сложности въ теченіи около 3-хъ мѣсяцевъ.

7. Хэнъ-лоѣ (S[7]) или Цуй, чиновникъ финансоваго отдѣленія (ху-сы́) ямыня Мэргэньскаго амбаня, маньчжуръ[1]). Знаетъ нѣсколько словъ по русски. Говорилъ, что уже теперь позабылъ по солонски (= манегирски, по нему), такъ какъ давно былъ въ Олóци. Съ нимъ, какъ и съ Нонгибу, говорилъ по китайски. Его имѣлъ подъ руками около мѣсяца, такъ какъ онъ въ февралѣ 1891 г. провожалъ меня въ Цицикаръ и жилъ со мною, покуда я не уѣхалъ оттуда.

8. Два молодые цилина (какъ они себя назвали) или солона (какъ ихъ назвали) съ рѣки Ганъ-бира (S[8]). Слышалъ все отчетливо (между прочимъ ч), но записалъ очень мало, такъ какъ они торопились къ своему офицеру, за которымъ они пріѣхали верхами сюда (въ Мэргэнь) изъ дому. Спрашивалъ по китайски, указывая по возможности то, о чемъ спрашивалъ.

9. Мелкій чиновникъ (6 степени, сяо-ци-сяо) Бао-чжунъ и цилинъ изъ деревни Надúму (sic) на Амурѣ (противъ станицы Димовой), присланные мнѣ изъ ямыня Синъ-ань-чэнˊскаго цзунъ-гуаня на 4-ой станціи отъ Айгуна (Сы-чжань, Калтархи-чжань) въ качествѣ цилиней (S[9]). Оба говорили по маньчжурски (такъ ихъ и спрашивалъ). У нихъ въ отрицаніи ачі слышался звукъ средній между ч и ц (обозначенъ посредствомъ ч). Второй зналъ немного и по русски. Бао-чжунъ и сообщилъ мнѣ грамматическій матеріалъ.

10. Нонохóнь[2]), назвавшій себя Манéгиромъ (S[10]) и приведенный ко мнѣ (въ Сы-чжань) въ качествѣ Ороньчона (О-лунь-чунь) или Цилиня. Говоритъ немного по русски. Былъ на Зеѣ, въ станицахъ Кумарской, Черняевой и др. Сказалъ, что Манегиры пишутъ по маньчжурски. Старался, чтобы я его спрашивалъ по русски (тогда насъ никто не понималъ, и онъ былъ спокоенъ).

11. Манéгиръ (S[11]) Бэйѣ, 30 лѣтъ, холостъ, зимой живетъ на Амурѣ. Сюсюкаетъ.

Перехожу теперь къ сообщившимъ дахурскіе матеріалы (9 человѣкъ). Всѣхъ ихъ спрашивалъ по китайски, кромѣ Доцúня, котораго спрашивалъ преимущественно по маньчжурски, и дахура Андрюшки, съ которымъ говорилъ и по русски.

Это: 1. Китаецъ Ванъ (D[1]), служащій въ одной Мэргэньской гостинницѣ, родомъ изъ Гуанъ-пинъ-сянь (близь Мукдэня). Мать его монголка; учился въ

---

1) Оттого, вѣроятно, у него и встрѣчаются въ словахъ маньчжурскія формы и окончанія.

2) Это значитъ «пятилѣтній мальчикъ», такъ называютъ его Манегиры (у нихъ нельзя называть человѣка по имени). Русскіе же зовутъ его Очокошка (Мк. *osóko* дядя) — «дядюшка».

Мэргэнѣ. Онъ сказалъ, что сообщаетъ слова монгольскія (да-цзы-хуа), чтò все равно, что дахурскія, такъ какъ дахуры свободно понимаютъ ихъ. Про иныя слова прямо говорилъ, что не знаетъ. Съ нимъ я имѣлъ дѣло нѣсколько дней, живя въ Мэргэнѣ въ этой гостинницѣ.

2. Вышеупомянутый (S[6]) дахурскій бошко Нонгибу (D[2]) или, какъ его называютъ китайцы, Но-инь-цзи-бу 諾 恩 (sic) 吉 布. Пишетъ по китайски. Съ нимъ я началъ переводить русско-китайскій словарь П. С. Попова на дахурскій языкъ, пропуская неинтересное и непереводимое по дахурски, но не успѣлъ дойти до половины. Между прочимъ, онъ перевелъ нѣкоторыя фразы и пословицы изъ этого словаря, причемъ сказалъ, что онѣ существуютъ въ такомъ видѣ и у дахуръ. Маньчжурскаго письменнаго языка не знаетъ.

3. Его родственникъ, мелкій чиновникъ (па-пинь-цзянь-шэнъ) изъ Мэргэньскаго ямыня Доцинь (D[3]). Молодой человѣкъ, но такой-же записной курильщикъ опіума, отчего производитъ впечатлѣніе довольно безпамятнаго и тупого человѣка. Однако онъ прежде много и хорошо учился. Не пишетъ по китайски, за то пишетъ и знаетъ по маньчжурски. Онъ перевелъ мнѣ отрывки (числомъ 11) съ маньчжурскаго языка на дахурскій. Онъ же писалъ оба текста, при чемъ я ему въ маньчжурскомъ позволилъ держаться собственнаго мнѣнія, чтобы имѣть вмѣстѣ съ тѣмъ и образчикъ теперешняго маньчжурскаго языка. Чтеніе я записалъ по слуху, не глядя въ текстъ, чтобы избѣжать вліянія послѣдняго. Произношеніе его не совсѣмъ ясно. Послѣдніе отрывки (съ VIII) взяты изъ его маньчжурской рукописи (Цакун ендуріңге, кит. Па-сянь-го-хай). Съ нимъ я занимался одновременно съ Нонгибу въ теченіи времени около 3 мѣсяцевъ, и они контролировали другъ друга, отчего иногда и есть незначительные варіанты[1]).

4. Мэргэньскій дахуръ Линъ-фу (D[4]). Говоритъ по китайски, не знаменный, а простолюдинъ (минь-жень).

5. Станціонный китаецъ Юй-лао-гэн 于 老 根 (D[5]). По общему признанію хорошо говоритъ по дахурски и въ постоянныхъ сношеніяхъ съ дахурами. Его имѣлъ подъ руками въ разное время недѣль около двухъ, живя въ Мэргэнѣ.

6. Дахуръ, прозванный русскими Андрюшкой (D[6]), изъ деревни Сяо-Доньчифá, чтò около 7 верстъ ниже Айгуна на нашемъ, лѣвомъ берегу Амура. Говоритъ немного по русски. Знаменный, бывалъ у меня въ теченіи 3 — 4 мѣсяцевъ.

7. Дахуръ изъ той же деревни, по прозванію Ванька (D[7]), постоянно фигурировавшій въ роли помощника шамана. По русски знаетъ два, три слова.

8. Айгунскій крупный подрядчикъ и мелкій чиновникъ (7 степени) Сунъ-гунъ (D[8]). Хань-цзюнь. Хорошо говоритъ по русски. Говоритъ и по маньчжурски, и по дахурски. Всѣ жители сосѣднихъ деревень (манчжуры, китайцы и дахуры) работаютъ на него и у него. Съ нимъ былъ въ постоянныхъ сношеніяхъ болѣе полугода.

---

1) Замѣчательно, что и типъ у нихъ различный: Нонгибу узколицый, Доцинь широколицый.

9. Шу - ванъ - шоу (D⁹), дахуръ изъ деревни близь Айгуна. Пишетъ по маньчжурски.

По солонски мною записано извѣстное количество словъ и всего только нѣсколько фразъ. Незначительное количество послѣднихъ объясняется тѣмъ что Солоны, бывшіе у меня, плохо знали по китайски, а къ другимъ языкамъ, по объясненной выше причинѣ, я не рѣшался прибѣгать. Какъ уже сказано выше, къ солонскимъ отнесены мною и слова ороньчонскія (иначе манегирскія; цилиньскія), такъ какъ я не видѣлъ между ними существенной разницы для выдѣленія въ особое нарѣчіе[1]).

Для дахурскаго языка мною записано нѣсколько больше: кромѣ переведенныхъ Доцинемъ отрывковъ еще фразы и пословицы.

Солонскія слова сличены мною со словами сибирскихъ тунгусовъ, приведенными въ упомянутыхъ уже сочиненіяхъ Маака, Кастрена и Шифнера, при чемъ, такъ какъ я главное вниманіе обращалъ именно на сличеніе съ этими тунгузскими словами, то иногда и были опускаемы соотвѣтствующія маньчжурскія слова. Слова же дахурскія сличены мною съ маньчжурскими и монгольскими[2]); изъ нихъ я приводилъ то или другое (т. е. маньчжурское или монгольское), смотря по тому, которое мнѣ казалось ближе по формѣ. На работу эту надо смотрѣть лишь какъ на посильное стараніе доставить нѣкоторый матеріалъ для выясненія вопроса о родствѣ всѣхъ этихъ языковъ. Для чего-нибудь большаго у меня не были ни времени, ни возможности. Поэтому я позволяю себѣ только упомянуть, что, очень можетъ быть, солонскій языкъ есть особая (сравнительно съ маньчжурскимъ) вѣтвь общетунгузскаго языка, а дахурскій, вѣроятно, ближе къ монгольскому, чѣмъ къ маньчжурскому языкамъ. Въ вопросѣ о заимствованіи очень важно помнить, что единственный письменный языкъ и для Солонъ, и для Дахуръ и въ оффиціальной и въ частной жизни маньчжурскій, между тѣмъ какъ въ разговорѣ всѣ (даже и китайскіе купцы) въ Мергенѣ прибѣгаютъ къ дахурскому языку.

Остается сказать нѣсколько словъ относительно самого изданія собранныхъ матеріаловъ. Фразы и отрывки я старался переводить какъ можно буквальнѣе, чтобы при пользованіи моимъ трудомъ легче было опредѣлить корневое значеніе даннаго слова. Всѣ объясненія словъ внесены мною въ списки словъ съ солонскаго на русскій и съ дахурскаго на русскій. Въ эти списки изъ отрывковъ я внесъ только тѣ слова, формы которыхъ вполнѣ были ясны. Слова, заимствованныя Солонами изъ дахурскаго языка отмѣчены въ спискѣ съ солонскаго тѣмъ, что послѣ русскаго значенія стоитъ: (дх). Объясненій такихъ словъ надо искать

---

1) Кромѣ того мною указано, какъ каждый называлъ свой языкъ, поэтому S¹ — S⁵ означаютъ слова бутха-солонскія, S⁶ и S⁷ ороньчоно-солонскія, а S⁸ — S¹¹ манегирскія (ороньчонскія).

2) Въ транскрипціи монгольскихъ словъ я придерживался чтенія Ковалевскаго въ его извѣстномъ словарѣ.

въ слѣдующемъ спискѣ, т. е., съ дахурскаго на русскій. Глаголы солонскіе переводилъ я неопредѣленнымъ наклоненіемъ, хотя они сообщались мнѣ съ окончаніемъ 3 лица единственнаго (ран, рен, тан, тен и т. д.) или множественнаго (тѣ-же окончанія, но безъ *н*) чиселъ. Въ самомъ концѣ моего труда приведенъ коротенькій списокъ словъ баргу-монгольскихъ, записанныхъ мною въ Цицикарѣ отъ двухъ Баргутовъ, отбывавшихъ тамъ военную службу. Такъ какъ монгольскія слова въ нихъ легко узнаются, то я ихъ и не приводилъ для сличенія (кромѣ двухъ, трехъ), а указалъ только слова, взятыя изъ китайскаго или маньчжурскаго языковъ. Тѣ баргутскія слова, которыя оказались сходны съ дахурскими или солонскими, я привелъ и въ третьемъ (т. е. съ русскаго) спискѣ въ скобкахъ [ ], а слова, вполнѣ тожественныя, отмѣчены тамъ знакомъ *.

Нѣсколько солонскихъ словъ найдено мною въ слѣдующихъ двухъ сочиненіяхъ: «Цзинь-го-юй-цзѐ»[1] 金國語解. — «Объясненіе словъ, встрѣчающихся въ исторіи Цзиньской (Чжурчженьской) династіи» и «Юань-ши-юй-цзѐ» 元史 語解 — «Объясненіе словъ, встрѣчающихся въ Юаньской исторіи»[2]. Какъ извѣстно оба эти сочиненія (вмѣстѣ съ «Ляо-ши-юй-цзѐ» — «Объясненіе словъ въ Киданьской исторіи») составлены особыми комитетами при настоящей династіи въ видѣ приложеній къ оффиціальнымъ исторіямъ этихъ династій. Въ основу приняты извѣстные нынѣ языки: монгольскій, маньчжурскій, солонскій, тибетскій и др.; объясненныя на основаніи этихъ языковъ древнія слова приводятся въ двоякомъ видѣ: въ исправленномъ видѣ (т. е. какъ слѣдовало бы по мнѣнію комитета писать эти слова) и въ древнемъ начертаніи (какъ прежде писались). Исправленное чтеніе передается и маньчжурскими буквами. Вотъ нѣсколько то словъ и показалось составителямъ солонскими, почему они ихъ такъ и исправили. Благодаря этому и попало въ эти сочиненія нѣсколько солонскихъ словъ. Привожу ихъ такимъ образомъ: сначала транскрипцію слова, изображеннаго маньчжурскими буквами, потомъ передачу его же китайскими гіероглифами[3].

Амтаха (а-му-та-ха 阿 穆 塔 哈) звѣроловный 打 牲 者. $Г_0$, л. 4*.

мірe (ми-лэ 密 哷) плечо 肩. $Г_1$, л. 25*.

меоке (мо-ю-кэ 墨 由 克) селеніе, волость 鄉 里. $Г_0$, л. 2.

талін (тэ-ли-инь 特 體 因) мелкое озеро, озерная низина 淀 湖. $Г_0$, л. 8.

дахурі (да-ху-ли 達 胡 里) земледѣлецъ 耕 種 者. $Г_0$, л. 4*.

тікде (ти-кэ-дэ 提 克 德) густой мракъ 連 陰 之 謂. $Г_{11}$, л. 25*.

---

1) Ху1. 544, т. VI. Обозн. ниже черезъ Г. Мелкія цифры означаютъ цзюани (0 предисловіе), л. — листы.

2) Ху1. 981 по каталогу Университетской библіотеки. Ниже обозначенъ черезъ Ю.

3) Не будучи вполнѣ увѣренъ въ точности передачи китайцами этихъ солонскихъ словъ, я не внесъ ихъ въ свой списокъ.

діlі (ду-ли 廸里) голова 頭. $Г_9$, л. 5*.

ду (ду 都) высокій 高. $Г_0$, л. 1.

ċаӊгуӥ (сянъ-гунь, сянь-унь 相温〇穩) управляющій дѣлами чиновникъ 理事官[1]). $Г_6$, л. 1.

сігун (си-гунь 錫衮) солнце. $Ю_4$, л. 13*. См. въ спискѣ шігун, сігун.

сігуне (си-гу-но 西沽訥) худой и длинный 瘦長. $Г_0$, л. 4.

сіӊсіјел (си-инъ-си-ѣ-лэ 西英西葉勒) хлопотливый, суетливый 行走勤者. $Г_0$, л. 7*.

шаӥціӥ[2]) куӥ (ша-инь-ци-инь-ку-инь 沙因齊因庫因) охраняющій крѣпостцу человѣкъ 守寨人. $Г_0$, л. 3*.

шороӊ (шо-лу-инъ 碩嚕英) пикъ 山之高峻. $Г_0$, л. 8.

кацiка (ка-ци-ка 喀齊一) маленькая собака 小犬. $Г_0$, л. 10.

Въ заключеніе пріятнымъ долгомъ считаю выразить свою искреннюю благодарность В. В. Радлову, помогшему мнѣ своими указаніями относительно лучшаго способа изданія собранныхъ матеріаловъ, и въ особенности К. Г. Залеману, отъ начала до конца работы помогавшему мнѣ какъ совѣтами, такъ и чтеніемъ корректуръ.

А. О. И.

---

1) Однако это слово очень напоминаетъ сянъ-гунъ 相公, что въ кит. романахъ и маньчжурскихъ переводахъ этихъ романовъ значитъ просто *ты* въ обращеніи къ чиновнику и вообще почтенному лицу.

2) Шанцін маньчжурское слово, по китайски шань-чжай.

Порядокъ буквъ, принятыхъ въ нижеслѣдующихъ спискахъ словъ, слѣдующій:
a, о, е, э, ә, ы[1]), i, v[2]), ы, о, у, ai, ei, oi, ui, ao, ay, еу, оу; п, п'[1]), б, б̆, ф,
в, w, м, м̆, т, т', т̤[2]), д, с, с̆, ҫ[2]), ш, ш̆, з, н, н̆, л, л̆, л̣, р, р̆, к, к̆, г, г̆, ӈ, ӈ̆, h[1]),
х, х̆, ӈ (нг, нг), ч, ч̆, ч̣, ц, ц̆, ц̣, ӡ, ӡ̆. Смягченіе гласныхъ обозначено посредствомъ j, согласныхъ знакомъ ⌣ (напр. ̆ба = бя, ̆бе = бѣ, ̆бо = біо, ̆бу = бю
и т. д.). Долгія гласныя означены знакомъ ‾ надъ гласной, рѣзкое произношеніе
означено чертой подъ буквой (напр. г̲ звонкое г), носовое — знакомъ ‿ подъ
буквой же.

Нѣкоторые буквы имѣютъ особое произношеніе, которое и объясняемъ здѣсь:
о — означаетъ звукъ средній между а и о[3]),
е — звукъ русскаго оборотнаго э,
э — открытый звукъ э, почти о,
ә — звукъ между ö и ӭ,
ы — звукъ средній между э и ы,
v — » » между i и ы,

п' ⎱
   ⎰ — согласные съ легкимъ придыханіемъ между ними и гласнымъ
т'   звукомъ.

w — звукъ средній между в и у,
т̤ — » » » т и ч (какъ въ японскомъ языкѣ),
ҫ — » » » с и ш,
л̣ — палатальное л,
л̆ — среднее между л и р,
ӈ — русское г въ словѣ Господь,
h — легкое, едва слышное придыханіе,
ч̣ — среднее между ч и ц,
н — обыкновенно н конечное, какъ въ русскомъ словѣ кабанъ,
ӈ — носовое н (г отдѣльно не слышно),
нг и нг — въ первомъ н имѣетъ менѣе носовое произношеніе, чѣмъ во второмъ, и г слышно болѣе сильно, чѣмъ во второмъ,
ц — чж (дж),
ӡ — цз (дз).

---

1) Только въ дахурскихъ словахъ.
2) Только въ солонскихъ.
3) У одного индивидуума; если же одинъ произносилъ а, другой о, то я такъ и писалъ, хотя
иногда, очеввидно, звукъ былъ не а и не о, а средній.

СОКРАЩЕНІЯ.

———

букв. — буквально,

(дх), дх. — дахурское слово, заимствовано изъ дахурскаго языка,

кит. — китайское слово, заимствовано съ китайскаго,

(Ман.) — маньчжурское слово, съ маньчжурскаго,

(Монг.) — монгольское, съ монгольскаго,

см. — смотри,

ср. — сравни,

Мк. — Маакъ: «Путешествіе на Амуръ». СПб. 1859 г., именно «Прибавленіе. Тунгузскій Словарь».

Пот. — Тангутско-Тибетская окраина Китая и Центральная Монголія. Путешествіе Г. Н. Потанина 1884—1886. СПБ. 1893.

Sch. [1]) — Alexander Czekanowski's tungusisches Wörterverzeichniss, herausgegeben von A. Schiefner (Mél. Asiat. t. VIII, p. 335—416).

Cast. — M. Alexander Castrén's Grundzüge einer tungusischen Sprachlehre.... herausgegeben von A. Schiefner. SPt. 1856.

S^1 [2])
S^2
S^3 } Бутха-Солоны,
S^4
S^5

S^6 } слова ороньчоно-солонскія,
S^7

S^8
S^9 } Манегиры (Цилинь),
S^{10}
S^{11}

———

1) Цифры означаютъ страницы.
2) См. выше стр. VI—IX.

D^1 — китаецъ Ванъ,

D^2 — дахуръ Нонгибу,

D^3 — дахуръ Доцинь,

D^4 — дахуръ Линъ-фу,

D^5 — китаецъ Юй-лао-гэн,

D^6, D^7, D^8 — амурскіе дахуры,

D^9 — китаецъ (хань-цзюнь) Сунь-гунъ.

Сокращенія[1]) у Маака:

М. = Манягры, — О. = Орочены, — ВТ. = Вилюйскіе Тунгусы, — СА. = Тунгусы на среднемъ Амурѣ, — НА. = Тунгусы на нижнемъ Амурѣ.

Сокращенія у Шифнера:

A. Anadyr-Tungusen, C. Castrén, Č. Tschapogirisch, G. Goldi, G'. Gerstfeld in Castren's Grundzügen, Jen. Jenisseier, Ḳ. oder Kond. Kondogiren, M. Manäger (nach Maack), M'. Manäger (nach Maximowicz), MA. mittlerer Amur, Midd. Middendorf in Castrén's Grundzügen, Mǯ. Mandshu, Nor. norilsche Tungusen, O. ochotskische Mundart, O' oder Ohl. Ohltscha (nach Maximowicz), P. Pallas..., Sp. Spassky in Castrén's Grundzügen, UA. unterer Amur, Werch. Werchojanskische Tungusen, WT. Wilui-Tungusen nach Maack.

---

1) Внесенныя и у меня въ спискахъ словъ, равно какъ и сокращенія Шифнера.

I.

ОБРАЗЦЫ.

А. СОЛОНСКІЕ.

1. Ajá[1]). S[4]. — Здравствуй! Кит. хао-ма 好 麼.
   Ші aijá (ajá). S[8]. — Здравствуй! Кит. ни-хао-ма 你 好 麼.
   Абҕарá. S[10]. — Здравствуй!
2. Цактыꙋ цабчо́ ачаҕо́. S[4]. — Здравствуй (букв. ѣлъ обѣдъ или нѣтъ)[2])!
3. Ajакáнꙁі. S[10]. — Прощай.
4. Насун оҕікчá. S[4]. — Сколько тебѣ лѣтъ?[3])
   Уоҕíн нахуцí. S[11]. — Сколько тебѣ лѣтъ?
   Адечí. S[8]. — Сколько тебѣ лѣтъ?
5. Герібé аҕó. S[4]. — Какъ тебя зовутъ?[4])
   Шíні гербу (или нерé)-ні. S[8]. — Какъ тебя зовутъ?
   Ні-гéрбу-бíчі. S[10]. — Какъ тебя зовутъ?
   Jéму гербíчí. S[11]. — Какъ тебя зовутъ?
6. Міні гербу́ . . . . S[10]. — Мое имя . . . .
7. Цу́к-ду гу аijé. S[4]. — Все ли дома благополучно (кит. цзя́-ли-ду-хао 家 裏
   都 好)?[5])
   Шíні цу́-де аjá. S[8]. — Все ли дома благополучно (кит. цзя-ли-ду-хао 家 裏
   都 好)?
8. Шíні енінé шамінé цу́-де бісіҥгí (бішіҥгí). S[8]. — Живы ли (букв. находятся
   ли въ домѣ) родители[6])?

---

1) Большинство словъ объяснено въ спискахъ словъ, гдѣ ихъ и надо смотрѣть.

2) Ачаҕо = ача (не, нѣтъ) + аҕо, ман. акун.

3) Насун (монг.) возрастъ, лѣта жизни; оҕікча = уоҕін съ окончаніемъ прошед-
шаго времени. Ср. Мк. okí, okíwa — сколько. Нахуцí = насун + ці (= чі) частица
вопроса и восклицанія.

4) Ср. Мк. ni gärbis — какъ тебя зовутъ? Нере (монг.) имя. Относительно jéму —
Ср. Sch. ékum (стр. 411), ew (409) was.

5) Гу — ман. губці все, всѣ.

6) Мать и отецъ. Ср. оҥéн и амін. Шамінé = шíні амін.

1

9. Алецáу. S¹⁰. — Спасибо.
10. Вараҫóу. S¹⁰. — Я хочу ѣсть.
11. Ашінан. S¹⁰. — Я хочу спать.
12. Морíн тергéн jабó áҥгарен. S¹⁰. — Лошади (и телѣги) еще не пришли.
13. Тергáн jабучá. S¹⁰. — Поѣхалъ въ телѣгѣ. (См. 21).
14. Кавáн бучá. S¹⁰. — Чиновникъ умеръ.
15. Амíн буҫé. S⁴. — Отецъ умеръ.
16. Цу-лáн енурéн. S⁸. — Вернуться домой. Cast. 65 ʒûlâ, zu Hause, daheim.
17. Тергáн тухучá. S¹⁰. — Запрегъ телѣгу.
18. Бéган декдечá. S¹⁰. — Луна взошла.
19. Бéган манаучá. S¹⁰. — Луна закатилась.
20. Хотон-дé ценегéр. S⁹. — Отправлюсь въ городъ.
21. Терыгáн теукҫá jабурéн. S¹¹. — Ѣхать въ телѣгѣ.
22. Емергечá. S¹⁰. — Пришелъ.
  Іртéн омычé. S⁸. — Пришелъ.
23. Делечá (ꙡеꙡечá) декдеҫá. S¹⁰. — Солнце взошло.
24. Делечá (ꙡеꙡечá) долбочó. S¹⁰. — Солнце зашло.
25. Атéне оҫíні S⁹. — Умѣешь или нѣтъ?

B. ДАХУРСКІЕ.

Пословицы[1].

1. 經過大江大浪 цзинъ-го-да-цзя́нъ-да-ланъ. Ḥíге мурí ḥíге далаjéн асулесéн[2]). D². Прошелъ огонь и воду.

2. 暗中取利 ань-чжунъ-цюй-ли. Дотóн асіребé. D². — Въ мутной водѣ рыбу ловить (букв. извлекать выгоды).

3. 一個將軍一個令 и́-гэ-цзя́нъ-цзюнь, и-гэ-ли́нъ. Нéке ʒáҥ-ʒуи́, нéке хафáн. D². }
  一個師傅一個傳授 и-гэ-ши-фу, и-гэ-чуа́нь-шоу. Нéке сéфу, нéке сордóл. D². } Всякій молодецъ на свой образецъ.

4. 病來如山倒病去如絲繞 бинъ-лай-жу-шань-дáо, бинъ-цюй-жу-сы-жао. Аýре кучурáҫе áула галугенуá (галугенуҧá), аýре jаhóсо сідьім кучуҧануҧа (кучуҧануá). D². — Болѣзнь входитъ пудами (букв. какъ будто опрокидывается гора), выходитъ золотниками (тянется по ниткѣ).

---

1) Большинство словъ объяснено въ словарѣ.
2) Асулебé — монг. асхараху литься, вытекать?

5. 怕 瞅 別 出 來 па-чоу, бѣ-чу́-лай.

Кı́мнéсе[1]) ajéсе бу гацı́ре темó. D[2].— Волковъ бояться (букв. если боишься вражды), въ лѣсъ не ходить (букв. не выходи).

6. 好 事 不 出 門 惡 事 傳 千 里 хао-ши-бу-чу-мынь, э-ши-чуань-цянь-ли.

Саı́н-баı́тá халӡásу ул-гара[2]), мō бáı-та ма́нга газı́рá селгѐбе. D[2].—Добрая слава лежитъ, а дурная далеко бѣжитъ (букв. хорошее дѣло не выходитъ изъ воротъ, а дурное передается за тысячу ли).

6. 習 慣 成 自 然 си-гуань-чэнъ-цзы-жань.

Такýрӟі соро́со ур(у) накá[3]). D[2]. — Привычка вторая натура.

Фразы.

1. Сı́ саı́н-абеıjé. D[6]. — Здравствуй (кит. ни-хао-ма).
2. Саı́н-á. D[6]. — Прощай.
3. Joкı́н нас(у)тáı[4]). D[4]. — Сколько тебѣ лѣтъ?
4. Хорı́н наı́мантéı. D[4]. — 28 лѣтъ.
5. Сı́ jамáр нерé. D[6]. } Какъ тебя зовутъ?
   Сı́н-пере-jó. D[4]. }
6. Сı́ саıjéн. D[6]. — Какъ твое здоровье?
7. Бı́ саı́н. D[6]. — Я здоровъ.
8. Jaмурé áıле. D[6]. — Какая это деревня?
9. Танé гéрı болобаıjá[5]). D[6]. — Можно войти въ твой (вашъ) домъ?
10. Танé гéрı аморӟá. D[6]. — Можно отдохнуть въ твоемъ (вашемъ) домѣ?
11. Гетехé[6]) сań já. D[6]. — Все ли дома благополучно (кит. цзя-ли-ду-хао).
12. Éге (Ḃıге) ачı́ге хао беıjé (бḃıjé). D[4].—Живы-ли родители (мать и отецъ)?
13. Сı́ хáна аӡáбıцı[7]). D[2]. — Ты гдѣ живешь?
14. Сı́ хáна ıцı́бéсı. D[2]. — Ты откуда пришелъ (ѣдешь)?
15. Сı́ хаıдá ıцı́бéсı. D[2]. } Ты куда ѣдешь?
    Хаıдéчıбı. D[6]. }
16. Бı́ хуáıна jaуıjá. D[2]. — Я поѣду сзади.

---

1) Ман. кı́муń съ монг. частицей еце (есе).
2) Монг. улу гарху.
3) Ман. урунаку непремѣнно, дѣйствительно, всеконечно.
4) Монг. имѣющій возрастъ.
5) Монг. болоıjа (болху), танé — монг, танı́, танаı́.
6) Монг. гердекı́ домашніе.
7) Ман. баńзı́мбı? монг. ацı́ + бıцı?

17. Сі ордо́ (эмы́н) já҇y [1]). D². — Ты поѣзжай напередъ.
18. Аі́ле угéи у́лі-іці́. D². Кит. 無 人 敢 去 у-жень-гань-цюй. — Никто не смѣетъ подойти.
19. Сі́ні ердéму терéсу[2]) ду́ара угéи. D². Кит. 你 的 本 事 不 在 他 以 下 ни-ды-бэнь-ши-бу-цзай-та-и-ся. — Твои способности не ниже его.
20. Сарóро гаці́рзáн. D⁴. — Взошла луна.
21. На́ра гаці́рзáн. D⁴. — Солнце взошло.
22. Бі у́лecimбі. D². — Я не пойду.
23. Медеку угéи. D⁶. — Не знаю.
24. Бу усу́лзí. D⁴. — Не говори.
25. Терé іці́сéн. D². — Онъ ушелъ.
26. Нама́нду беи. D⁶. — У меня есть.
27. Бі і́дебéи. D⁶. — Я хочу ѣсть.
28. Н̃а҇у́н усу҇у́ гуру́ бісіjá. D⁴. — Понимаешь ли?

Отрывки.

I a.
(Маньчжурскій текстъ.)

[Manchu script text]

I b.
(Дахурскій текстъ.)

[Daur script text]

---

1) Ман. = монг. jабу.
2) Терéсе. D³.

Баіреңге; бі донзіці, ере Букуі хечен-де Бутхаі-Солон Барху ꞑалма бі.

Мімбо такурараде

Хесе Солон Барху гісун-бо фонзі
таці сехеңге-бо гіңгулеме дахафі, вошіхун Фентен Барху ему ꞑалма, Солон
ему ꞑалма уңгіре-бо баімбі. Барху Солон гісун-бо арахаку, ере хечен-ці ду-
раці опораку.

Гуівеіні; бі соносу́, е́не Бу́куі хо́-
тон-де́ Батха́н Хоңко́ру Ба́рху ку беі.

На́маі та́карасу́

Хесе́ Хоңко́р Баргу́ усугуі́ју́ хасо́
соро́ хелсені́ гіңгуꙙзі́ дахазі́, дергі́
Фінте́н Ба́рꙙу нек-ку́, Хоңкорі́ нек-ку́
ірелегеве́і го́ібеі. Ба́рꙙу Хоңкорі́ усу-
гу́і кісе́н угеі́, е́не хото́н-насе́ худуꙙзі́
боло́ угеі́.

Прошеніе. Какъ я слышалъ, въ этомъ городѣ (Цицикарѣ) есть Бутха-Солоны и Баргу (-Монголы). Такъ какъ при моемъ отправленіи мнѣ было дано при-
казаніе изучать языкъ Солоновъ и Баргу, то поэтому прошу почтенное отдѣленіе [1])
прислать мнѣ одного Солона и одного Баргу (-Монгола). Не записавши словъ солонскихъ и баргутскихъ, я не могу выѣхать изъ этого города.

Примѣчаніе. Въ этомъ отрывкѣ 6 маньчжурскихъ словъ: такарасу́ (таку-
рамбі), хесе, гіңгуꙙзі́ (гіңгулембі), дахазі́ [2]), дергі́ и Фінте́н (фентен), отчасти съ
дахурскими (монгольскими) окончаніями; 5 словъ общихъ и неопредѣленныхъ:
бі, Бу́куі, Батха́н, Хоңкору́ и Ба́рху. Остальныя 17 — монгольскія: хелсені́ —
монг. хелексен съ част. винит. пад.; ірелегеве́і — монг. ірегулху́; худуꙙзі́ —
монг. ку́ду́лку́ — двигаться.

II a.

II b.

---

1) Военное отдѣленіе (Бинъ-сы) ямыня Цицикарскаго цзянъ-цзюня.
2) Отношу къ маньчжурскимъ, хотя въ монгольскомъ и есть *дагаху*, такъ какъ
ближе къ *дахафі*. Фінте́н вмѣсто фенте́н произносятъ и маньчжуры.

Амасі маріре цалін. Боолараҥге. Те міні німеку уцен охо. Умаінаці опораку офі, бі Вошіхун гурун-і гемун хечен-де генере-бо накафі, амасі марімбі. Баіреҥге. Мерген-і бабо туакара меірен-і цаҥгін мімбо туашатаме бенехе Дагур цуве (цуо) налма Доцін, Ноҥгібу ере цуве налма кемуні мімбо Аіхун-де ісібуме бенере-бо баімбі. Гуа налма-бо уме бенебуре. Цаі, міні німеку уцен охо тургунде, худаі налма-і сецен-де тефі јабуме мутераку. Вошіхун гурун-і албан-і сецен-де тефі јабуме, елхекеі амасі маріці, умесі ачанамбі.

Хуаіјанда морківеі толде. Бáолавеіні. Еде міні аурé хунду́ болсóн áзі, херзі болосе угеі áзі, бі Дергі гурун-і Безін хотон-де іціуéі хézі, хуаіјандá бедеребéі-бі. Гуівеіні. Мергéн газіреі[1]) саҥіҙу́ áмбаҥ нáмаі ершезі укуіцісéн Дáхуру коірó ку, еденí кемуні нáмаі Аігун хотон-дé кургезí укуіцівéі гу́беі (бі). Бісін-ку́ бу укуіцітеҙáі. Сіраме міні áуре ку́нду болсóн турҙунде маіман куіју́ тергедéіні сáузі јаóсы шадáу увéі áзі, Дергі гуруні алабéі терҙедé саузі еҥгелірé хуаіндá бедерéсе, тені боротí ҙуі-гісéн.

По поводу возвращенія назадъ. Сообщеніе. Теперь моя болѣзнь усилилась, и я, не будучи въ состояніи ничего подѣлать, оставляю поѣздку въ Пекинъ и возвращаюсь назадъ. Прошеніе. Прошу по прежнему отправить для сопровожденія меня вплоть до Айгуна двухъ дахуровъ Доциня и Нонгибу, командирован-

---

1) Въ текстѣ газірео (газіреу).

ныхъ для сопровожденія меня (до Цицикара) Мергеньскимъ амбанемъ. Отправлять другихъ людей (изъ Цицикара) не требуется. Затѣмъ, вслѣдствіе ухудшенія моего болѣзненнаго состоянія, я не могу ѣхать въ купеческой телѣгѣ, и было бы очень удобно, если бы я помаленьку вернулся назадъ въ казенныхъ (станціонныхъ) телѣгахъ Высокаго государства.

Примѣчаніе. Словъ маньчжурскихъ 11: морківéі (марíмбі), баолавеíні, дергí, гурун-í, бедеребéі (бедерембí), амбаŋ, ершеѯí (ершембí), кемунí, сíраме, турѯундé и тенí; словъ общихъ 8 (7): мінí, (бí), Бéѯін, Мергéн, Дáхуру, Аігýн, мáіман и алабéі (монг. = ман. албан-і); остальныя (31) монгольскія: укуіцісéн (посланный) прош. вр. отъ укуіцібé, монг. ўкцілгекў (ўкчў ілгекў); кургеѯí — монг. кýргекў доставить; ѯуі-гісен — монг. ѯокіксан (ѯокіху).

III a.

Тацікуі цусе мінí гісун-бо донѯí.
Ученики, слушайте мои слова.

III b.

Тáшікуі кекурé мінí усугуі сонсó.

1 слово маньчжурское (ташікуі), 1 общее (мінí) и 3 монгольскихъ.

IV a.

Мінí ама аікабадé ененгі бедерецí, урунаку сімбо тантакí.

IV b.

Мінí ачá аікабадé (въ тек. ечіге·аіка) éнедурý ѯаѯірéсе, óннака (въ тек. оронака) шамéі ѯанцібéі.

Когда мой отецъ сегодня вернется, то непремѣнно накажетъ (побьетъ) тебя.

2 слова маньчжурскихъ (аікабадé, óннака = урунаку), 1 общее (мінí) и 5 монгольскихъ.

V a.

V b.

Ама еме-бо х̇аошула́, ахун део(доу)-де сен̇гіме, гучу гарган-де хаꙁі́ла.

Ечіге́ егеі с̇аошуꙗꙁі́, а́ге до́у-де са-наꙗꙁі́, гучу гарган-де́ акдо́н.

Будь почтителенъ къ родителямъ, не́жнолюбящъ въ отношеніи братьевъ и дружелюбенъ съ друзьями.

6 маньчжурскихъ словъ: с̇аошуꙗꙁі́, а́ге, доу, гу́чу, гарга́н и акдо́н (акду́н) и 3 монгольскихъ.

VI a.

Jaja н̇алма соктохо ман̇гі, бечунеме ц̇амарамбі.

VI b.

Н̇амарꙁі́ ку сортосо́н хуаінасы̇, ку-те́і тогіꙗц̇ібе́і[1]), багіꙗц̇ібеі.

Всякій человѣкъ, когда напьется, шумитъ и буйствуетъ (съ другими, букв. съ людьми).

1 общее слово (сортосо́н) и 5 монгольскихъ.

VIIa.

VIIb.

---

1) Чогіꙗц̇ібеі (Ц̇огіꙗц̇ібеі) въ текстѣ, но произносилъ тогіꙗц̇ібеі.

VIII a.

VIII b.

Даосы налма Фулган буракі-де цаі-
лафі, гебу аісі-бо буjераку, ненехе
Форгон-де Jao Шун-і сооріш-бо улаха.
Цеу-хан хулхін¹) офі, туа-де деізі-
бухе. Цеу-гурун-і абкаі Фецергі дасан
цакун тангу ана охо амала, Цеу гурун-і цу-хеу(хоу) афахадарі надан гу-
рун-бо баргафі, ілан біра-бо дендехе.

Учун-і усугу.

Даоші ку хулан туараласе цаілзі,
нере-аісі туаралацу uwei, ордоніці
Форгонде Jao-хан Шун-хан сооріні ула-
сен. Цоу-хан хулхін азі, галі-дé ту-
ередéсен. Цоу-гурун-і тенгері²) ду-
аргі дасан наіман цао хуан болсон
хуаінасé, Цоу гурун-і цу-хéі алалцівéі
туалан доло гурун-і баргезі, гуарбéн
хуаргéі хоjéсен-де.

Пѣсня. Даосы удалился на красной пыли и, не желая славы и выгодъ, въ
прежнее время передалъ (оставилъ) престолъ Яо и Шуня. Чжоускій царь, будучи
невѣжественъ, сгорѣлъ въ огнѣ. Послѣ того какъ Чжоуская династія управляла
имперіей 800 лѣтъ, ея удѣльныя князья силою оружія образовали 7 государствъ
и раздѣлили 3 рѣки.

Примѣчаніе. Въ этомъ отрывкѣ 8 маньчжурскихъ словъ (аісі, учун, Форгондé,
сооріш, уласен(уламбі), хулхін, гурун и баргезі), 6 словъ общихъ (даоші, цаілзі,
Jаохáн, Шунхáн, Цоу-хан и цухéі), остальныя (25) монгольскихъ; изъ нихъ
туараласé — монг. торо-пыль, туаралацу — монг. дуралаху; хуáн (ниже хон) —
монг. он (годъ), хоjесен — монг. хобіjаху дѣлить, раздѣлять.

IX.

Нejá неjá (въ текстѣ неje), неіjá неіjá, неіjé неⳒjè!

Jeгéi jeгéi, jaгéi jaгéi!

Нерікý нерікý, неіjý неіjý!

Лejá (въ текстѣ ле-je) лejé леіjáу леіjáу (въ текстѣ
лее-jao), лeіjé лeіjé!

Варіантъ А. (сообщ. D³)

Наjaí наjaí наіja!

Неjaí неjaí неіja!

Нарірá наjáí наіjó!

Нарікé нерéрі нáріка.

Варіантъ В. (сообщ. D⁴).

Неijá неijá неijá-ja-já!

Беі араі харéі харéі iканá, харéі-áі!

Хавá канé, авá канá!

Аваjá хеіл̇удá

Санá дотóр барзáмбі.

Примѣчаніе. Пѣсня эта, очень популярная даже и въ нашемъ Забайкальѣ, не поддается переводу. Всѣ прямо говорятъ, что ея нельзя перевести. Никто даже не брался передать ея смысла ни по китайски, ни по маньчжурски. По общему признанію, это наборъ словъ, смысла которыхъ не понимаетъ пѣвецъ: ему весело и онъ поетъ эту пѣсню [1]). Понятны только три послѣднія слова варіанта В (въ душѣ сокрушаюсь), да для наріра, наріка и т. д. D³. предложилъ нерембі (雨帽) носить при себѣ (по Зах. накидывать дождевой плащъ; нереку дождевой плащъ).

X a.

X b.

[Текстъ на маньчжурскомъ письмѣ]

_____

1) Хотя она поется протяжно, заунывно.

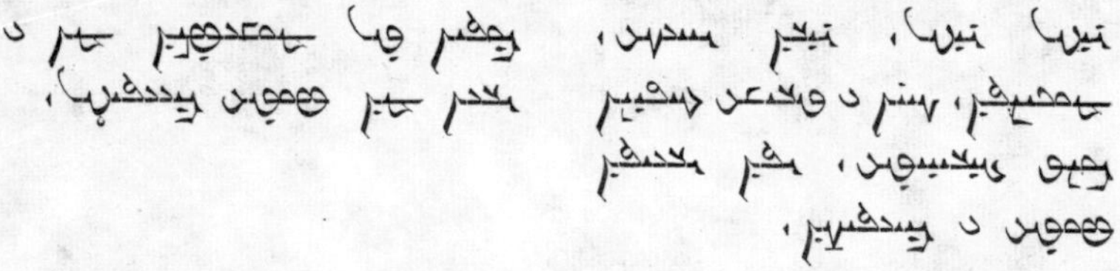

Гуніхаку, ерін форгон ваʒіфі, Цін-ші-хуаң еџен офі, абкаі феџергі-бо еџелехе. Тумен ба голмін хечен арафі, міңган аṅа еџелекі сеці, адараме абкаі феџергі хан омбікаі! Тесе-бо туваці, ундехен унтухун бісіре, јадаліңгу бучеме, абкаі феџергі-бо темпемдумбі. Аіну гуніхаку-де јаса хабтаршара-де[1]) сіденде, гелі енчу ṅалма-де хулашамбі. Еменуңге гебу аісі џалін-де гунін-бо ваціхаме, мутенбо туцібуме те-і ерін-де боо-беі меітехе.

Сансáң уђеі ерін форгóн бардаʒі, Цін-ші-хуáң еџéн болʒі, теңгері дуарђі еџелéсен. Тумы́н газіри ортó котóн кіʒі, ṁаңгáн хон еџејалесéн, керé теңгері дуарђі хан болʒі шатбéі. Теденí уʒ̆есы́, картусы́ хосóн авеіні, ебеденí (въ тек. ебері-ні) укʒí теңгері дуарђі (дорђі) темпелџеуеіні. Јý сансáң увеідé нíде каромýро кіђý сідеṅдé, басé бíсін ку-дý калаџцібéі. Неккéн неккéн нéре аісí толдé санáі барʒí, шаделé молó гаргáбеі, едé ерíṅдé баобéі меітесéн.

Неожиданно назначенное судьбою время окончилось и Цинь-ши-хуанъ(-ди), сдѣлавшись государемъ, овладѣлъ имперіей. Когда (= разъ что) онъ, построивши Великую (букв. длинною въ 10000 ли) стѣну, хотѣлъ владѣть (въ лицѣ своего потомства имперіей) тысячу лѣтъ, то какъ онъ могъ быть царемъ имперіи (вселенной)! Когда посмотришь на подобныхъ людей, то они пусты какъ доски и, умирая въ крайности, спорятъ другъ съ другомъ о вселенной. Къ чему неожиданно въ одинъ мигъ еще мѣняются съ другими. Нѣкоторые, ради славы и выгодъ, напрягая свои мысли и употребляя (все свое) искусство (способности), въ настоящее время раздѣлили на часть драгоцѣнность[2]).

Примѣчаніе. Въ этомъ отрывкѣ 6(7) маньчжурскихъ словъ (ерíн, форгóн, сідеṅдé, ебері, аісí, едé, меітесéн), отчасти съ дахурскими (= монгольскими) окончаніями, какъ и выше; 7 словъ общихъ (Цін-ші-хуáн, еџéн, еџе-лéсен, тумы́н, ṁаңгáн, хан, темпелџеуеіні[3]), бао-бéі); остальныя 35 словъ монгольскія. Изъ нихъ бардаʒí — монг. баракдаху окончиться (дѣепр.), авеіні — прич. (монг. аху) + іну (ні); укʒí — монг. ӱкӱкӱ; барʒí — монг. бараху.

---

1) По Зах. јаса хабташамбі; јаса хабташара (хабталара) сіден-де въ мигъ, мгновеніе ока (букв. въ промежутокъ времени нужнаго для миганія глазъ).

2) Имперію, власть надъ ней.

3) Монг. темецелцеку, такимъ образомъ въ этомъ словѣ является смѣсь маньчжурскаго съ монгольскимъ.

XI a.

XI b.

У-ӡаӊ еӊен аку охо. Веи-шуі біраде Ѐаӊ (Ӡаӊ?)-таі-гуӊ сабураку охо. Луі-шаӊ алін-де јуаӊ-шуаі Хаӊ-сіӊ аібіде генехені? Варгі Шу баі Куӊ-міӊ аібіде біні? Ере гесе гебу туціке ендуріӊге мергесе сеӊгі суку-бо акдуламе мутехеку, даму ургуӊеме ту́шанбо накафі, алін-де бедерехе. Ӡаӊ-ӡы-ја еӊен-і Фуӊнере-бо гаіхаку. Јаӊ-ӡы-

У-ӡа́ӊ еӊе́н уһе́і болсо́н. Веі-су́і хурагаде́ Ѐаӊ-таі-гуӊ узірдеӊу́ уһе́і болса́н. Луі-ша́ӊ а́ула-де јуаӊ-шуа́і Хаӊ-сіӊ јамы́ре газі́ре іпісе́н? На́ра вапуге́і Шу-і газіре́і Куӊ-міӊ јамы́р ҕазі́ре беі. Еӊе адалі не́ре гарса́н ендурі́ адалі мерге́н-соло́ чосе арсају́ акдуӣзі́ шадаса́н уһе́і, даму́ тушаӊа́се хезі́ баісезі́ ауӣде́ будеребе́і. Ӡаӊ-ӡы-ја́ еӊе́н лаӊ ере цуве (цуо) налма бейебо хафу улхіфі те-і ерін-де цалафун ентехеме гоідамбі», семе дер семе учулеме ва-зіха маӊгі. . . .)

фуӊневéі уасéн уӊéі. Јаӊ-зы-лаӊ éне коїрку беје-мољо хафузі гурузі, едé ерінде цалафуӊ ентехемé гуаідебéі», (хеļзі дереоļзі уцуļзі барсáн хуаі-насы. . . .)

Царь У-цзянъ умеръ. На рѣкѣ Вэй-шуй Сянъ-тай-гунъ сдѣлался невиди-мымъ (изчезъ). На горѣ Люй-шань главнокомандующій (юань-шуай) Хань-синъ куда отправился? Кунъ-минъ изъ (царства) Западнаго (дах. букв. гдѣ солнце заходитъ) Шу гдѣ находится? Подобные прославившіеся святые мудрецы не были въ состояніи сдѣлать вѣчнымъ своего тѣла и только, съ радостью отказавшись отъ службы, удалились въ горы. Цзянъ-цзы-я не принялъ пожалованія отъ (своего) государя. Янъ-цзы-лянъ (и?[1]) эти двое вполнѣ постигли самихъ себя и въ настоящее время (ихъ)долгая и счастливая жизнь вѣчно продолжается». (Когда кончилъ пространно пѣть такимъ образомъ. . . .)

Примѣчаніе. Въ этомъ отрывкѣ 14 маньчжурскихъ словъ (ендурі, туша-нáсе, акдуļзі, даму, будеребéі, фуӊневéі, хафузі, едé, ерінде, цалафуӊ, ентéхеме, гуаідабéі = гоідамбі, дереоļзі отъ дер-семе, учуļзі); 14 словъ общихъ (кромѣ собственныхъ именъ, еще ецен, адалі, мергéн, бејé); остальныя 26 словъ мон-гольскія; изъ нихъ хезі — монг. гегекӳ бросить, покинуть, бájасезі — монг. бáјасху радоваться, аусéн — монг. ӳккӳ давать (здѣсь брать, см. нáда аубéі въ спискѣ словъ).

XIIa.   ## XIIb.

«Гунін банін-бо хуваітараку (хуаі-тараку), Iн-Jаң цуве (цуо) сукдун-бо узіфі, дан-окто-бо уребумбі. Баіта акуде, ціб-сере алін-де амгамбі. Абкаі гесе елхе; саін ехе-бо карулараңге ендурі хуту-ці іну гетукен. Інеңгідарі чуң-ґан нуре-бо арафі, цакун дуң-ні ендурі-се ісхунде солімбі», (сембі).

«Сана балині којеве[1) уңеі, Iн-Jаң коіре сукдуні тецезі даң-октоі уребубеі. Баіта уңеі-де, цібе елугу (вътек. ціб ел-у) аула-де вантабеі. Тенгері адалі амела; саін мојо каролавеіні ендурі сіркулосе геткун. Удур туалан чуң-ґан нуре кізі, наіман дуңні ендур солоі некенде ісхунде сололцібеі», (елсон).

(Говорятъ, что) Не связывая (своихъ) мысли и природы и (питая) элементы силъ Инь и Янъ, упражняются въ изготовленіи пилюль. Не имѣя дѣлъ, засыпаютъ въ безмолвныхъ горахъ. (Они) спокойны подобно небу; (ихъ) воздаяніе за добро и зло (добрыя и злыя дѣла) еще явственнѣе (понятнѣе, чище) (воздаяній) духовъ и демоновъ. Ежедневно, изготовивши вино чунъ-гянь, (эти) духи восьми пещеръ угощаютъ другъ друга.

Примѣчаніе. Маньчжурскихъ словъ 13 (балін, сукдун, окто, уребубеі, баіта, цібе, елугу=елхе, каролавеіні, ендурі, геткун, нуре, ісхунде, сололцібеі), общихъ 7 (Iн, Jаң, даң, адалі, саін, чуң-ґан, дуң) и 14 монгольскихъ; изъ нихъ: сіркулосе — монг. чіткур-еце (есе). Којеве — ср. VIII v. хојесен-де.

II.

СПИСКИ СОЛОНСКИХЪ И ДАХУРСКИХЪ СЛОВЪ.

1. СПИСОКЪ СОЛОНСКИХЪ СЛОВЪ.

Аіл. S[10]. деревня (дх).

ајá. хорошій. Въ этомъ смыслѣ употребляется всѣми жителями Амура.

ајá. S[4]. здравствуй; въ вопросит. формѣ ајé: S[4]. Ср. Sch. ајá-gut. Въ маньчжурскомъ яз. употребляется какъ междометіе удивленія или похвалы: ахъ!

ајакáнзі. S[10]. Прощай. Ср. Sch. ајакákun-gut. Зі частица восклицанія (еще ці, чі); однако на Амурѣ въ маньчжурскомъ языкѣ встрѣ-чается междометіе кунзі, означающее радость, веселое настроеніе[2)].

абá. S[4]. отецъ. Монг. аба, абáі. Ср. Мк. abai M. О. медвѣдь (т. е. букв. батюшка?).

абкі. S[6]. мухогонка (кит. инъ-шуа) (дах).

абһарá. S[10]. здравствуй. Ман. абгарі свободно живущій, праздный; Sch. awgará (С. С. abgara, O. abgor)-gesund.

авóн. S[10]. широкій. Ср. дах. áу.

---

1) D². хојеве. (Ман.?) Связывать по монгольски кулíку.

2) Имъ, напримѣръ, оканчивается каждый полустихъ одной изъ вывезенныхъ мною маньчжурскихъ пѣсенъ.

амá. S³. S⁶. S⁷. áма. Sˢ. отецъ¹). Ман.
ама. Ср. Мк. ami (М.) отецъ; Sch.
amiɲi (О. А. O′G. áma) Vater,
Schwiegervater; ‖ S⁷. дядя. ‖ S¹. Sᵗᵉ
ротъ. Ср. Мк. aɲma (НА) ротъ;
amɲan (ВТ.) ротъ. См. амýн. Монг.
амáн.

амасхáки S⁹. назадъ. Ср. Мк. amaškin
(ВТ.) сзади; Ман. амасі.

амаргý бэіjé. S⁹. задній. Ман. амаргі.

амеіlá. S⁹. аміlé. S⁵. сѣверъ. Ср. Ман.
амала, амаргі (амала ергі); монг.
умара ʒук.

амíн. S⁹. отецъ. См. ама. Sch.(M′)ámen

И.   амíн S⁹. отецъ

Р.   амінгíн

Д.Т. аміндýі

В.   амінмíн

П.   аміндýбкí

амеіlé. S⁵. сѣверъ. См. амеіlá.

амыла áчі. S⁹. безпокойный. Ср. дах.
áмела. Dᶾ. спокойный.

амыᵬéле. S⁴. сѣдло. См. емéле, емеᵬéі.

амо. S⁴. одинъ. См. Эмýн, емýн.

амý. S⁴. губы. См. емýн.

амýн. S¹⁰. ротъ. Ср. Мк. ömun (M) губа
(ротъ?). См. амá, амугáн, амгáн,
амᵬá — ротъ.

амунáн. S¹¹. испражняться. Cast. amo-
nam.

амýр. S⁷. рѣка.

амугáн, амгáн. S¹¹. амᵬá. S⁴. амаᵬá.
S³. ротъ. См. амýн, амá.

аталкáн. S¹⁰. снять шапку. Sch. 389
tálkal.

атéне осíні. S⁹. умѣешь или нѣтъ?
Ср. Ман. етембі—съумѣть. Мк. aʒin
(М) нѣтъ, aćin (ВТ.) нѣтъ.

атыркáн. S¹¹. жена. Ср. Мк. atirkan
(М.), atrikan (ВТ.) старуха; см.
ćагды етыркáн.

адалí. S⁹. подобно, -ый. (Ман.); ср.
Мк. adali (М.) равный.

1) См. амíн.

адечí. S⁸. Сколько тебѣ лѣтъ? Ср. Sch.
adý — wie viel; чі — частица вопроса и восклицанія.

адíне. S⁴. вѣтеръ. Ман. едуɴ. Ср. Sch.
ödýn (С. ädin, WT. ödin) Wind.

адíнен. S¹⁰. молнія (сверкаетъ?). Ср.
Мк. agdy (М.), agdi (ВТ.) гроза.

асí. S⁴. S¹⁰. S¹¹. асíн. S⁶. жена. Ср.
Sch. aši (= WT. O.A; O′. asi, G.
asa, M¹. aꙅe) Weib, Frau.

асí гадá. S⁴. жениться. Ср. Sch. aši-
laᵹiren — er wird heirathen.

áсімі. S⁶. спать. См. асінá.

асíн гурýрен. S⁹. Развѣ ты не понимаешь? не понимаешь ли? Ср. Мк.
aćin (ВТ.), aʒin (М) нѣтъ.

асінá. S⁴. асынé S⁵. áшінан¹). S¹⁰.
áᵬінан. S¹⁰. Аᵬінéн. S¹¹. спать. Ср.
Sch. ašinʒam (WT. aʒäm, С. âsinam,
âhinam, WT. ahinam) schlafen.

аɴá. S⁹. годъ (ман.). См. ангані.

аɴé ᷉бе (бі S⁴.). S¹¹. 1-ая луна.

аɴé (еɴé). S⁸. аɴíн. S³. S¹⁰. S¹¹. мать.
Ср. Мк. öɴі (ВТ., М.) мать; Sch.
oɲni (С. änä, änin, WT. М. öɴі, A.
öɴin, öɴé) Mutter. См. еᵬíн.

аɴдýр бурхáн. S⁴. богъ. См. еɴдурí.

аɴᵬоктó. S¹¹. носъ. См. онуктó, ꙩнoктó.

аɴчá. S⁴. аɴчýн. S⁵. щеки. Sch. аᵬćán
(С. ancan, UA. aićan) Wange. Ср.
Ман. аɴчуɴ серьги въ ушахъ.

алеɴáу. S¹⁰. спасибо. Ср. Sch. alárču
angenehm, süss.

алó. S¹⁰. рыба, рыбу ловить²). Ср. Мк.
olo (ВТ., М.) рыба; Sch. olló (WT.
óllo, С. oldo, A. olda, O. ólra, Ċ.
olro) Fisch.

алóці. S⁹. валенки. См. олóці.

1) Соб. по S¹⁰ хочу спать.

2) Послѣднее значеніе сомнительно. Вѣроятно спуталъ 打魚 да-юй (ловить рыбу,
но мѣсти.) съ 大魚 да-юй большая рыба.

алмара́н. S⁹. слѣдовать, подражать (= Ман. сонколомбі, что даетъ возможность сближать съ алꙗа́ слѣдъ).

алта́. S⁴. алта́н. S¹⁰. S¹¹. золото. (Ман. = Монг.). Ср. Мк. altan (М., О.) мѣдь.

алдама́. S⁵. плетеная, круглая корзинка.

алга́н. S¹⁰. S¹¹. алꙗа́н. S⁹. нога. Ср. Мк. algan (О.) нога, но algá (М.) неводъ. Sch. xálgan (С. halgan, algan, O′. halga, G. palga) Fuss.

алꙗа́. S⁴. слѣдъ. ‖ S³. ладонь. Монг. алага— ладонь. См. аранга.

араму́ш. S¹⁰. наштанники (отъ сапогъ до колѣна). Мк. aramus (М.) отдѣльные для каждой ноги панталоны.

аракі́. S¹⁰. S¹¹. араꙗі́. S⁴. водка (ханшина). Мк. araki (СА.) водка. Ман. аркі.

аранга. S⁸. ладонь. См. алꙗа́. Ср. Ман. фалангу.

арооктó. S¹¹. трава. См. орóкто.

арпуку́. S¹⁰. мухогонка. Ср. Мк. arpuki (М.) опахало; Sch. arpuki (М. särpakta—Pferdehaar.... Mӡ̌. arfuku Fliegenwedel) Pferdeschweif.

арсала́. S⁴. левъ (Ман.=Монг. арсалан).

арка́н. S⁶. спина. См. дах. аракы́н, арка́н.

аркі́ муре́н. S⁴. вино. Ман. аркі нуре. См. аракі.

ака́. S². S⁸. S¹¹. ака́і. S¹⁰. акі́н. S³. S⁶. старшій братъ. См. аха́, аху́н. Ср. Sch. акі (М¹. акі, А. О. С. ака. O′. G. aga, Mӡ̌. age) älterer Bruder, Oheim. ‖ S¹¹. ст. сестра. Ср. Мк. акі (М.), ökі (ВТ.) сестра (М. старшая).

аку́. S¹⁰. грязь.

акта. S¹⁰. быкъ (т. е. кладеный быкъ). Ман. = Монг. меринъ, кладеный. Ср. Sch. ákta gekratzte Stelle.

акта́ морі́н. S⁴. меринъ. Ср. Мк. akta murin (М.) меринъ.

акдыре́не. S⁵. радоваться[1]). Однако ср. Мк. agdy (М.), agdi (ВТ.) гроза, agdiriӡ̌ärän (ВТ.) громъ гремитъ; Sch. agdý (. . . Mӡ̌. akӡan) Donner.

акшука́н. S¹⁰. въ долгъ давать.

аге́іту. S¹⁰. дуракъ.

агіла́. S⁴. нижній. Ср. угіло́. S⁴. верхній (т. е. противоположность предметовъ обозначается перемѣною гласныхъ звуковъ).

аꙗіінан. S¹⁰. спать. См. асіна́.

аꙗíн гуруре́. S¹¹. не понимать. Ср. асíн гуру́рен.

аꙗó см. 1 стр., 5-ую Фразу.

аꙗу́(н). S⁴. а́ꙗун. S³. S⁸. а́ун. S⁸. шапка. См. àун.

аха́. S¹. S⁴. старшій братъ. См. ака́.

ахіне́н. S¹¹. спать. См. асіна́, а́ꙗінан.

аху́н. S⁷. старшій братъ. (Ман.). См. ака́.

анга́і. S⁷. ротъ. Ман. анга. См. ама́.

анга́ні. S⁴. аꙡга́н. S¹¹. годъ. Ср. Sch. aꙡani (= WT. М.; С. аꙡані, anꙡan, А. О. Mӡ̌. anija) Jahr.

а́ꙡгаре́н. S¹⁰. еще не.

ангіда́. S⁹. правый. Ср. Мк. aꙡidab (ВТ.) направо; Sch. aꙡeda.....rechts.

аꙡгіра́н. S⁹. слѣдовать. См. алмара́н, алꙗа́.

ача́. S². ачá. S¹. отецъ (дх.).

ачаꙗó. S⁴. или нѣтъ? Сложное изъ ача + аꙗо.

аꙡа́у. S¹⁰. нѣтъ. Въ отвѣтахъ, напр. вм. нашихъ: нѣтъ, не хочу; нѣтъ, не ходилъ. Мк. aćin (ВТ.), aꙗin (М.) нѣтъ.

'онокто́. S¹⁰. носъ. См. а́ꙡꙗокто, онукто́. Ср. Sch. oꙡoktó (= WT.; C. onokto, hoꙡokta, А. oꙡat.....) Nase.

Еме́ле. S⁸. сѣдло (дах.). См. емеꙗе́л.

емергеча́. S¹⁰. пришелъ[2]). Ср. Мк.

---

1) Записанъ среди глаголовъ, означающихъ душевныя движенія: сердиться, смѣяться и т. д.

2) Съ окончаніемъ обоихъ прошеди. временъ? См. Castr. 33.

ämam (ВТ.) придти, ömöẕöm (ВТ.) идти; Sch. omoẕém ich komme, omorän er kam; ‖ S¹⁰. принесъ. Ср. Мк. ömöbum (ВТ.) принести.

емеӈе́ӆ. S¹⁰. сѣдло. Мк. ömögöl (М.) сѣдло. См. емы́ре, емыге́ӆ.

емы́ре. S¹. сѣдло.

емыге́. S¹. S². жена (дх.).

емыге́ӆ. S⁹. сѣдло. См. емеӈе́ӆ; Монг. емегел, емѣл.

емо́, оӈе́н. S⁶. мать. Ср. Ман. еме — мать; Мк. öӥ (ВТ., М.) мать.

е́му мі́нга́н. S⁷. тысяча (Ман.).

е́му тангу́. S⁷. сто (Ман.).

е́му туме́н. S⁶. десять тысячъ (Ман.).

ему́н. S⁶. одинъ. См. эму́н, уму́н.

ему́н. S¹¹. губы. См. аму́. Ср. Мк. ömún (М.) губа (ротъ?).

(дамуӈа) емука́ӆ. S¹¹. курить (соб. кури) — табакъ. Ман. дамба́гу омі́мбі; ср. Мк. иҭẕam пить.

емке́. S⁷. одинъ (Ман.).

етырка́н см. атырка́н, ẕагды́ етырка́н.

есу́ро. S⁸. метелка (дах.).

е́ша. S¹⁰. глаза. См. jéса.

еӈе́. S⁷. мать. См. емо́.

еніне́. см. Фразы (стр. 1, 8-ая).

енуӈу́. S⁴. болѣзнь. Ср. Sch. enúmuk (С. änuкu) Krankheit, Schmerz; Мк. önuẕäm (ВТ.) страдать, хворать.

еӈдурі́. S⁹. богъ (Ман.).

еӈду́ріӈге. S⁹. божественный, мудрый (Ман.).

'еӈге́. S¹¹. колѣно. Ср. Sch. хоӈо́н (С. hänän, WT. höӈon, UA. öӈen.....) Knie.

еӆе́. S⁹. здѣсь. Ср. Мк. ödú (М.) здѣсь; Sch. edú (= O. A; C. êdu) hier; Ман. еде; Castr. 65 älå — hier.

еӆлеӈа́у. S¹¹. я сытъ. Ср. Ман. елембі — я сытъ.

ерегы́ӆ. S⁶. быкъ (дх.).

ерде́му аçі S⁹. бездарный. Ман. ердему -+ Мк. аçіn (ВТ.) нѣтъ.

ерселе́. S¹¹. желѣзо. См. сѣле.

еркі́. S⁸. S¹⁰. S¹¹. штаны. См. 'оккі́. Ср. Мк. örki (М.) верхніе штаны. Sch. horki (WT. hýrki, A. hörki, M. örki, Midd. yrki.....) Hosen.

ерӈіӆе́. S⁹. низъ. Ср. Мк. hörgiŝki (ВТ.) внизу; Sch. xorgíla (С. härgîlä) unten.

ерчу́. S⁶. грудь (дх).

еке́. S². старшая сестра. См. ака. Ср. Sch. aké (....G. éga) ältere Schwester; монг. exe — мать. См. ехе́.

екте́ дамуӈа́. S¹¹. опіумъ. Ср. Ман. окто; дамуӈа́ (табакъ) см. дамга́.

еӈі́н. S⁸. мать. См. аӈе́, аны́н.

ехе́. S⁴. старшая сестра. См. еке́.

ечіге. S⁸. отецъ (дх).

еẕіӆе́. S⁹. западъ.

Эвэ́ӈ. S⁷. хлѣбъ. Ман. ефен.

эмэ́ӆэ. S⁶. сѣдло (дх.)

эму́н. S⁶. одинъ. Ср. Мк. ömún (М.) одинъ, ùmukón (БТ.) одинъ; Sch. omukán ein.

Эни́. S⁴. мать. См. аӈе́.

(Деӆеча́) jуре́н. S⁸. востокъ. Ср. Мк. ilin (ВТ.) востокъ. Sch. judirek (O. ӊulrem aufgehen) Aufgang, Cast. 129 — sygun juren — Osten.

іма́. S².¹) S⁶. козелъ. Монг. ımän, Ман. ıman.

іманара́. S⁴. снѣгъ идетъ. См. мана́. іньӈä; Ман. німарамбі – снѣгъ идетъ; Sch. imánna...Schnee; Мк. ämana (М.) снѣгъ.

іма́гін. S¹⁰. зеленый. Ср. Мк. niӈä (НА.) зеленая краска; Sch. ímoki (М'. imekin) frisch (ср. кит. цинъ-цао 青 草 зеленая трава).

ӡдан іме́ре. S⁴. курить табакъ. См. імке́, іме́ре.

імы́к. S⁶. пить. См. імке́.

іму́рту. S⁶. масло. Sch. imurän (С. imuӷän Butter) geschmolzenes Fett.

---

1) S². собственно сказалъ баранъ, но, очевидно, ошибся (спуталъ 羊 съ 山羊).

(му) ímpéне. S⁵. (му) імké. S³. пить
(воду). Ман. омімбі пить. Ср. Мк.
umӡam пить, umibkanäm повть.

іté. S⁴. канъ.

ісáӆ. S⁴. глаза. См. jéса.

іза. S⁶. мыло (кит. и-цза 胰子).

інахí. S⁴. собака. См. нінакíн. Ман.
індахун. Ср. Мк. inakin (CA.), ni-
nakin (BT.) собака.

інактырéн. S¹¹. інектерé. S³. смѣяться.
Ср. Мк. інäktäӡom (BT.) смѣяться.
См. інтерéне, нактырéн.

інéн. S¹⁰. íненгí, íненí. S¹⁰. іненгí. S⁴.
день. Ман. іненгí. Ср. Мк. інäӈдо-
lin (М.) полдень, inäӈi (М.) день.

інтерéне. S⁵. смѣяться. См. інактырéн.

іні. S⁷. его (Ман.)

іныгé. S⁵. іныíнге. S⁵. інгé. S¹⁰. інгí.
S¹¹. языкъ. Ср. Мк. siӈmu (НА.)
языкъ; Castr. 135 inni, 74 iӈi —
Zunge. Ср. Ман. іленгу.

інӊá. S¹⁰. земля (на улицѣ). Ср. Sch.
іӈa (C. іӈå Stein) Land.

інӊá. S¹⁰. снѣгъ. См. іманарá.

ілáн. S⁶. S⁷. S¹¹. jілáн. S⁹. S¹¹. іӆáн.
S⁴. jелáн. S⁸. три. Ман. ілан. Ср.
Мк. ílan (BT.), ilán (М.) три; Sch.
illen (WT. illan, C. ilan, OA. elan,
O'G. ella) drei.

ілáн ̆бе. S⁴. S¹¹. 3-ья луна. Мк. ilambä
(М.) апрѣль.

іӆáн. S⁴. три.

ілатáр. S⁹. по три.

іӆáга мачéс̆. S¹⁰. пріятель.

іӆекчá. S¹⁰. ноздря. Ср. Мк. iliksa
(BT.), ilikɵa(M.), inokɵa (CA.) сопли.

терігé іӆберé ̆беijé. S⁴. извощикъ,
кучеръ (кит. гань-чӡ-ды). Кит. гань
趕 даетъ возможн. сближать іӆберé
съ ilbam (Sch. 361. C. verjagen).

іӆӆáн. S¹⁰. встать, стоять. Ср. Мк.
iliс́am (BT.) стоять, встать; Sch.
ilým (C. ilim) stehen.

іӆчí. S¹¹. уголь. Ср. Мк. äla (BT.), äla
(М.) уголь; ilaс́ibun (BT.) кочерга.

іӆӡáн. S¹¹. земля (полъ въ фанзѣ).

ірéн. S⁸. девяносто (дх.).

іріӈгí. S⁴. языкъ. См. іныгé.

іртéн омычé. S⁸. пришелъ. Ср. Мк.
ötöӡöm (BT.) идти; Sch. omoӡem
ich komme, omočaš du bist gekom-
men; іртéн ср. монг. ireku, Мк.
irämam (BT.) посѣтить.

іркекíн. S⁹. 1-ое число. Ср. Мк. ir-
kákin (М.) новый. іркекíн ӈур¹). S⁹.
2-ое число; іркекін іӆáн. S⁹. 3-ье
число. (По образцу кит. 初 и Ман.
іче).

ікáнан. S¹⁰. испражняться.

ікте. S⁴. ікté. S³. S⁵. S¹⁰. S¹¹. зубы.
Ср. Sch. íkta (=WT.M.; O. it) Zahn.

іхáн. S⁷. іхáн̆. S¹¹. быкъ (Ман.).

ічá, іу̃á. S⁴. локоть. Ср. Sch. ičan (=
Midd., WT. ičon, C. icän, O'. uiče;
s. xuiča) Ellbogen.

ічерéн. S¹⁰. смотрѣть. Ср. Мк. ісäӡäm
(BT.) видѣть; Sch. ičetčem (C. icä-
čim, O. ittem, A. ittum) sehen.

ічекéӆ. S¹⁰. посмотри. Ср. Sch. ičétkal
sieh.

Ооné. S⁴. подмышка. Ср. Sch. ogoný
(...Aoӈnan, Mӡ. oho) Achselhöhle.

(бітігé) оорáн. S⁴. писать. Ман.
арамбі. Ср. Sch. óӡam ich thue,
mache; oran er macht. См. уарáн.

оjóн генерé. S⁴. выдти замужъ. Ср.
Ман. генумбí (вм. генéнумбí) вы-
хожу замужъ.

оуó. S⁴. хлѣбъ. См. эвэ́н и уӊóн, уóн.

омóӆ. S⁴. омолó. S³. поясъ. См. ому́ӆ.

омоӆé. S⁴. внукъ. Ман. омоло.
омоӆé унáзі. S⁴. внучка.

омýн. S¹¹. одинъ. См. эмýн.
омýн аӈганí. S¹¹. одинъ годъ.

ому́ӆ. S⁸. S¹⁰. S¹¹. поясъ. Ср. Мк. omul
(М.), omalä (НА.) поясъ.

омуктáн̆. S¹¹. яйца. Ср. Мк. omukta
(BT. М.) яйцо.

(дамгá) омнáн. S¹⁰. курить табакъ.
Ср. Мк. umӡam пить. См. імерé.

---

1) Ӈур см. ниже.

— 20 —

одáран. S¹⁰. стрѣлять (изъ лука, изъ ружья). Castr. 110 hôdâm—schiessen.

одонá. S⁴. идетъ дождь. См. удын уденéн. S¹⁰.

óсікта. S⁴. ошіктó. S⁵. звѣзда. Ср. Sch. ôsikta (C. ôsikta, WT. ohikta, M′. osikta....) Stern.

осó. S². óзо. S². озó. S¹. вода (дх.).

нáру онохó. S⁸. югъ (дх.).

онуктó. S⁸. носъ. См. ѻноктó.

онꙗá. S³. указательный палецъ. См. унаꙗá.

оȋоȟде. S⁴. курма. Ср. Мк. öꙟörokta (НА.) синяя мужская куртка.

олокý, улукý. S¹⁰. мѣшокъ для табаку. Ман. фулху (произносится даже Фолого).

олóці. S⁷. сапоги, S¹¹. кожаные лапти (кит. ýлу), Ср. Ман. олошон бродни.

óрі сірáн. S⁴. сердиться. См. аурісчаȷáȟе. Ср. монг. урín гнѣвъ.

орíн. S⁶. S⁷. S¹¹. ʼорíн. S⁸. двадцать. Ман. орін. Ср. Мк. urin (М.) двадцать.

орóкто. S⁴. арооктó. S¹¹. трава. Мк. oroktu (ВТ.) трава; Sch. orókta (= C.; WT. oroktu, G. órokta) Riedgras.

оругýн. S⁴. большой палецъ.

оркýн. S⁸. S¹⁰. орхýн. S³. веревка. Ср. Мк. orkún (М.) Фитиль.

óкі. S⁶. голова (дх.).

окíн. S³. старшая сестра. См. акá, окці.

(морín) октé. S⁸. ѣхать верхомъ. Ср. Мк. uktyrän галопъ.

ѻккí. S³. штаны. См. еркí.

окці. S¹. старшая сестра. См. акá.

оꙗікта. S¹⁰. небо. См. óсікта.

оꙗікчá. S⁴. сколько. См. Фразы (стр. 1, 4-ая).

Уáсе онці. S⁵. кирпичъ. Ср. Ман. васе (кит. ва 瓦) черепица, Феісе жженый кирпичъ.

уантабéі. S⁸. спать (дх.).

уарáн. S⁹. работать. См. оорáн.

уеілé уачá бэіјé. S⁹. преступникъ. Ман. веіле араха ȟалма (=бејé).

уíȟ. S¹. уíȟ. S⁷. уȟíȟ. S². дочь (дх.)

уíȟ. S⁷. девять. Ман. ујуȟ. Ср. Мк. ujumbä (М.) октябрь.

уȋȟ-дý (дóу). S¹. младшая сестра (дх.).

уíȟцу. S⁷. уíȟцуȟ. S⁶. девяносто. Ман. ујуȟцу.

(ча-хý 茶 壺) уȋȋчóне. S⁵. вода скипѣла. См. уȷурéн. Ср. Sch. uláköl (C. ulâm, ulôm) koche.

уб. S¹. мать (дх.).

уобéі. S¹. пить (дх.).

уóн. S¹⁰. хлѣбъ. См. эвэȟ, уꙗóн.

уогé. S⁵. тыква.

уоꙗíн. S¹¹. сколько. См. Фразы (стр. 1, 4-ую).

ујýȟ бе S¹¹. ујýȟ бе S⁴. 9-ая луна. Ср. Мк. ujumbä (М.) октябрь.

(мýју) уȷурéн. S⁹. кипятить воду. Ср. Cast. hujum kochen.

умýн. S¹¹. одинъ. См. эмýн.

умбукé. S¹⁰. шишка на шапкѣ (по кит. мао-га-да).

умшóȟ бе S⁴. уȋшȟун бе. S¹¹. одиннадцатая луна. Ман. омшон ба.

умкý. S¹⁰. платокъ. Ман. фуȟку. См. уȟкý, хýȟку.

утагáн. S¹⁰. чемоданъ¹). У Мк. однако utakán (СА.) поросенокъ, но есть hutakan (ВТ.) мѣшокъ, кошель для табаку.

утáці. S⁶. дѣдушка. Ср. Sch. atyrkán (WT. M′. atrikan Alte, ötörikan Alter, M. atirkán Alte, C. atirkan Alte, ätirkán Greis, A. atekan, O. atykan) Greis.

утé. S⁴. S¹⁰. утэ̂. S⁹. сынъ ‖ утé. S¹⁰. утэ̂. S¹⁰. отецъ. Ср. Мк. uto сынъ. умýн утэ̂. S⁹. одинъ сынъ, ꙗур утэ̂. S⁹. два сына. См. ýȟту. S⁶.

утýма. S⁶. утумó. S¹. S². хлѣбъ (дх.).

удын уденéн. S⁹. одонá. S⁴. идетъ дождь. Ср. Sch. udún (WT. C. údun,

---

1) Указалъ ему на мой кожаный.

O. odón) Regen; udúllen (O. odóllin) es regnet.

усі́. S⁴. ушіхáн. S¹⁰. ремень. Ср. Sch. uši, (C. u̯ši, Mӡ̇. uše) Riemen, Zügel.

унаӊá. S⁴. унаӊáн. S⁸. S¹¹. онӊá. S³. указательный палецъ; ‖ унаӊáн. S¹⁰. палецъ. Ср. Sch. umokačán (C. unakan Finger, M. uнakan, M. онakan Zeigefinger, WT. uнakačan Finger, Zehe) der zweite und vierte Finger.

унáӟі. S⁷. S¹¹. унáці S⁷. сестра S¹⁰, дѣвушка S¹¹, дочь S⁷. Ср. Мк. onaӡ́i (M.) взрослая дѣвушка; Sch. xunnát (C. hunnát, O. xunađ) Mädchen.

унáӟі утә̇. S⁹. дочь.

унáӟін некý(н S³.) S⁴. младшая сестра.

унínмáтаі. S¹⁰. торговать. Ср. Мк. unujimaćim (BT) купить.

уніӊáн. S⁸. четвертый палецъ. См. унаӊá.

унтá. S⁴. унтγ́. S¹⁰. керачγ́н уктá. S¹¹. сапоги. Ср. Мк. untá (M.) зимніе сапоги.

унтý(н). S⁵. бубенъ. Ср. дх. хунтγ́ру; Ман. унтун; Мк. untuwun (M.), uӊtuwun (M.), umčäfu (CA.), umćохо (HA) шаманскій бубенъ.

ýнту. S⁶. сынъ. См. утé.

уӊкý. S¹¹. платокъ. См. умкý.

уӊчі́. S¹. учкó. S⁵. учікé. S⁴. уцікáн. S⁶. ножъ. См. дх. óнці, óнчі.

улá. S¹⁰. улá (уллá). S¹¹. улдá. S⁴. одѣяло. Мк. ulá (M.) одѣяло, покрывало.

уларі́н. S⁴. уларі́н. S¹¹. красный. Монг. улан ┼ рін — окончаніе прилагательныхъ.

уларі́н лéбо. S¹¹. морковь. Переводъ кит. хунъ-ло-бо 紅蘿蔔.

ýле. S¹¹. улé (улó). S¹⁰. уллі́. S⁶. улдә̇. S⁴. мясо. Ср. Мк. ula (BT), ulŏ (M.) мясо; Sch. ulló (WT. úlla, M. ullö, C̣. úlra, A. ulda, C. u̯ldä . . . . . .) Fleisch.

улептéн. S¹⁰. пепелъ. Ср. Мк. uluptán (M.), huloptan (BT.) зола.

уліré. S⁹. шить. Ман. улімбі продѣвать нитку въ иголку.

улогетéн. S¹⁰. обмануть. Ср. Sch. ulakitten (WT. ulakičöm, C. ulŏktim lügen, C. ulök Lügen) lügen.

улдá. S⁴. одѣяло.

улдә̇. S⁴. мясо. См. улé.

уллі́. S⁶. мясо.

улгéн. S⁴. улгéн. S¹¹. свинья. Ман. улган.

улгýр. S⁹. слово. Sch. 386 C. u̯lgú̯r Wort.

улгучáнан. S¹⁰. улгучáнен. S⁹, улгучéнерé. S⁴. говорить. Ср. Sch. ulgočan (C̣. ulgučaxul sage) sie sagten; ulgučanen er benachrichtigt.

уré. S¹⁰. громъ. Ср. Ман. урамбі раздается гулъ, эхо; Sch. ureliren Echo; Мк. ultaran (M.) звукъ, эхо.

уребтýн. S¹⁰. набрюшникъ. Ср. Мк. uriptun (M.) нагрудникъ.

уré-де туктірéн. S⁹. всходить на гору; уре-дукі аурéн. S⁹. спускаться съ горы. Ср. Sch. urö (WT. ur ojon, O. ur, O′. hura) Berg, Bergrücken. Sch.tuktýkal (WT. tuktim, O′. togtambé) steiginauf. См. еурі́н.

урі́н. S⁴. двадцать. См. орі́н.

уріле. S⁹. сыновья (много), дѣти. Ср. hurul — дѣти.

урубурéн. S¹⁰. учиться (о солдатахъ). Ман. уребумбі.

урунéн. S⁹. радоваться. Ср. Ман. ургуӊембі; Sch. urunšam (C. u̯ruнsäm, WT. urúnom) sich freuen.

урункýн. S⁹. короткій. Ср. Sch. urunkún (WT. urúmkun, C. urimkun) kurz.

ур(у)гуптýн. S¹¹. урӊу-ӊебтéн. S⁸. широкое кольцо на большомъ пальцѣ (для натягиванія лука). Ср. Мк. urgóptun (M.), uнakaptun (M.), кольцо съ большаго пальца.

уруӊýн. S³. S¹¹. урӊýн. S³. орогýн. S⁴.

большой палецъ. Ср. Мк. urugun, uruhun (M.) большой палецъ.

уркé. S^{10}. S^{11}. уккé. S^{4}. дверь. Ср. Sch. úrka (= M., WT. úrko, C. urkä, O'. Mž. učé, O. urkupyn) Thür.

уркýн. S^{4}. веревка. См. оркýн, урхýн.

урҕýн. S^{8}. большой палецъ. См. уруҕýн.

урҕу-ҕебтéн. S^{8}. кольцо на большомъ пальцѣ. См. уругуптýн.

урхýн. S^{11}. веревка.

укýр. S^{10}. S^{11}. укурý. S^{1}. S^{2}. уҕýр. S^{4}. быкъ (дх.).

уктыленé S^{9}. бѣглецъ. Ман. укамбі убѣжать, укандцу бѣглецъ, Мк. hučahinam (BT.) убѣжать.

укшíн. S^{10}. солдатъ. Ман. уксін латы, латникъ. Ср. Мк. uksin (M.) короста, парша[1]).

уккé. S^{4}. двери. См. уркé.

уккýн. S^{8}. молоко. Ср. Мк. úkun (BT), ukún (M.) жен. грудь, сосецъ, молоко; Sch. ukún (. . . . . C. ukun, O'. ku, G. kuꬻ) Mutterbrust.

угіló. S^{4}. верхній, уҕілé. S^{9}. верхъ. Ср. Sch. uhýla (C. ugilä) oben.

угілé боҕá. S^{4}. небо.

угіáран. S^{10}. лечь. Sch. uklážiren (WT. hukulažöm, C. huglan, hukäläm) er liegt.

уҕíн. S^{2}. дочь. См. уíн (дх.).

уҕілé. S^{9}. верхъ. См. угіló.

уҕірí морíн. S^{9}. верховая лошадь. Ср. Sch. uhyrím (WT. ugýrim) ich er hob.

уҕіктáн. S^{10}. ногти. Ср. Мк. uꬻikta (BT.), oꬻikta (M.) жила. Sch. также.

уҕóн. S^{11}. хлѣбъ. См. уóн.

уҕýр. S^{4}. быкъ. См. укýр.

учікé. S^{3}. ножъ. См. уꚗчí.

учіхéн кукý. S^{7}. сынъ (дх.)

учýꚗ. S^{9}. пѣсня (Ман.)

уꚗкó. S^{5}. уꚗкáн. S^{6}. ножъ. См. уꚗчí.

Еідé турáні. S^{11}. браниться. Ср. Sch.

---

1) Покрываетъ тѣло, какъ панцырь?

turán Wort; Мк. taráčäm, пов. turatkal говорить; еще ман. еітерембі.

Уішун ´бе. S^{11}. 11-ая луна. См. умшóꚗ ´бе. Мк. umsumbä (M.) декабрь.

Аудé. S^{8}. двери (наружныя) (дх.).

àун. S^{10}. S^{11}. áҕун. S^{8}. аҕý(н). S^{4}. шапка. Ср. Sch. aúun (M. áun, C. áwun, NA. afun, WT. abyn, O'.G. afo) Hut.

áула. S^{6}. гора (дх.)

аулахáі. S^{10}. одѣть (одѣнь) шапку. Образованъ отъ аун посредствомъ частицы ла (= ман.—монг.).

аурісчаіáне. S^{5}. сердиться. См. opi сірáн.

Еуó. S^{2}. мать (дх.).

еурíн. S^{8}. спускаться, сойти. Ср. ман. ебумбі.

Jаувáн jayijá. S^{6}. jаукáн jабурéн. S^{11}. идти пѣшкомъ (Монг.=Ман.)

jабó. S^{10}. пойдемъ, идти (Монг.=Ман.).

jабукáі. S^{10}. ступай; jабугáн. S^{10}. домой идти.

ілáꚗ jамázі. S^{11}. триста. См. німázі.

jáсыле. S^{3}. jасьле. S^{5}. глаза. См. jéса.

jáлі. S^{3}. мясо (Ман.).

jaló ошíкте. S^{5}. «Три звѣзды»—созвѣздіе Орла. См. ілáꚗ.

jára ачá jýре. S^{9}. безвредный. Монг. japa рана, ача ср. Sch. ačin (= WT.; A'. ata, ača, O. ačča) ist nicht.

jaҕíн. S^{4}. jеҕíн. S^{8}. jеьíн. S^{11}. jeíн. S^{7}. уíн. S^{6}. девять. Ср. Sch. jöhýn (C. jägin, M. jagin, O'.G. xuju) neun.

jaҕýн улурé. S^{3}. jooҕà улірéн. S^{4}. ходить пѣшкомъ. Формы jаувáн, jаукáн, jayijá, jaҕýн объясняются отъ корня jабу (Монг.—Ман.) перемѣ- ною б въ ҕ, һ. См. дахурскіе тексты.

Jeíн. S^{7}, jеьíн. S^{11}. девять. См. jаҕíн.

jému. S^{10}. какой. См. Фразы. (Стр. 1, 5-ая).

jéса. S^{11}., jéꚗе. S^{8}. jáсыле. S^{3}. jасьле. S^{5}, ісáі. S^{4}, éꚗа. S^{10}. глаза. Ср. Мк. jasa (HA) глаза; Ман. jaса; Sch.

ésa (C. êsa. C̓. eša, WT. äha) Auge.

jeлáн. S⁸. три. См. iлáн.

jeлáн ȝiреꚃéi. S⁹. трижды. Ман.
iлан ꚃергi.

jeꚃíн. S⁸. девять. См. jaꚃíн.

Jiманáран. S⁹. идетъ снѣгъ. См. iма-
нарá.

jiлáн. S⁹. S¹¹. три. См. iлáн.

jiлатáр. S⁹. по-три. Ман. iлата.

jiрáн. S¹¹, jiрóн. S⁴. девяносто (дх.).

Joшухý, Joшхý. S¹¹. замокъ. Ман.
joce, jooce.

jooꚃá улiрéн. S⁴. идти пѣшкомъ. См.
jaꚃýн улурé. Ср. Мк. ulim (М.) ѣсть
(улiрéн чит. улурéн?).

Jурéне. S⁵. встать (отъ сна). Ср. Sch.
judirek (O. нulrem aufgehen) Aufgang. См. ӱрéн.

Паꚃчiбé. S⁸. сердиться. Ман. ɸан-
чамбi.

печка. S¹⁰. печка (рус.).

пi, S⁶. S¹⁰. кисть писчая (кит. би 筆).

пы́нса. S¹¹. плошка (кит. пынь-цза 盆
子).

пýшeлe. S¹⁰. купецъ.

пуꚃeлé. S¹⁰. лавка. Ман. пуселi отъ
кит. пу-цза 鋪子.

Бáшу. S¹¹. холстъ. Ман. босо.

баꚃдáн. S¹¹. стулъ, Ман. (съ кит.)
бандан.

баꚃдéн сiрꙋ́. S⁶. большой столъ.

балтý. S¹⁰. хозяинъ.

балчiрáн. S⁸. написано. У Sch. есть
baldyżeren, но значитъ другое: er
wäscht.

бараꚃдá. S⁵. западъ. Монг. барӯн
правый, западный.

барí. S⁷. возьми (дх., монг. барíху).

баркáн. S¹. богъ (дх.).

багдарíн. S¹⁰, богдарíн. S¹¹. бѣлый.
Мк. bagdama (ВТ.), bagdarin (М.)
бѣлый.

бáга. S⁶. небо, еще боꚃá. S⁹, угiлé
боꚃá. S⁴. Ср. Мк. ba mamgun (НА)
млечный путь; buꙅá (М.) мѣсто;
Sch. boáw (. . . O῾G. boa) Gegend.

ꚃáꚃa. S⁵., ꚃe. S⁷., ꚃéꚃa. S⁴, S⁹. S¹⁰.,
ꚃéга. S¹⁰., бiꚃá. S⁴. луна. Sch. béga
(WT. bäga, Mꙅ̌. bija, A. ꚃäꙅ́) Mond.

бéле. S⁸. рукавицы (дх.).

белдéр. S⁴., бы́лкé. S⁷. нога. Ман.
бетхе.

бi. S⁸. я. Ман. = Монг.; Sch. bi
(=WT. C. O῾G. O.) ich.

Единственное число.

И.	Бi S⁹. я	وَ
Р.	мíнгí	مِنِکِ
Д. Т.	мíнду	مِنْدُ
В.	мíнебó	مِنَوَ
П.	мíндукí	مِنْدُکِ

Множественное число.

И.	мíтý мы	مِتَ
Р.	мíткí	مِتْکِ
Д. Т.	мíткíду	مِتْکِدُ
В.	мíткíбó	مِتْکِوَ
П.	мíткídукí	مِتْکِدُکِ

бiтегé. S¹⁰. пить (sic!), но бiтеꙅ́é (бi-
теꙅ́é). S¹⁰. писать.

бiты́ꚃé. S¹⁰., бiтéхе. S⁸., бiтхе. S⁴.
книга. Ман. бiтхе; Мк. bitiꙅ́a (М.)
письмо, письмена.

бiсíꚃгí, бiшíꚃгí. S⁸. есть ли? живы
ли? См. Фразы (стр. 1, 8-ая); ман.
бiсiреꚃге.

бiрá. S⁴. S¹¹. рѣка. Sch. böra (WT.
birá, Mꙅ̌. bira) Fluss.

бiрахáн. S¹⁰. гора (sic!).

бiргáн. S¹⁰., бiргáн. S⁷. рѣчка. Ман.
бiрган.

бiꚃá. S⁴. луна. См. ꚃáꚃa.

бojé. S⁹. человѣкъ. Ср. Sch. bojó, boӧ
(WT. buja, M. böija...) Mensch.

бокé. S¹⁰. тушь (Ман.). Ср. Мк. bökä
(М.) чернила.

богдарíн. S¹¹. бѣлый. См. багдарíн.

боꚃá. S⁹. небо. См. бáга.

(горó) боꚃó. S⁹. (далекое) мѣсто.

буі̆ цуанемéне S⁵. человѣколюбіе. Ср. бојé — человѣкъ.
буі̆ле S⁵. губы. Монг. буіла—десны.
буда ідé. S¹. ѣсть (дх.).
(амíн) бусé. S⁴. (отецъ) умеръ. См. бучá; Ман. бучехе умеръ. Ср. Мк. bušädäm (BT.) болѣзнь, хворать.
бýлке S⁵. зеркало. Ман. булеку.
буркáн. S¹¹. богъ (дх.).
бургáн. S⁴. роща. Ср. ман. буцан — роща.
(кавáн) бучá. S¹⁰. (чиновникъ) умеръ.
баіталарáчі. S⁵. безполезный; баіталара (Ман. причастіе) + ачі (= Мк. ačin).
беі[1]). S⁶. есть (дх.).
Фохорí. S⁷. штаны. Ман. факурі. Ср. Мк. furu (HA) мѣх. штаны.
Вáса. S²., вáса. S¹¹. чулки. Кит. ваца 襪子; Ман. васе.
вáран. S¹⁰. убивать. Ман. вамбі. Ср. Мк. wäŋnäm (BT.), wânäm убивать; Sch. wáldyren.
варацоу. S¹⁰. хочу ѣсть.
вынгі. S⁷. свинья. См. улгéн.
вусіхá. S⁷. звѣзда. Ман. усіха.
Wáлдерен. S¹⁰. браниться.
Маевáн. S¹¹. сердце. См. мéван.
мао S¹⁰. S¹¹. кумирня (кит. 廟).
манá. S¹⁰. снѣгъ. См. іманарá, інӈа.
(бéган) манаучá. S¹⁰. луна зашла. Ср. Sch. manáuran. . . . es ging zu Ende.
мáӈала. S⁶. S⁴.¹, маӈалá. S²., мáхала. S¹, махалá. S⁷. шапка (дх.).
махá. S¹. мясо (дх.).
мáнган S⁶. тысяча. См. мінгá.
мáнгі̆ле. S³. мáнгіл. S⁴. лобъ (дх.)
мангó. S⁹. лодка. Ср. Мк. mamu, maŋo (CA) лодка. См. монгó.
мачáн. S⁴. ружье. Ман. маочан (кит. няо-цянъ 鳥槍).
мèван. S¹⁰. грудь, маевáн. S¹⁰. сердце. Ср. Мк. mäwan (BT. M.) сердце; Sch. méwan (WT. mäwan, J. mewo, G. mewa, O′. meo Herz) böse (по Мк. mäwan ačin (BT.) негодяй).
менеукéл. см. кýді менеукéл.
ментухýн. S⁹. глупый (Ман.)
меӈгýн. S¹⁰, меӈгýн. S¹¹, муӈгý. S⁴. серебро. Ман. меӈгун. Sch. móŋun . .(C. mäŋun... O′. móŋgu...) Silber.
міт́у. S⁹. мы. Sch. mity (A. mur) wir.
мíрі. S⁴. плечо. (См. дх.), Sch. mira (C. mira, Mǥ. meiren) Schulter.
мінгá. S⁴. S⁸. S¹¹. тысяча, еще мáнган. S⁶. éму мінгáн. S⁷. (Ман.=Монг.)
мінгецíн. S⁹. подобно (-ый) мнѣ.
мō. S⁴. S¹⁰. дерево, S¹¹. палка, S⁵. прутья, ср. Мк. mo (BT.) дерево; Sch. также[1]); ‖ S⁸. вода. См. мӯ.
мóдо. S⁶. дерево (дх.).
мóса. S¹¹. роща. Ср. Sch. 407 moja-Holz, Sch. 404 mólin — Wald.
морí. S¹. S². S⁷, мóрі. S⁶, морíн. S⁴. S¹⁰. S¹¹. лошадь (Ман. = Монг.); морі́ті јабурéн. S¹¹. ѣхать верхомъ. Castr. moriči, morindi — zu Pferde.
мóгу. S¹¹. грибъ (кит. 蘑菇). Ср. Мк. mogo (HA) грибъ.
монгó. S¹⁰. лодка. См. мангó.
мочоурáн. S⁹. возвращаться, ворочаться. Ср. Sch. mučudam (O. močuren) er kehrt zurück; mučuren er kehrte zurück.
мӯ. S⁴. S⁶. S⁷. S⁹. S¹⁰. S¹¹. вода. Ср. Sch. mu (= WT. M.) Wasser.
мý-дамга[2]). S¹⁰. кальянъ (кит. шуй-янь-дай 水烟袋). См. дамга табакъ.
мунéке. См. тáла мунéке. Ср. Мк. moŋoro (CA.) сосудъ изъ дерева, muksu (CA.) сосудъ изъ дерева, mulu (CA.) корзина, сосудъ изъ дерева, но muŋak (BT.) собраніе, сборище.

---

1) Почти бі.

1) Ман. моо.

2) По кит. шуй-янь (по мѣст. суй-янь) — водяной табакъ — называется табакъ, который курятъ въ кальянахъ. Онъ не боится подмочки.

мургурéн. S[10]. молиться богу. Ср. Мк. murgum (М.) кланяться; ср. Монг. мӳргӳмӳі.

мукуатáшı̄. S[10]. задница. Ср. Мк. mukóto (ВТ.) задница.

мукдахáн. S[11]. бить. Ср. Sch. múgda (M̆. mugdehen) Stamm; mukdakán...Dem.

муӊгу́. S[4]. серебро. См. меӊгу́н.

мáісa (Кит.) гулí(н). S[11]. лапша. Мáісa —пшеница 麥子, гулí(н)—см. хулíн, ҕолó; Монг. гурíл, гулíр.

Тао, тавó. S[11]. огонь. См. тоҕó.

таухéл̄. S[10]., теныҕéл̄. S[11]. садись. Ср. Sch. tookol, tógokol (A. tögettum sitzen) — setze dich.

таттáн. S[9]. учиться. Ман. тацімбі.

татгéл̄. S[10]. одѣть (пов. накл.) платье. Мк. tättim (ВТ.) одѣвать. См. теттéн.

тасхá. S[4]. тигръ (Ман.). Ср. Мк. tasxa (НА.) тигръ.

тананҕí. S[11], туанҕí. S[4], тороӊгангí. S[8]. пятьдесятъ. Ср. Мк. tunaӡar (ВТ.) пятьдесятъ.

тансы́. S[5]. одѣяло. Кит. тань-цзы 毯子; еще ср. у Мк. tättim одѣвать, tänina потникъ.

талá. S[9]. тамъ. Мк. tála (ВТ.), talá (М.) тамъ.

тáла мунéке. S[9]. берестовые буракí[1]). См. талé, талу́; мунéке.

талірé. S[4]. громъ гремитъ. Ср. Мк. talin juran (М.) молнія; Sch. taliнúran (= M. G′., M̆. talkijan, O′. taɫé) Blitz.

талé (тал). S[5]., талу́. S[10]. береста. Sch. talö (C. WT. talu, O′. G′. talo) Birkenrinde. Ман. толхон.

тараҕá. S[10]. чесать волосы. Ср. Мк. tarakъ (М.) лысый.

тарíн. S[9]. ихъ. Castr. tar — jener. Сабсу тарíн iлáн бэjé. S[9]. трое человѣкъ: Сабсу и прочіе.

———

[1]) Баргу(-монголы) называютъ бересту тáла монí, токтá монí.

таррáн. S[9]. пахать. Ман. тарімбі.

таргáн (тарҕáн). S[10]. пашня. Ман. тарíн, Монг. тарíја.

таҕірéн. S[9]. знать. Мк. tagym (ВТ.). узнавать; Ман. такамбí.

тáціху. S[9]. училище. Ман. тацíку.

тебкосу́н. S[5]. гвоздь. Мк. tipkasu (М.) желѣзный гвоздь.

тебгурáн. S[10]. черная береза.

тему́ҕé. S[4]. верблюдъ (Монг.=Ман.).

теттéн. S[9]. одѣвать. См. татгéл̄, терыгексé.

теныҕéл̄. S[11]. садись. См. тэҕірэ́.

терыгé. S[4]. телѣга. См. тергé.

терыгексé. S[9]. одежда. См. теттéн. Ср. Sch. tetýha (C. tätigä...) Kleidung.

терыгáн, тергáн. См. подъ тергé.

теру́. S[11]. теру́. S[10]. подушка. Ср. Sch. tyrú (M̆. ćirku, WT. tiru . . .) Kissen; Мк. tiru (ВТ., М.) подушка.

тергé. S[1]., тергéн. S[10]., терыгé. S[4]., терҕé. S[11]. телѣга. Монг. терге(н). Мк. tyrgán (М.) телѣга.

тергáн jабучá. S[10]. поѣхалъ въ телѣгѣ.

терыгáн теуксá jабурéн. S[11]. ѣхать въ телѣгѣ. Ср. теуксá съ Ман. тефí и съ тэҕірэ́.

текé. S[3]. сидѣть, садиться. Ср. Ман. техé — сидѣлъ, сѣлъ. См. тэҕірэ́.

тегул̄чáн. S[10]. сердиться. Ман. туҕулáн. Ср. Мк. tikylibkanim (ВТ.) сердить; Sch. tykunӡären — er zürnt.

тегдерéн. S[10]. дождь идетъ. Ср. Sch. týgda (Kur. = Midd., M. tigda, O.′G. tugda) — Regen.

тегеттéн. S[10]. сидѣть. См. тэҕірэ́.

тэҕірэ́. S[5]. сидѣть. Мк. tyhyӡäm (ВТ.) сидѣть, жить; Ман. тембí.

т′оо. S[6]. огонь. См. тоҕó.

тобчí. S[3], S[8], S[10]. S[11]., тóбчі. S[4]. пуговица (дх.). Мк. torći (М.) пуговица.

томонáн. S[9]., S[10]., тумунéн. S[11]. плевать. Ср. Мк. tuminam (ВТ.) плевать; Sch. tumýn (WT. tumin, C. tômin, tumin) — Speichel.

тондо́. S⁹. безпритворный, прямой. Ман. тондо.

то́ло. S⁵. большое зеркало на одеждѣ шамана (дх.). Монг. толі.

толма́. S⁵. ведро (дх.).

тороӈгангі́. S⁸. пятьдесятъ. См. тананꙂі.

тороӈꙂа́. S⁸. пять. См. тунга́.

токоука́л. S¹⁰. осѣдлать (пов. накл.) коня. Ср. Мк. tögömči (M.) сѣдельная подушка. Ман. тохомбі.

токола́. S¹⁰. земля (полъ въ Фанзѣ), туꙂа́ла. S⁴. земля. См. туллá. Ср. Мк. tukála (BT., M.) глина, песокъ; Sch. tukala (..G. tóala, M. toxola Sumpf) — Erde, Boden.

токторо́н. S⁹. утверждаться (на чемъ-либо). Ман. токтомбі.

тоꙂо́. S⁴. S⁵., т'оо. S⁶., табо́, таво́. S¹¹. туа́. S⁷. огонь. Ман. тува (туа́). Мк. togo (BT., M.) огонь; Sch. tohó (...C. togo...) Feuer.

тохола́. S¹⁰. стѣна (земляная?). См. токола́.

туа́. S⁷. огонь. См. тоꙂо́.

туангáн. S⁶. пять. См. тунга́. Ср. туангéн.

туангара́. S⁶. чашка.

туангéн. S⁶., ему тангý. S⁷. сто. Ман. таӈгун.

туанꙂі́. S⁴. пятьдесятъ. См. тананꙂі.

тумé. S⁴., тумó. S⁸., тýмен. S⁶., тумéн. S¹¹., ему тумéн. S⁷. десять тысячъ (Ман. = Монг.).

тумунéн. S¹¹. плевать. См. томонáн.

тумкꙋл (тумкуꙋл). S¹⁰. вязать, связывать. Ср. Sch. túmkol — wickel auf (Birkenrinde, Zwirn); Мк. toӈoló (M.) петля.

тýду. S¹¹. картофель (кит. тý-доу 土豆).

тулла́ S¹¹. земля (на улицѣ). См. токола́. Ср. Мк. tur (M.) земля.

сідé турáні. S¹¹. браниться. См. подъ еідό.

туксé. S¹¹. облако. Sch. túkšu (WT. Midd. tuksu, O'.G. táuaxsa, Мꙁ. tuǧi) — Wolke.

тукші áчі. S⁹. безоблачный.

тукшý. S¹⁰. звѣзда (? См. туксé).

туꙂáла. S⁴. земля. См. токолá.

туꙂулáн. S¹¹. сердиться. См. тегул-чáн.

(тергáн) тухучá. S¹⁰. запрегъ телѣгу. Ман. тохомбі.

тунгá. S¹¹., тунꙂá, S⁴., тунгáн. S⁷., туангáн. S⁶., торонꙂá. S⁸. пять. Ср. Мк. tuӈa (BT.) пять; Sch. tuӈa (WT. C. toӈa, O'. túnꙂa, Мꙁ. sunꙂa) — fünf.

таібό S⁵. балка (у крыши). Ман. (= Монг.) таібý матица, балка.

Дамбагý (Ман.). S⁷., дамгá. S¹⁰., дáнга. S¹., дангá. S²., данꙂá. S⁴. табакъ. Мк. damga (M.), damgi (CA.) табакъ.

енуꙂý дасарá даіпý. S⁴. докторъ. ЕнуꙂý см. выше, дасарá также и по маньчжурски, даіпý — кит. дáі-фу 大夫 — докторъ.

дарі́. S⁷. трубка. См. дáіра.

даꙂахý. S⁹. близко. Ср. Мк. dagakun (M.), dahakun (CA.), dagamakikan (BT.) близко.

дангá. S²., дáнга. S¹., данꙂá. S⁴. табакъ. См. дамбагý.

де. S⁴. трубка. См. дáіра.

дебтелé. S⁸. крыло¹). Ср. Мк. dok-tylá (M.) крыло.

дэві́. S⁷. лодка. Мк. ꙅaba (BT.), ꙅau (M.) лодка изъ бересты. См. дх.

десó. S⁴. стѣна (дх.).

дéза. S⁸. тарелка (кит. дѣ-цза 碟子).

дендíн (дензíн). S¹⁰. крыша (кит.?).

делечá, дėлечá. S¹⁰. солнце. Sch. de-lečá (C. dilacá, WT. dilǎčá)—Sonne.

делгý (дулгý). S¹¹., долꙂó унаꙂá. S⁴. долꙂó уніꙂáн. S⁸. дóло онꙂá. S⁸. 3-ій (средній) палецъ. Мк. ꙗolgún (M.)

---

1) Указалъ ему крыло для стиранія пыли.

длинный палецъ (на рукѣ). См. дóло
онѕá.

деⷧпé. S⁴. подстилка. Ср. Ман. дерхі
циновка (на канѣ и постелѣ).

дерáм. S⁹. грубый. Ср. Мк. diran (ВТ.)
толстый (о веревкѣ).

дерé. S⁴. дерé. S¹⁰. лицо. Ман. дере.

дереб́о. S⁸. подушка. См. дах. Ср.
терý.

дересýн. S¹¹., дерешіýн. S¹⁰. рогожка
(дх.). См. дерсýн.

дерí. S¹⁰. трубка. См. дайрá.

дербý. S⁴. подушка. См. дереб́о.

дерсýн. S⁵., дерз́о. S¹. S². дерз́о. S⁸.
рогожка (дх.). См. дересýн.

декíн. S⁸. сорокъ. См. дéѕі.

декылé. S⁸. родъ жилета, безрукавки
(кань-дянь-цза). Ср. Мк. dököli(М.)
верхнее платье, халатъ.

(деⷧечá — см. деⷧечá) декдеѕá. S¹⁰.
(солнце) взошло. Ман. декдембі.

(б́еган) декдечá. S¹⁰. (луна) взошла.

дегíн S⁶. четыре. См. дігéн.

дéѕі. S⁴., дерѕí. S¹¹., дерѕíн. S⁶., декíн. S⁸.,
дехí. S⁷. сорокъ. Ман. дехі; Мк. di-
ginӡar (ВТ.) сорокъ.

дерѕíн. S¹¹. четыре. См. дігéн. Ср.
деѕíн.

деѕіⷧ деѕіⷧірé. S⁴. птица летящая¹).
Ср. Мк. däxi, döki (М.) птица; Sch.
dohí (С. dägi . . .) — Vogel; doguát-
ten — er fliegt; dogýlle — er ist
davon geflogen. Ман. дéјенге лету-
чая (отъ дéјембі).

дехí. S⁷. сорокъ. См. дéѕі.

діⷧаптýн. S¹¹. браслетъ²). Ср. Мк.
giláptun (ВТ.) браслетъ.

дуⷧ. S¹⁰. дуⷧі. S⁹. голова, дуⷧі S⁴. черепъ. Ср. Sch. dyl (WT. dili, O. del,
A. dil, UA. ӡil) — Kopf.

дігéн. S⁴., діѕíн. S⁸., дыѕíн. S⁷. четыре.
Ср. Sch. dygín (WT. digin, O. dygen.
A. dügün, О´.G. dui, Мѯ. duin) —
vier.

---

1) По кит. фэй-няо 飛 鳥.
2) Показалъ мѣдный.

дб̄. S⁹. сердце.

доосóн. S⁴. соль. Мк. dausoӈ (СА.)
соль; Ман. дабусун, монг. дабусун.

добтóн. S¹⁰. чулки. Ср. Мк. dokton
(ВТ.) короткій сапогъ, чулокъ.

дóло онѕá. S³. 3-ій палецъ. См. долѕ́о
унаѕá. Ср. Мк. doli ćumćo (НА.)
длинный палецъ, dolin (М.) средина;
Sch. dulú — der mittlere Finger.
См. делгý.

долб́о. S⁴. ночь. S¹⁰. почта (sic!). Ср.
Sch. dolbani (= A., WO. dolboni,
М'. dolboné, Мѯ. dobori) Nacht;
dolbo — bei Nacht.

(деⷧечá) долбочó. S¹⁰. (солнце) зашло.
Ср. Sch. dolbača—spät, dolbalčá—
Sonnenuntergang.

долѕ́о унаѕá. S⁴.) 3-ій (средній) па-
долѕ́о уніѕáн. S⁸.) лецъ. См. делгý.

доⷧзіѕá. S⁹. слушай. Ман. донзімбі.
Ср. Sch. dolčašin—hört... WT. doldim...hören, doóldyren. . er hörte.

дӯ. S². S⁷., доу. S¹. младшій братъ
(Ман. = Монг.).

дуӣн б́е. S¹¹., дуӣн б́е. S⁴. 4-ая луна.
Ман. дуін б́а. Мк. dujin bä (М.) май.

дуоⷧдерéн. S¹¹. слушать. Sch. doóldyren (WT. doldim) — er hörte.

дуз́э. S⁸., десó. S⁴. стѣна (дх.).

дуⷧімбуѕá. S⁴. средній. Ман. дулімба
(дулін -+- ба), буѕа = боѕá = ба
мѣсто; Ср. Мк. dolin (М.) средина;
dulu (ВТ.) средній; Sch. dulin — in
der Mitte, dulýnin — Mitte.

дулгý. S¹¹. 3-ій палецъ. См. делгý.

ӡáli дуранѕіб́еі. S⁹. какъ удобно.
Ср. Sch. ӡali (С. ӡali, Мѯ. gali)
Verstand. Дуранѕіб́еі ср. Монг. ду-
рабер, дуран-јер.

дꙋр. S¹¹. два. См. џур, џýру.

даі. S³. S⁵. трубка (кит. 袋).

даіба. S⁵. крышка(на котлѣ).См. дáіѕу.

даірá. S²., дáіре. S⁸., даірí.S¹⁰. дарí.S⁷.,
дерí. S¹⁰. трубка. См. даі; Мк. dairi
(М.) трубка.

дáіѕу. S⁸. крышка (на чайной чашкѣ).

См. да́іба. Ср. Мк. dahim (ВТ.) покрывать (dašmi, пов. daškal).

доу.̣S⁸. младшій братъ. См. дӯ.

Ċаове́н. S¹¹. хә̀шанъ (буддійскій монахъ). Ср. säwoŋ и др. подъ словомъ ċевукі́.

ċао-ха́і. S¹⁰. младшій братъ (кит. ¹) 小孩).

са́ві. S⁴. туфли, башмаки. Ман. сабу.

самасꙁі́. S⁵. платье шамана (== дх.). Ср. Мк. samäšik (М.) шаманское платье.

ċан. S⁶. уши. См. ċе.

ċанꙿна́н. S¹¹. дымъ. Ср. Мк. saŋhän (М.), saŋija (НА.) дымъ. Ман. шаꙿнꙿганъ (шанꙿjанꙿ).

са́реміkте. S³. сармукто́. S⁸. брови. Ср. Sch. saremýkta (M. G. sálmykta, UA. sarämta, G′. saremto) Brauen; Мк. sarmukta (М.), sarämta (НА.), harymykta (ВТ.) брови.

сарпо́. S². S⁸., ċарпо́. S¹¹., чарпу́. S¹⁰. палочки для ѣды (куай-цза 快子); щипцы для огня (хо-куай-цза). Мк. ċarpu (М.) палочки, служащія вмѣсто вилокъ.

сармукто́. S⁸. См. саре́міkте.

ċактууре́н. S¹¹. подстилка. Ср. Мк. soktokú (НА.) коверъ.

ċагды́ етырка́н. S¹¹. старикъ. Ман. сакда старикъ; Мк. sagdani (М.) бабушка, sagdami дѣдушка; hagdi (ВТ.) старый; atirkan (М.), atrikan (ВТ.) старуха; Sch. atyrkán.... Greis.

саꙁала́. S². S³. S⁵., сахала́. S⁷., саха́р. S¹. борода (и усы S²) (дх.).

са́ꙁала. S⁷. усы (дх.).

ċе. S³., S⁴., ċен. S⁸. S¹⁰. S¹¹. уши. Ср. Мк. siän (ВТ.), sijäŋ (НА.), säŋ (М.) ухо; Ман. шан.

---

¹) Буквально маленькій мальчикъ, парнишка. Китайцы, наоборотъ, чужаго парнишку называютъ при личномъ разговорѣ младшимъ братомъ.

ċевукі́. S¹⁰. богъ (бурханъ). Ср. Мк. höwökîn (ВТ.) богъ; sau (СА.), sauo, säwoŋ (НА.) идолъ; säwoki (М.) идолъ; Sch. sewakí..... Herr. См. ċaowén.

сергі́. S¹⁰. песокъ. Мк. sirgi (М.) песокъ. Castr. 130 sergi — Land.

сеꙁі́н. S¹¹. телѣга. Ман. сецен.

ċе́ле. S¹¹., ерселе́. S⁴., п̇ело́. S¹⁰. желѣзо; Ман. селе; Мк. hölö (ВТ.) желѣзо; Sch. s̓élö (Midd. s̓élö, sälö, šela, G′. šela) Eisen.

сі. S⁹., ші. S⁸. ты. Ман. сі; Sch. si — du; Мк. si (ВТ.) ты.

Единственное число.

И.	сі. S⁹. ты.	
Р.	сінгі́	
Д. Т.	сі́нду	
В.	сінебо́	
П.	сі́ндукі́	

Множественное число.

И.	сӯ вы.	
Р.	сунгі́	
Д. Т.	су́нду́	
В.	су́нево́	
П.	су́ндукі́	

сімкіре́н. S⁹. кашлять. Мк. simkin (М.) кашель, himkiċim (ВТ.) кашлять.

сіде́. S². зубы (дх.).

сіді́ме́. S¹¹. просо (кит. ми-цза 米子; хуанъ-ми; ме == кит. ми, сіді ср. сіꙁарі́н желтый?)

сіды́ꙁу́н. S¹¹. ремень. У Мк. tiꙅir (М.), tölöċi (М.) ремень. Castr. tidar, ċidar.

сісіꙁі́, сісіꙁе́. S¹¹. войлокъ. Ман. ċiċre постилка, тюфякъ; Мк. sisxa (НА.) коверъ. Ср. Монг. іші́ге войлокъ.

сіні́. S⁷., ші́ні. S⁸. твой. Ман. сіні; Мк. hiŋі (ВТ.) твой.

сіла́н. S⁴. синій, S¹¹. зеленый. Ср. Мк. silá (М.) синій.

сіле́. S¹. столъ. См. сіре́.

сіленку́н. S⁹. узкій. Ср. Sch. sylím-
kun — eng.

сілбо́. S⁵. палка для вѣшанія одежды[1]).

сіра́н. См. орі сіра́н.

сіре́. S⁴., сіле́. S¹., сіра́. S⁶., шіре́. S².,
шіре́. S⁵. S⁸. S¹⁰. S¹¹. столъ (дх.).

сірꙗекте̌. S⁴. капуста.

сінгада́. S¹¹. молчи.

сіꙗарі́н. S⁴., сінгарі́н. S¹¹. желтый.
Мк. siꙗarín (M.) желтый.

соктоора́н. S⁹. напиться. Ман. соктомбі.

сонꙗоро́но. S⁵. плакать (о ребенкѣ).
Ман. Сонгомбі, Мк. hoꙗom (ВТ.)
плакать.

сӯ. S⁹. вы. Ман. суве, суо̄.

суанда́. S⁵. чеснокъ (Ман.).

суі́ткі́. S⁵. мизинецъ. Ср. дх. суі́ткó.

суса́і. S⁶. S⁷. пятьдесятъ (Ман.).

су́су мо́до. S⁸. палка, трость. Ман.
чу́се-мбо бамбукъ.

су̀н. S¹⁰. халатъ. Мк. ꙗun (M.) ниж-
нее платье.

суꙗца́ бі́. S¹¹., суꙗза́'бе. S⁴. 5-ая луна.
Мк. sunꙗabä (M.) іюнь.

суліꙗа́. S⁹. востокъ.

су̀ра́. S¹¹. блоха. Мк. sorá (M., у Дах.)
блоха.

су́ку. S⁵., цуге́. S⁴. топоръ. (Отъ Ман.
=Монг.). Sch. húko, hukó (C. suꙗkä
....Midd. šuꙗko, ꙗukö) Axt.

сухарі́. S¹⁰. сухари (рус.).

суі-jaꙗ-да́і. S⁴. кальянъ (кит.; 水烟
袋).

спі́чкі́. S¹⁰. спички (рус.).

Ϛі. S⁵. уши. См. ϛе.

ϛа́ра. S⁸. желтый (дах.).

ϛарпо́. S¹¹. куай-цза. См. сарпо́.

ϛігу́н. S⁵. солнце. Ман. шун.

Шаміне́. См. Фразы (8-ая).

ша́ра (шаре́). S². желтый (дх.).

шарбага́н. S¹⁰. палецъ на ногѣ.

шѐло́. S¹⁰. желѣзо. См. ϛеле́.

шіні́. S⁸. твой. См. сіні́.

шілута́н. S⁴., шілукта́н. S⁸. песокъ.
Ср. Castr. hꙗläftän — Asche, Ман.
фуленгі.

шіре́. S⁵., S⁸. S¹⁰., S¹¹., шіре́. S². столъ
(дх.).

Шіркꙗꙗ. S¹⁰. Амуръ. Мк. Silkär (M.)
Амуръ.

шокꙗохе́. S¹⁰. дахурская шапка изъ
войлока. Ср. Мк. soksokä (M.) пуговица на женской шапкѣ.

На́ла. S³. S⁵., ꙗа́ла. S⁴. S¹⁰., 'га́ла. S¹⁰.
См. гарі́, гале́. рука. Ман. гала;
Sch. nála (WT. M. O. A. ꙗala, C.
ꙗala, nala) Hand.

намаꙗі. S⁴., ꙗама́ꙗі. S¹¹., німа́ꙗі[1]). S⁸
сто. Sch. ꙗamaꙗі (C. namaꙗi, O. A.
ꙗämá) — hundert.

нада́. S⁴., нада́н. S⁷., надан. S⁸., ꙗада́н
S¹¹, наде́н. S⁶, надо́. S⁵. семь. Ман.
надан; Sch. nadán (= WT., A. G.
M. nada)—sieben; Мк. nadaꙗ (M.)
семь.

нада́н'бе. S⁴. S¹¹. 7-ая луна; Мк.
nadambä (M.) августъ.

наданꙗі́. S¹¹, наданꙗу́. S⁶. S⁷., нада-
рангі́. S⁸., надарінꙗі́. S⁴. семьдесятъ.
Мк. nadaꙗі (M.), nadanꙗar (ВТ.)
семьдесятъ. Ман. наданꙗу.

наде́н. S⁶. семь. См. нада́.

надо́ ошікте. S⁵. Б. Медвѣдица (букв.
семь звѣздъ).

насу́н. S⁴. возрастъ. См. Фразы.

нана́. S¹⁰. кожа. Sch. nánna (C. A.
nanda, O. nandra, M. A. nantä, O. G.
nanta) Fell.

ꙗа́нсе. S⁵., ꙗа́нсе. S³., пі́нза. S⁴. носъ.
Однако Sch. (O.) наꙗꙗá Schmutz. См.
онꙗокто́.

ꙗара́ві бэjе́. S⁹. мущина. Castr. ꙗе-
rawi — Mann, Mannsperson.

на́рі. S⁷. солнце (дх.).

на́ран іненꙗі́. S⁹. ясный день.

---

[1]) На веревкахъ подвѣшивается къ бал-
камъ подъ крышей.

[1]) Ясно разслышалъ.

нарем. S⁶. пшено (кит. сяо-ми-цза 小米子).

нактырен.. S⁹. смѣяться. См iнактырен.

набан. S¹⁰., набан. S³. канъ (родъ теплыхъ наръ). Ман. нахан.

нахун. S⁸. зеленый. Ман. йохон.

небу́. S⁴. небун. S¹¹. младшiй братъ, (S¹¹. и младшая сестра). См. некун.

неелрене. S⁵. бояться. См. цаларiн.

неыкере. S⁵. маленькое зеркало на одеждѣ шамана.

нѐмо. S⁸. ящичекъ. Ср. Мк. нumur (СА.) корзина.

немкун. S⁹. тонкiй. Ср. Мк. nömkúkan (ВТ.) мелкiй.

(терега́) неабурiн. S¹¹. извощикъ. См. iабере.

нерыга́, нербга́. S¹¹. гречиха. Ср. Ман. мере — греча.

нѐрукте. S¹⁰. коса. См. нурiкте и нiруктэ.

нербга́. См. нерыга́.

некун. S³. S¹¹., небун. S¹¹, небу́. S⁴., нукiн. S⁶. младшiй братъ (S¹¹. и младшая сестра). Ср. Мк. nökun (М. ВТ.) младшiй братъ, младшая сестра; Sch. nókun...jüngere Schwester, nokunдimer (C. näkun)—jüngerer Bruder.

некте. S⁹. низкiй. Ср. Мк. näjamkukán (ВТ.) низкiй; Castr. naptar — niedrig.

нечiхун (дх.) унаżi. S⁴. дочь. См. унаżi.

нiмаурен. S¹⁰. ходить въ гости. Ср. Мк. нimor (ВТ.) гость.

нiмаżi. S⁸. сто. См. намаżi.

нiде. S³., S⁷., нiде. S⁶., нiдэ́. S¹. глаза (дх.).

нiнакiн. S¹⁰. собака. См. iнахi.

нiнгiн. S⁶., нiнгуй S⁷., нiнбо́. S⁴., нунгун. S⁸., нунбун. S¹¹. шесть. Ман. нiнгун; Sch. нuhun (WT. M. нunun, O. нunyn, O'. G. нungu, ningu) — sechs.

нiнгун бе. S⁴. 5-ая луна. Мк. нunbä (М.) iюль.

нiнбунгi. S⁴., нiнцу́. S⁶. S⁷. (Ман.), нуунбi. S¹¹., нунгунгi. S⁸. шестьдесятъ. Ср. Sch. нúhunżar (М. нunuнi, G. нungungu, O'. нungunżo, Mż. ninżu) neunzig (sechszig?).

нiнза. S⁴. носъ. См. нансе.

нiнцу́. S⁶. S⁷. шестьдесятъ. См. нiнбунгi.

нiруктэ. S¹⁰. волоса. См. нурiкте.

нiрубан. S⁴. рисунокъ (Ман.).

нiчукун (дх.) байта. S⁹. бездѣлица.

нойон. S⁴. S¹¹. господинъ (S⁴.), чиновникъ (дх.).

норба́. S⁴. кулакъ. Мк. nurga (М.) кулакъ, norga (М.) рука. См. нуруга́.

нобаргiн. S⁹. его.

Единственное число.

И.	(нѣтъ) S⁹. онъ ¹).
Р.	нобаргiн
Д. Т.	нобандун
В.	нобанман
П.	нобандукi.

Множественное число.

И.	(нѣтъ) S⁹. они ²).
Р.	тарiн
Д. Т.	тарiлдо
В.	тарiло
П.	тарiлдокi

нонгорiн. S¹¹. черный. См. коннорiн.

нуунбi. S¹¹. шестьдесятъ. См. нiнбунгi.

нуректе. S¹¹., нурiкте. S⁴., нурукто. S³.

*нурукте. S⁴., нерукте. S¹⁰. *нiрук-

---

1) Castrén даетъ нuнan.

2) У Castrén'a (стр. 22) соотвѣтствуетъ *tar* jener; множ. числ. *taril*, которое склоняется слѣдующимъ образомъ: G. tarilнi, D. tarildu, A. tarilwa (мое тарiло очевидно образовалось изъ tarilwó), Ab. tarilduk и т. д.

тэ̀. S^{10}. волоса (S^3., *S^4., *S^{10}), коса (S^{11}., S^4., S^{10}.)

нуругá. S^{11}. кулакъ. См. норѣá.

нукíн. S^6. младшій братъ. См. некýн.

н̇унѕу́н ѷе (бі). S^{11}. 6-ая луна.

нуӈгá. S^{11}., нунѣá. S^{10}. капуста. См. дх. ці̇ѣá ноѣа.

н̇унгу́н. S^8. шесть. См. нíнгу́н.

н̇унѕу́нгí. S^8. шестьдесятъ. См. нíн-ѕунгí.

н̇унѕу́н. S^{11}. шесть.

Ла. S^{11}. свѣчка (кит. 蠟).

ланту́. S^4. S^5. молотокъ (кит. лан-тоу 榔頭, ман. ланту́).

ло́бо. S^{11}. рѣдька (кит. 蘿蔔).

ло́за. S^4. лошакъ (кит. 騾子).

локко́л. S^{10}. (повелит. накл.). снимать платье. Ср. Мк. lukim раздѣваться; Sch. lúkkal — wirf fort.

ло̇нко́. S^{11}. горшокъ. Ман. лонко мѣдный котелокъ съ крышкой.

Р̇áкта. S^{10}. большая черная сосна. Ср. Ман. ѕáкдан.

ро́кто. S^{10}. сѣно. См. оро́кто.

Каjéр. S^{10}. красный. (У Sch. есть хаjéma, но значитъ: rein, xajakátten — er glänzt. Блестящій?).

каптаѕ́óн., S^{11}., каптусу́н. S^8. доска (дх., монг. хабтасун).

каптурѣá. S^8. кисетъ. См. хаптýрѣа.

кавáн. S^{10}. чиновникъ. См. хафáн.

катá. S^6, хатаѕáн. S^{10}. соль (дх.).

катуѕáн. S^{10}. дочка. Ср. Монг. хатун.

кадáла. S^8., хадáла. S^6., мо́рін ѕадалá. S^4. узда. См. дх.; Мк. kadál (M.) узда; Ман. хадала.

казáкъ. S^{10}. казакъ.

к̇áна. S^5. трава (дх.).

каньтáза. S^{10}. пальто (съ кит.).

кáлга. S^{10}. ворота, заборъ, хáлга. S^4. ворота (дх.).

карá. S^8., харá. S^2. черный (дх.).

карá мо́рін. S^{10}. вороная лошадь.

карто́шка. S^{10}. картофель (рус.).

какá. S^{10}. кошка. См. кеке́.

какарá. S^6. S^{10}. S^{11}. курица (S^6. и пѣтухъ) (дх.).

кемке́. S^{10}. S^{11}. огурецъ. Ман. хенке; Мк. хӧӈ̇ko, хуӈko (НА.) огурецъ; мѣстн. кит. хуанъ-го (= ванъ гуа 王瓜).

ке́се. S^9. указъ. Ман. хесе.

ке́лі. S^6. брюхо (дх.).

керачу́н укта́. S^{11}. сапоги[1]. См. унтá.

кеке́. S^6., какá. S^{10}., хе́хе. S^4. кошка. Ман. кесіке́.

кенгы́ре̇. S^4. грудь.

к̇е́ѕа. S^{11}. коробка (отъ кит. хэръ 盒兒, хэ-цза — коробка).

кообы́н. S^3., ко́бун. S^{10}. очагъ (кит. хо-пы́нь — жаровня 火盆).

коомуге́. S^{11}. шея. См. комогá, ко́ма.

ко́онді. S^{10}. земля (планета)(кит.?). Ср. Мк. koӈdan (M.) дыра.

ко́буӈ. S^{10}. очагъ.

ко́ма. S^4. комогá. S^{10}., коомуге́. S^{11}. шея. Мк. komaká. (M.) шея.

кото́. S^4. S^{11}. ножъ (дх., Монг. хутуга). Мк. koto (M.) ножикъ. Sch. (С. М. С̇.) тоже.

кото́н. S^{10}. городъ (дх.).

коннорíн. S^{10}., хоннорíн. S^4., S^{11}., ноӈгорíн. S^{11}. черный. Ср. Sch. koӈnṓmo (С. koӈnorin, M′. koӈnore, C′. kolnorin) — schwarz; Мк. хоӈnomo (BT.), hoӈnorin (M.) черный.

кочо́ро. S^1., ѕочо́ро. S^8., гочо́рі. S^6., хочо́ро. S^2. сапоги (дх.).

куалáн. S^8., кулáн (кулáн). S^4., хуáла. S^2. хуалы́н. S^5. хуáр. S^1. канъ (родъ теплыхъ наръ). Ср. Ман. хулан–дымовая труба[1]; Мк. kola (НА) труба.

куалíмпо. S^6., кулімпá. S^{11}. овесъ (дх.).

куахаӈ. S^{11}. сынъ. Sch. kuakán (= С̇.; kuӈâkan, WT. kuӈakán, O. koӈakan) Kind.

---

[1] Показалъ ему свои кожаные.

[2] Она, какъ извѣстно, проходитъ подъ каномъ и нагрѣваетъ его.

куіргі́н. S¹¹. цѣпочка ²).

куучі́. S¹¹. халатъ на ватѣ.

кумка́. S¹¹. вошь. Мк. kumka (ВТ. М.), kumkakan — вошь.

кутӡ́. S⁴. тридцать. См. ниже подъ г.

ку́де. S⁸., коудё. S⁴. мѣшокъ. Кит. кóу-дай 口袋.

ку́ді менеукéӏ. S¹⁰. таскать вещи. Ср. Sch. mannúkal — beschleunige. Кýді — мѣшокъ?

ку́ды. S¹¹. мѣшокъ. См. ку́де.

ку́ше. S¹¹. бакенбарды. Мк. kuʙa (М.) бакенбарды.

кунíн. S¹⁰. S¹¹. овца (СъМан.=Монг.).

кула́н (кула́н). S¹¹. канъ. См. куала́н.

кулерéне. S⁵. лежать. Мк. hukulaӡöm (ВТ.) лежать.

ку́лí. S⁶. нога (дх.).

кулíмпа́. S¹¹. овесъ. См. куалíмпо.

(тергáн) курду́. S⁵. колесо (дх.). Ман. кӯрдун.

кузí. S¹¹. курительная свѣча (дх.).

каі-дáу. S¹¹. поѣхалъ верхомъ (кит.?).

коімáлі. S⁹. безразсудный. Ман. коімáлі лживый, хитрый; коімáлі уӡ-гучáнен. S⁹. безразсудно говорить.

коудé. S⁴. мѣшокъ. См. ку́де.

Гадáн. S¹⁰. купить. Sch. gadám (= WT., A. gadum, O. garem, C. gam) nehmen, erhalten.

гашкáн. S⁶. собака. Мк. kaćikan (ВТ., М.) щенокъ; Sch. kačikán — Kätzchen.

гандӳ́. S¹¹. огниво. Мк. gandy (М.) огниво.

галé. S¹., гáрі. S⁶., гарí. S⁷. рука. См. нáла.

гáга. S¹., гáӊа. S⁶. свинья (дх.).

гахáӏ. S¹⁰. возьми. См. гадáн. Ман. гаімбí, пов. гаӈу́.

гетӡӳ́н. S⁵., гедыӊéн. S¹¹., геӊігé. S⁸., гектé. S³. коса. См. дх., Мк. gadykän (М.), gödykän (М.) коса.

гéшан. S⁶., гéшен. S⁸. дверь, двери

(внутреннія S⁸). Кит. гӡ-шань 隔 扇 — перегородка (съ дверью).

генерéн. S¹⁰. ходить. Ман. генембí.

герібé. S⁴. имя. См. Фразы. Также гéрбу. S⁸. S¹⁰. герібé áці онӡá. S³. 4-ый (безъимянный) палецъ.

гектé. S³. ⎫
геӊігé. S². S⁸. ⎬ коса. См. гетӡӳ́н.

гідá. S⁹. копье (= Ман.). Мк. gida (ВТ., М., СА.) копье.

гіӏтерíн. S⁴. бѣлый. Castr. 134 (III) giltalli — weiss.

гіӏтарíн шатáн. S⁴. бѣлый сахаръ.

гінгулéрен. S⁹. почитать. Ман. гінгулембí.

госíн S⁶. тридцать (Ман. гусíн).

госірéн. S⁹. любить. Ман. госімбí.

госíре бэйé. S⁹. любящій человѣкъ (Ман.).

госікáр. S⁹. люби.

гоно́м. S⁹. длинный. Sch. gonomnak— vorübergehend; Ман. голмíн; Castr. ŋonim (83), ŋonnom (127, II) — lang.

гóлі. S⁴. мѣдь. См. гаолí.

гóлі. S⁶. рѣка (дх.).

горó. S⁹. далеко, -ій. Мк. goro (ВТ.) далеко. Sch. также.

горолó генерéн. S⁹. вверхъ ходить. Castr. gorolo — weit, fern.

гочóрі. S⁷. сапоги. См. кочóро.

гутíн. S¹¹. тридцать. Мк. gutin (М.). 30.

гудé. S⁴., гудегé. S¹⁰. брюхо (дх.).

гу́се. S¹¹. сундукъ. Мк. guʙa (М.) ящикъ (съ кит.).

гусíн. S⁶. тридцать (Ман.).

гулí(н). См. мáіʙа гулíн. Ср. ӊолó.

гурурéн. S⁹. S¹¹. понимать.

гуруцá. S⁹. понялъ (Ман. улхиха), асíн гуру́рен S⁹. не понимаешь ли (сі улхірахун), гурурекí S⁹. если понимаешь (улхіці), гуруӡéр унéн S⁹. желаю понимать (улхікі сембі); асíн гуру́рен, аӊíн гуруру́ — см. еще подъ асíн, аӊíн.

гургáкта. S⁴., гурӊактá. S¹⁰. S¹¹. бо-
рода, усы (S¹⁰. S¹¹). Sch. gurgákta
(= WT., M. gurgaktá, O′. goigakta,
G. goǵakta) Bart, Schnurrbart.

гугдá. S⁹. высокій. Sch. gúgda (=
WT., M. gugda Höhe, O. gutgai
Wuchs, Höhe) — hoch.

гáолі. S¹¹. мѣдь. См. гӧлі. Мк. gawli
(М.) желтая мѣдь (дх.).

гáолі зіӊá. S¹¹. мѣдныя деньги.

гóу морíн. S⁴. кобыла (Ман.=Монг.).

(Морíн)ӊадалá. S⁴. узда. См. кадáла.

ӊіптéн. См. цакты, ӟакты.

ӊоты́н. S⁸. тридцать. См. гутíн.

мáіза (кит.) ӊолó. S⁴. мука. См. гулíн.

ӊочóро. S⁸. сапоги. См. кочóро.

ӊургí. S⁸. пряжка на поясѣ (Ман. =
Монг.). Мк. gurgi (М.) пряжка.

Хабтергé. S¹¹. хаптуръӊа. S⁴., кап-
туръӊá. S⁸. кисетъ. Мк. xapturga
(М.) кошель для табаку.

хафáн. S⁴. S⁸. чиновникъ (Ман.).

хафасáр (хапсáл). S⁹. чиновники.

И. хафасáр, хапсáл S⁹.
   чиновники.

Р. хафасангí

Д. Т. хафасалдý.

В. хафасалвó

П. хафасалдукí

хамырá. S²., хамы́р. S¹. S⁶, хамурí.S⁴.
носъ (дх.).

хатаӊáн. S¹⁰. соль. См. катá.

хадáла. S⁶. узда. См. кадáла.

ханнáран. S¹⁰. брить голову. Ср. Мк.
kaŋnadäm (ВТ.) рѣзать.

хáлга. S⁴. ворота (дх.).

харá. S². черный. См. карá.

хаці́ра. S³. щеки.

хéхе. S⁷. жена (Ман.), S⁴. кошка. См.
кекé.

хотон-дé ценегéр. S⁹. отправляюсь
въ городъ, Ман. genembí. См. генерéн.

хóні. S¹. S⁶., хоні́. S⁴. S⁷. овца (Ман. =
Монг.).

хоннорíн. S⁴. S¹¹. черный. См. коннорíн.

хорó. S⁶. палецъ (дх.).

хочорó. S². сапоги. См. кочóро.

хуáла. S²., хуалы́н. S⁵., хуáр. S¹. канъ.
См. куалáн.

хуáина. S⁸. сѣверъ (дх.).

хýнзу. S⁸. зола (дх.).

хýнку. S⁸. кусокъ холста, платокъ.
См. умкý.

хулá. S²., хулáн. S⁸. красный (дх.,
монг. улáн).

хулíн. S⁸. мука (дх.). См. гулíн.

хáоле. S⁶. греча, гречиха (по кит. цяо-
май 蕎麥) (дх.).

Ӊгáла. S¹⁰., S¹¹., нгáла. S⁴. рука. См.
нáла.

цаларíн. S⁹., неелрéне. S⁵. бояться.
Ср. Sch. naleukátten (С. nåläm) —
er setzt in Furcht.

цáрін богó. S⁹. ясное небо. Ср. нáран
інеңӊí.

Чамчá. S¹⁰., чамцá. S¹¹. рубаха. См.
цамцí. Ман. чамцí, Монг. цамца.

чáдінку. S¹⁰. чашка. См. чáчуху.

чáшун. S¹⁰. бумага. См. цасýн.

чáшкі нгеекéл. S¹⁰. перейти черезъ
рѣку. Sch. časki (WT., M. časi) da-
hin; Мк. časki omä (ВТ.) подви-
гаться, приближаться. Ср. еще у
Sch. neéko — плоскій раздолъ.

чáза. S⁶. бумага. См. цасýн.

чалбáн. S¹⁰. береза. Sch. čálban (=
WT., Midd.; Mӟ. calfa) Birke.

чарпý. S¹⁰. куайдза. См. сарпó.

чакý. S¹., чáку. S¹⁰, чахý. S³. S⁸. чайникъ (кит. См. стр. 20 уілчóне.).

чанкó. S¹⁰. окно (кит. чуáнъ-ху 窗戶).

чачарáн. S⁹. убѣжать. Ср. Ман. су-
цумбі, Мк. hućahinam (ВТ.) убѣжать.

чачачá бэjé. S⁹. убѣжавшій человѣкъ, бѣглецъ.

чáчун. S¹¹. бумага. См. цасýн.

чáчуӈу. S⁵. S⁸., чáчуху. S⁴., чáчеку, S¹¹., чáдiнку. S¹⁰. чашка (чайная) (дх.).

чекалáу. S¹⁰. хорошая погода.

чечiӈý (чочоӈý?). S⁵., чечугá. S¹¹. плеть, кнутъ. См. чíчуга.

чечуӈá (—гá). S¹⁰. доска (плетка?) ¹).

чíбкéза. S¹. жилетъ (по кит. каньдянь-цза).

чíмеркí. S⁸. мизинецъ. См. цíмiткí.

iнí чiсýи. S⁹. самовольно, самъ собой (Ман.).

чiкí. S¹. S²., цiкé. S⁷. уши (дх.).

чiгéн-мурéн. S¹⁰. мочиться. Мк. ćikönäm (ВТ.) мочиться. См. цiӊенéн. Cast. ɫikänäm — pissen.

чíгелтéн. S¹⁰. penis.

чiӈá. S²., чiӈáн. S⁸. бѣлый (дх.).

чíчугá. S⁴., чечiӈý. S⁵., чечугá. S¹¹. плетка. Мк. ćićuga, ćaćuga (М., СА) кнутъ.

чолпýн. S⁵. созвѣздіе. Мк. ćolpon (M.) Венера (планета).

чоɫчохý. S⁵. поперечныя жерди на крышѣ.

чогдонó. S¹⁰. спина. Sch. sogdönno (C. sogdondo, M. sogdono) Rücken.

чоӈá. S³. войско. Ман. чооха.

чоӊӈó. S⁵. окно. См. чонкó.

чонкó. S¹⁰. свинья.

чонкó, S¹¹., чуáнху. S⁴. окно (кит.).

чубулáкта. S¹⁰. мыть лицо.

чýка. S¹⁰. трава. Sch. čúka (C. cŭka) Gras.

чуӈутурíн. S¹¹. синій. См. слѣдующее.

чуӈурíн. S⁴. зеленый. Ср. Мк. čuturin (M.) зеленый.

чаi. S⁶. S¹⁰. чай. Мк. ćai (ВТ.) чай.

чоiдогó. S⁴. мизинецъ. См. цíмiткí.

Чаӈулын. S⁵. чумичка, плетеная поварёшка.

чiнзó. S⁴. перецъ (кит. цинь-цзяо 秦椒).

---

¹) Одинъ изъ присутствовавшихъ плеткой ударилъ по кану, чтобы лучше разъяснить, о чемъ спрашиваю (канъ забранъ досками). Но S¹⁰. стоялъ на своемъ, что не плетка, а доска.

Цамцí. S⁷. халатъ. См. чамчá. Мк. ćamča (M.) верхній покрой.

цасýн. S⁴., чáшун. S¹⁰., чáчун. S¹¹., чáза. S⁶. бумага (дх.).

царáткi. S¹¹. 4-ый палецъ. Мк. ćaratkin (M.) безъимянный палецъ. Castr. XIV (Gerstf.) ćerapki — der vierte Finger.

цéнцi. S⁶. халатъ. См. цамцí.

цíмiткí. S¹¹., чíмеркí. S⁸., чоiдогó. S⁴. мизинецъ. Мк. čimitkin (M.) мизинецъ, Castr. XIV (Gerstf.) ćemitki — der kleine Finger.

цíза. S⁴. флагъ (кит. ци-цза 旗).

цiкэ́. S⁷. ухо, уши. См. чíкí.

цiӊенéн. S¹¹. мочиться. См. чiгéн мурéн.

цугé. S⁴. топоръ. См. сýку.

цуí-дéӈ. S⁶., S¹¹. спички (кит.).

Ца. S⁴. десять. См. цан.

цаарá. S⁵. шапка шаманская.

цабкéн. S⁶., цабкó. S⁴. восемь. См. ниже.

цабкорінӈí. S⁴. восемьдесятъ. См. ниже.

цабкýн. S⁸., ӟабкýн. S¹¹. восемь. См. цабкéн. Sch. ӟарkún (C. ӟarkún) — acht. См. ниже.

цабкунгí. S⁸. восемьдесятъ. См. ӟабхунгí. S¹¹.

цабхýн. S⁷. восемь. Ман. цакун.

цабхуӈӈý. S⁷. восемьдесятъ. Ман. цакунцу. См. цакаӊцýн.

цан. S⁸. S⁹. десять. См. ӟан, цуан. Мк. ӟän (ВТ., М.) десять. Castr. ӟân — zehn. Ман. цуван (цуан).

цан амó. S⁴., цан емýн. S⁸. одиннадцать.

цан цур. S⁴. двѣнадцать.

цан тороӊӈá. S⁸., цан тангýн. S⁶. пятнадцать.

ӟай ӟiрӈéi. S⁹. десять разъ.

цалбарáн. S⁹. молиться (Ман.=Монг.).

(мíні) цакá. S⁷. (мои) вещи (Ман.).

цакаӊцýн. S⁶. восемьдесятъ. См. выше.

цакты́ џі́бте́. S⁵.S⁸., цакты́ џібте́н.S⁴.,
цакты зібке́. S³. џо̏бте́н. S¹⁰. ѣсть.
См. подъ з. Ман. џембі (прич. џетере). Мк. з̌äptilä (ВТ.) пища; з̌а-
buŋnam (ВТ.) ѣсть; Sch. з̌ébkol,
з̌apkol — iss, з̌aptile Essen.
џакда́. S¹⁰. сосна. Ман. џакдан. Sch.
з̌agdá (M. WT. з̌ágda, C. зagda,
dágda) Fichte.
џага́. S¹⁰. чохъ (мѣдная монета). Ман.
зіха; Мк. ćаха (M.) монета.
џаџі.̏подбородокъ. Ср. Мк. з̌ögі (ВТ.)
нижняя челюсть.
џаџуй̏ бе.S⁴.8-ая луна. Ман. џакун̏ба.
џергі, зірџе́. S⁹. степень, разъ.
џібте́н. См. џакты́ —.
џіџа́. S². S⁴. чохъ. См. џага́.
џіџунџə́. S⁵. востокъ. Буквально это
должно значить лѣвый, лѣвая сторо-
на¹). См. Sch. з̌ögу́nnida...O. з̌ägun-
da — linkshin. Мк. з̌ägin böіjä (M.)
лѣвая сторона, даже з̌ägäntäki (M.)
сѣверъ. См. зеџінгіде́.
џо̏бте́н. S¹⁰. ѣсть, обѣдать. См. џакты́
и подъ з.
џō̏. S⁷. два. См. џуо.
џоана́н. S⁹. думать. Мк. з̌aldam (ВТ.),
з̌äldäm думать. Ман. џобомбі.
џоло́. S⁸. S¹⁰., џо̏ло S⁴. ²) камень (дх.).
Sch. з̌olo (M.) Stein.
џу. S⁴. џӯ. S³.S⁷. домъ. Sch. з̌u (M. C.
з̌ӯ, O. đu, A. đo) Zelt, Jurte.
џула́н енуре́н. S³. вернуться домой. См. з̌у.
џуа́н, џаѝ.S⁶.десять.См. выше и ниже.
џуа́н̏ бе. S⁴. S¹⁰. 10-ая луна. Ман.
џуан̏ба.
џуа́н, џаѝ емы́н. S⁶. одинадцать.
џу́о. S³. два (Ман.).
џу́о̏ бе. S⁴. S¹¹. 2-ая луна. Ман.
џу́о (џуве)̏ба.

---

1) Китайцы и др. югъ считаютъ перед-
ней стороной.
2) А џоло́ по нему солнце. Очевидно
онъ спуталъ китайскія слова шѝ-тоу (камень) съ жѝ-тоу (солнце) и не хотѣлъ со-
знаться, хотя многіе разъясняли ему.

џуванџі ана́. S⁹. 10-ый годъ (Ман.).
џуѝ. S⁷. десять. См. выше.
џуѝ ему. S⁷. одиннадцать.
џула́н енуре́н. S⁸. вернуться домой.
См. џу.
џулілé. S⁸. западъ.
џуѕл̏лé. S⁵. югъ. Ман. џулергі — передній, южный. См. з̌улеіл̏á.
џу́р. S⁴., џу́ру. S⁴., S⁶. два. Мк. з̌џrä
(ВТ.), з̌џг (M.) два. Ман. џуру —
пара. См. з̌ур.
џуруџу́н̏ бе. S⁴. 12-ая луна. Ман.
џоргон̏ба. См. з̌уръџу́н̏бе.
(џаџá) џугутта́н. S¹⁰. мѣнять (деньги).
џугутте́н. S¹⁰. смѣяться.
з̌абку́н. S¹¹. восемь. См. подъ џ.
з̌абхунгі́. S¹¹. восемьдесятъ.
з̌ан (џа́н). S¹¹. десять. См. подъ џ.
з̌ан ему́н. S¹¹. одинадцать.
з̌алі́. S⁹.¹) мысль. Sch. з̌ali (C. з̌ali,
М з̌. gali, WT. з̌aldam—ich denke)
Verstand; Мк. з̌äldäm думать.
з̌áкта. S¹⁰. каша, ѣда. См. џакты́.
з̌áкты џіпте́н. S¹¹. ѣсть.
з̌áхуѝ бе.S¹¹. 8-ая луна. Ман. џакун
̏ба.
зеџінгіде́. S⁹. лѣвый. См. џіџунџə́.
Мк. з̌äginin (M.), з̌ägŋynidab (ВТ.)
лѣвый, Sch. з̌ögу́nnida....linkshin.
зібте́н. S⁹. ѣсть. См. џакты́.
зібтере́ џака́. S⁹. съѣстные припасы. Ман. џетере џака.
зібке́. S⁹. ѣшь. Sch. з̌apkol, з̌éb-
kol — iss.
зібча́. S⁹. ѣлъ.
зібџа́. S⁷. шуба. Ман. зібча.
з̌оло́. S¹¹. камень. См. џоло́.
з̌у (џ̏у). S¹⁰. S¹¹. домъ. См. џу.
з̌улеіл̏á. S⁹. югъ. См. џулл̏é
з̌улџу́џу бэіjé. S⁹. передній.
з̌ур (џур) jамáзі. S¹¹. двѣсти. См.
џур и німáзі.
з̌уръџу́н̏ бе. S¹¹. 12-ая луна. См. џу-
руџу́н̏ бе.

---

1) Въ монг. з̌ali значитъ: обманъ, фо-
кусъ; мечта.

2. СПИСОКЪ ДАХУРСКИХЪ СЛОВЪ.

аїнцíн (аӈцíн). D¹. госпожа.

áïлe. D². деревня. Монг. аіл, аїл.

аíлђа. D². выговоръ, произношеніе.

ajá некдáу. D². ахать. Ajá — ахъ!, некжау, несомнѣнно, нéке одинъ и дау — Монг. дагу, дӯ — голосъ.

áбе. D². есть, находится. Монг. аху.

неïђендé¹) ула-абíлéн. D². безпрерывный.

абкí. D². мухогонка. Ср. арпукý. S¹⁰.

áма. D². D⁴. ротъ. Монг. аман, ама.

áмала. D³. спокойный, безмятежный. Монг. амугулаӊ, амур.

амíнá какарá. D⁶. пѣтухъ. Ср. Ман. амíла — самецъ птицъ.

áмо. См. некцí áмо таċéн уђéі.

амун-кý. D⁶. женщина. Монг. емеген –+– ку (кӯмӯн).

амбáн. D⁴. амбáнь, генералъ (Ман.).

адáзу, адóзу. D⁶. дуракъ.

адáн. См. неïрé уђéі уантаѕí адáн. Монг. јадáн.

асíребé. См. дотóн асíребé.

асóбе. D². спрашивать. Монг. асагуху, асакху.

бі ᴨамáда асооіjá. D². я у тебя спрошу.

асулебé. См. пословицы (1-ая).

ашíк. D². дядя. Ман. ецíке, есхен — младшій братъ отца.

áӈа (Ман.) сáра. ⎱ D⁴. 1-ая луна. Монг.
анé (Ман.) сáра. ⎰ сара.

анађáн сартé-хон. D². высокосный годъ. Ман. анаган (-і ба высокосная луна), сартé — Монг. саратаі имѣющій луну (высокосную), хон — годъ (Монг. он).

аӈдабé. D². жить. Ср. аѕабіці (Фразы).

аӈдáне. D². пѣтухъ.

¹) Монг. нігенде-улу.

алабéі терых (терыђе). D². казенная телѣга. Монг. албан-у терге(н).

аларцíці цíрлце іцíѕі алалцібé. D². воевать. Монг. алалцаху убивать другъ друга, сражаться.

алíбé. D². принимать. Ман. алімбí.

албé газíр. D². казенное, присутственное мѣсто. Монг. албан-у газар.

албé герí. D². казенный домъ.

албýгетé саïдабé сардінгí. D⁴. сторожъ при станціонномъ домѣ (по мѣсти. кит. кань-фаръ-ды-лаотýръ). 1-ое слово по Монг. албан-у гер-те, 2-ое сакіцу аху; 3-ье происходитъ отъ Ман. сакда старый (съ частицей ніӈге).

áлта. D⁴. золото (Монг.).

аѕíбé. D². мѣнять. Монг. аралціху.

арá. D⁴. ахъ!

аракын. D². спина. Монг. ару. См. аркáн.

арігі. D⁴. водка, ханшина. Монг. аракí, арікі, Ман. аркí.

арба. D⁹. овесъ. Монг. арбаі, Ман. арфа.

арса. D³. кожа. Монг. арасу.

аркáн. D². спина. См. аракын.

арђí чомó. D². бокалъ. См. арігі, чомо Ман. слово.

арчó аудебé. D². боль (болитъ?) подъ ложечкой.

арцібé. D³. брать (áрці — бери). Монг. арчіху стирать, вытирать, но здѣсь очевидно отъ абцáху (абчі ірекý) уносить, брать.

акá. D². D⁴. старшій братъ (Монг.).

акóро. D²., акорó. D⁴. штаны. Ман. факурí.

ађá (акá). D⁴. старшій братъ.

ᴣіӊа́ уӊе́і аӷа́са. D². безденежье. 1-ое
слово Ман. 2-ое и 3-ье (= аксан)
Монг.

а́нга. D². балаганъ¹).

ача́. D². D⁴. D⁶. отецъ. Монг. ечіге.

ачіцан. D⁶. мышь. Ср. Мк. асікісан
(М.) мышь.

аці́рᴣі ваᴣі́ре (-рсе́н прош. вр.). D².
вводить. Монг. ачараху привести.

аᴣі́рсын уӊе́і D². безвредный.

Еме́ле D⁶. сѣдло. Монг. емегел, емёл.

еме́ге (емы́х). D⁴., емы́ге. D². женщина, жена. Монг. емеген.

еміне́ какара́. D⁶. курица. Ман. емі-
ле самка птицъ.

емы́і пусы́ле. D². аптека. Мон. ем-
ун, емыӊ; Ман. пуселі отъ кит. пу-
цза 鋪子 лавка.

емы́не. D². передній, югъ. Монг.
емуне. См. емы́ін.

емы́не бе́jе́де (Ман.) а́бе. D². впереди. А́бе находиться.

емы́ін бо́і. D³. югъ. Бо́і=бе́jе́(Ман.
=Монг.)=боӷа́(сол.)=ба(Ман.).

емы́ге. D². жена. См. еме́ге.

емуӷу́нху. D². баба. Монг. емеген +
хун (хӱмӱн).

ете́ муда́н, ете́нек муда́н. D². впервые. Ман. емте, мудан.

таіта́і (кит.) ете́ӊу (ете́у). D². бабка.

му́рі еделге́бе́. D⁴. переправиться
черезъ рѣку. Монг. мурен, гетӱлкӱ.

е́се. D³. эти (Ман.=Монг.).

есу́ру. D⁴. мести.

е́не. D³. этотъ (Монг.).

И.   е́не D³. этотъ

Р.   нѣтъ²)

Д. Т. ененде́

В.   еныjу́

П.   ене́су

---

1) У Маака упоминаются лѣтники —
хомара́-ангхо́.

2) См. примѣчаніе къ те́ре.

И.   е́де D³. эти

Р.   нѣтъ¹)

Д. Т. еды́нде

В.   едынсолбі

П.   едыне́се

е́не гаᴣі́р. D². здѣсь, въ этой мѣстности (Монг.).

е́недуру́. D³. сегодня. Монг. ене-
дур, ене едур.

енде́. D². здѣсь (Монг.).

Бі енда́беі. Я здѣсь. Монг. енде́,
аху.

ендыі́ре. D⁶. иди сюда. Монг.
енде, іре.

еӊдурі́. D⁷. богъ (Ман.).

ендугу́. D⁶ яйцо. Мон. ӱндӱгӱн, ӱн-
дӱген.

(бі) енкулце́бе. D². (я) ожидаю, буду
ждать²).

еле́ге баі́бе́. D². навѣстить, явиться
къ начальству³). Ман. елхе баімбі.

еле́ге баі́пі. D². явлюсь, иначе —
елегебаіjа́. D².

еле́ге баісе́н. D². явился по начальству.

елеӷе́ уӊе́і. D². безпокойный. Ман.
елхе.

ерегы̄і̇. D². быкъ (букв. самецъ отъ
ере?).

ердебе́. См. ердеᴣі́. Монг. ебдекӱ раз
рушать, ломать.

ерде́м уwе́і (уӊе́і). D². бездарный
(Монг.).

ерде́м укуці уӊе́і. D². безсильный.
Монг. хуцун.

ердесы́н уwе́і. D². безвредный. Монг.
ебдереші угеі.

---

1) См. примѣчаніе къ те́ре.

2) Монг. кӱліекӱ, Ман. ереме гунім-
бі, ерехунцембі.

3) Кит. цинъ-ань 請安.

ердезі даі́ дасазі ҕíбе. D². возобновлять. Монг. ебде(ре)кӱ, даі́ снова, Ман. дасамбі, кіку̅ (Монг. дѣлать).

ердыртéн (ередыртéн) бурí. D². ветошка. Монг. ебдерекӱ, бу̅рі.

ергу́нку, ерҕу́н. D². мущина. 2-ое слово монг. ере + ху̅н (человѣкъ), 1-ое удвоенная форма.

ерчу́. D²., D⁶., ерчу D⁴. грудь. Монг. ебчіҕу̅н.

экѐ. D⁴. старшая сестра. Монг. еке мать.

éкці. D². старшая сестра. Мон. егечі.

ецы́ге, ачá. D⁴. отецъ. Мон. еціге.

еҕéн бáіта ісікéу чаоϕáҕ герí. D². тронная (букв. зало, въ которой Государь правитъ дѣла). 1-ое слово Ман. = Монг., 2-ое Ман., 3-ье Ман. іціхамбі (-ра), 4-ое кит. 朝房, 4-ое Мон. гер.

еҕелесéн. D³. Прош. время отъ еҕелебé овладѣть (Ман. = Монг.).

Эмѐлэ. D²., D⁴. сѣдло. См. емéле.

эмы́н. D². См. емы́не.

Сí ордó (эмы́н) jáҕу. D². ты впередъ поѣзжай. Монг. урíда, jабу.

Эці у́ле гуáҕла. D². ни во что не входить. Монг. jун-чí (jагун-чу), улу; кит. гуань 管.

Ызíн. D⁴. царь.

ызíн хотóн. D⁴. столица. Монг. езен, хотон.

Іу́ санá ҕоҕубéі. D². безпокоиться. Монг. санá, зобаху

імá. D². козелъ. Монг. jамáн, Ман. німан.

(бі) ідебéі. D⁶. (я) хочу ѣсть. Монг. ідеку.

(бáіта) ісікí ҕаабé. D². (велѣть?) заниматься дѣломъ. Ман. баіта, іціхамбі. Ҕаабé. D². сказать, Монг. ҕакіку.

ішікен ҕéза. D². блюдечко. Монг. уҕухен (маленькій), ҕеза кит. слово (см. стр. 26).

íза. D². мыло (кит., см. стр. 19).

íҕці таҕдé. D⁵. барабанъ.

ілáці (Ман. ¹) хорó. D⁴. 4-ый палецъ. Монг. хуругу(н).

іреҕéн. D². народъ. Ман. ірген.

ічібé. D⁶. ходить. Монг. ечіху. Прош. вр. іҕісéн. D¹.

іцікен бáіта (Ман.). D². бездѣлица. См. ішікен — маленькій.

санá (Монг.) іҕцí. D². какъ удобно. Ман. іці — согласно.

Оí хорó. D². указательный палецъ. Отъ оïбé. D². шить.

оïбé. D². шить. Монг. оjуху.

оjу́нго уҕéі. D². бездѣлица. Ман. оjонго важный.

(бі) ó̅баі. S⁶. (я) хочу пить. Монг. у̅ху.

ómo. См. мáо ómo. Монг. ем — лекарство.

но óмоло (Ман.). D². внукъ. Но мальчикъ.

омпáбаі. D⁴. мыться. Ср. Ман. обомбі.

отáчі. D⁴. дѣдъ. Въ Монг. отачі, оточі лекарь. См. сол. утáці.

óсо. D². вода. См. óзо. Монг. усу́н.

óсо баціꙗдéн. D². вода закипѣла. Монг. буцалху.

óсо гуꙗáн газíр. D². бродъ. Монг. гуіхун мелкій.

óзо. D⁴. D⁶. вода. См. óсо.

(мóрі) оносóн. D². верховой. Монг. унуху ѣздить верхомъ.

(мóрі) óнді ²) jаубé. D⁴. (ѣздить) верхомъ. Дѣепр. отъ онобé.

óнчі. D⁶. ножикъ. См. óнці.

óнпі. D⁴., óнцы. D². ножъ. См. сл. уꙗчí.

óлозо. D⁶. конопля. Ман. оло, Монг. у̅лу̅су̅н.

орібé. D². визжать (Ман.=Монг.).

ороокóꙗ. D². къ вечеру. Ср. широнгольское (Пот. II, 411) орей, орой вечеръ. Монг. ороі поздно, -ій.

óрто. D². D³. длинный. Монг. урту.

---

1) третій.

2) Отчасти звучало какъ óнці.

ордо́. D². прежде, напередъ. Монг.
уріда.

ордоні̨і́. D³. прежній. Монг. уріда́кі.

о́ркі. D². легкія. Монг. агушкі, калм.
öшкі; ср. Мк. öpta (ВТ.) легкое.

о́кі, окі́. D⁴. голова (о́кі), черепъ (по
кит. нао-дай—окі́). Монг. окі вер-
хушка.

(на́ра) уанобе́і бо́ї́. D³. западъ (букв.
сторона, въ которой спитъ солнце).
Монг. унтаху.

уа́за. D⁸. чулки. Кит. ва-цза (См. стр.
24).

уі̄мбе́. D⁴. 9-ая луна. Ман. уjу́н ба.

уі́п. D². дочь. См. уҧі́н.

уі́н омоло́ (Ман.) D². внучка.

уі̇̄н-ду́. D⁴., уі́н до́у (дӯ). D². младшая сестра. Монг. дегу, дў; Ман.
доу.

уі́н ко́уке. D⁴. дочь. Монг. хўхен.

уі̄нсі́н бе. D⁴. 11-ая луна. Ман. омшон ба.

(а́лта) 'уі̄ло́у (веі̄ло́у) газі́р. D². золотые пріиски. Ман. веілембі —
работать.

уо̄ (уо̄беі). D². пить. См. о́баі. Монг.
ӯху.

(да́нҕа) уобе́ (-бе́і). D⁴. курить
(табакъ).

уоре́. D³. самъ. Монг. ўбер.

уоре́ іцісе́н (іцібе́). D³. самъ пошелъ (пойду).

уе́іле. D². преступленіе (Ман. ве́іле).

уе́іле нецісе́н (-бе́). D². беззакон-
ничалъ. Ман. нечімбі.

(бі не) уеі̄тебе́. D³. (я) беззаконничаю (не — теперь — Ман. сл.).

уеілете́. D². беззаконничать (повел.
накл.).

у́беі. D⁶. умереть. Монг. ўкўў.

у́бутуру. D¹. глупый.

ута́ці D². дѣдушка. См. ота́чі.

уту́ма. D²., уты́ма. D⁴. хлѣбъ. Калм.
öтмöк. Ср. Пот. II, 421 Сч. итими́.

уту́м ҕі̨ҕу ху. D². булочникъ.

(букв. человѣкъ дѣлающій хлѣбъ).
Монг. хіхў, кікў.

уду́р. D⁶. день. Монг. еду́р, ўду́р.

уду́р туала́н. D³. ежедневно, каждый день (Монг. едур бурі, едур
тотом). Монг. тала — по.

усу̣ъзібе́. D²., усу̣ъзібе. D². говорить. См. узгу̣ъці.

усу̣ъзі, сі(=ты) усу̣ъзі. D². говори.

бі усу̣ъзіjа́. D³. я буду говорить.

усу(гу)ъзі. D³. говори¹) (Ман. гісуре), бу усу(гу)ъзі́. D³. не говори
(уме гісуре), усу(гу)ъзісе́н D³. говорилъ (гісурехе), усугу̣ъзіво
а́сан D³. говаривалъ (гісурембі-
хе), усугу̣ъзісе́н а́сан D³. прежде
говорилъ (гісурехе біхе), усугу̣ъ-
зісе́н ку D³. говорившій человѣкъ (гісурехе на́лма), усугу̣ъ-
зітеха́і ці̨е́ D³. хотя говорилъ
(гісуреці́бе), усугу̣ъзіjа D³. буду
говорить (гісуреці́), усугу̣ъзіў
уве́і D³. не говорю (гісуреракy),
усугу̣ъзісе́н D³. если говорю (гі-
суреці), усугу̣ъзіjа́ елбе́і D³. хочу
говорить (гісуреці́ сембі).

усу́гу. D². слово. Монг. ўсўк буква,
шрифтъ.

усу́гу у́су̣ъці́бе́і. D⁴. говорить.

усу̣ъў барзі (монг. барі̨ці) на́даъ-
зі (-бе́). D². балясничать. Монг.
нагадху, нагадулцаху.

ушхі́н хоро́. D⁴. мизинецъ. Монг.
ўцўхен. См. ішікен.

узгу̣ъці́. D⁸., узгу̣ъці-бе́і. D⁶. говорить. Ср. усу́гу усу̣ъці́бе́і.

у́мо. D². тетка.

уні́н. D⁶. корова. Ман. унен, Монг.
унӗ.

унӗ-су. D⁶., уні́-су́. D⁴. молоко.
Монг. сў(н).

уннако́ танімо́к (ку́). D². безжалостный (человѣкъ).

улаҕі́н. См. кўбу улаҕі́н.

улаҕу́. См. зіҕа́ улаҕу́.

1) См. стр. 8—9, VII.

у́ле. D². не, нѣтъ. Монг. улу.

уребу́р, урубу́р. См. каоцін уребу́р чоӊа́.

урубу́ре меı́н. D². учебная команда. Ман. уребуре мејен.

уры́м. D⁴. масло. Монг. ӯру́ме жареныя пѣнки.

укоцı́у. См. укуцібе́, терегу́ле укоцı́у хаФан.

уку́ узіде́. D¹. показывать. Монг. ӱкку́ давать, ӱзеку́ смотрѣть.

укуру. D⁴. D⁶., уку́р. D⁸. быкъ, корова (D⁴.). Монг. ӱкер, ӱхӱр.

укуцібе́. D². отослать, провожать.

угéи. D². D⁶., уӊéи, уӊеі D². D³., уwéи. D³. не, нѣтъ (Монг. ӱгеи).

угı́, уӊı́н. D⁶. дѣвица. Монг. укін, ухін.

уӊé. D⁶. слово. Монг. ӱге.

уӊу́ле, уӊе́ле¹). D². зима. Монг. ебул, ӱбӱл.

учı́кен (ушхы́н). D⁶., ішı́кен, іцı́кен. D². малый. Мон. ӱцухен.

у́зі саı́н. D². первостепенный. Ман. уӊуі первый, саı́н хорошій (Ман.= Монг.).

узібе́. D². смотрѣть, видѣть. Монг. ӱзеку́.

узı́ (узé). D¹. глядѣть (пов. накл.).

узı́зі саібе́. D². блюсти. См. саӊіӊу́ (охранять).

Аісіла́ра. D². писарь (букв. помощникъ). Ман. аісіламбı́ (—ра́ прич.).

а́іле. D⁶. деревня. Монг. аіл. аı̆л.

аб. D⁴. мать. См. еуо́, эуэ́.

а́оре. D¹. каменистая гора. См. аула. Ср. сол. уре.

а́у. D². широкій, въ ширину. См. сол. аво́н. Ман. он.

аутте́. D². больно. См. аудебе́.

а́уда. D⁴., ауде́. D³., ауды́. D¹. дверь (на улицу), ворота (D⁴.). Монг. егуден, ӱден.

ауды́-ду́р. D². верѣя.

аудебе́. D². D⁶. болѣть.

аурте́. D². заболѣлъ.

ау́за. D⁶. трава. Монг. ебесун.

а́ула. D². D⁴. D⁶. гора (малая. D²). Монг. агула, ӯла.

аулéн угéи (уду́р). D². безоблачный (день). Мон. ӱлен.

а́ура, а́уре. D². атмосФера, воздухъ. Монг. агар.

ау́ре. D². болѣзнь. Ср. Монг. ӯрı́ху (уӯре) получить шрамъ.

ау́ре дасабе́. D². лѣчить болѣзнь.

аурте́. D². заболѣлъ (отъ аудебе́).

аурты́ ху. D². больной человѣкъ.

Эуэ́. D⁶., еуо́. D¹. мать. См. аб. Отъ Ман. еме́, сол. емо́ (S⁶). Сл. сол. уо́, еуо́.

(О́зо) оубаı́. D⁴. хочу пить (воду). См. о́баі.

Jаобаı́. D⁴. сидѣть (sic!).

jаобе́ (прош. вр. jаоса́н). D². бѣгать, ходить. Монг. jабуху, Ман. jабумбı́.

jауван jауіjа́. D². идти пѣшкомъ.

jауӊа́н чуӊа (Ман. чооха). D². пѣхота, пѣшее войско.

jама́р. D⁶., jамуре́. D⁶. какой. Монг. jамар, jамбар.

сана́да jамурӊу́ла цака ідеіjа́. D². аппетитъ. Монг. сана̄ (дат. пад.), цака — Ман. сл. (вещь), монг. ідеку — (желат. накл.).

jасé у́ı аудебе́. D². боль въ сочленіяхъ. Монг. jасун-у уіjé суставы. См. аудебе́.

jалаӊа́зі ӊарӊа́бе. D². выбаллотировать, выбрать. Ман. ілгамбı́ различать, отдѣлять; Монг. гаргаху — вывести, вынуть и т. д.; здѣсь для образованія глаг. вида (= рус. предл. изъ, вы; кит. чу 出).

(саı́н цака́) jалегéзі гарӊа́бе. D². выбирать (хорошія вещи).

jалы́н бе. D⁴. 3-ья луна. Ман. ілан ба. См. подъ і.

jарӊасу́н уӊеı́. D². безвредный. Монг. jарга — обломокъ.

---

¹) Когда скоро произносилъ — уӊу́ле, когда раздѣльно — уӊеле.

jaң-пáȯ. D². ружье (кит. сл.).

jісу́. D¹., jісу. D². D⁴. девять (Монг.).

jíρе. D¹. D²., jíρе. D⁴. девяносто. Монг. jере.

jiң. D⁵. беркутъ (кит. сл. 鷹).

jокíн. D⁴. сколько, какой? Монг. jакін — какъ? какимъ образомъ?

joxí. D². что? Монг. jагун, jӱн.

jу́ме. D⁶. рожь (отъ кит. сл. юй-ми 玉 米 — кукуруза?).

Пáньза. D². батогъ (кит. сл.).

н'áра. D⁶. сани. Кит. пá-ли 爬 力, ср. Мк. рага (М.) сани.

петкуну́р (= кит. чоу — вонючій) вáте. D². вонь. Мон. ӱнӱр запахъ; Ман. вахун вонь. (Пет = вате? вонючій?; но вáте, судя по китайскому чоу-вэй-ръ, должно соотвѣтствовать Монг. амта вкусъ).

пі. D⁴. писчая кисть. Кит. бі 筆, Ман. Фі.

пын. D⁶. потолокъ (кит.).

эмбі́ пусы́ле. D². аптека, (Монг. ем (род. п. емbyин), Ман. пӱселі лавка, отъ кит. пу-цза —) лавка лекарственная.

пу́за, пу́за. D⁴. поясъ. Монг. бусе. См. бы́зе.

пу́зыл. D⁶. лавка. См. пусы́ле.

пуццібé. D². брызгать. Ср. Ман. пуксеме.

паотáі. D². бастіонъ (кит. 炮 臺).

пао-куарáн. D². артиллерія. Кит. пао пушка, Ман. куваран ограда, дворъ и т. д.

Бajíн. D². богатый. Монг. бajан. Ср. Мк. bai (BT.) богатый; Sch. bai— reich, WT. M. bajan.

бáтур. D². богатырь (Монг.).

бадá. D⁴. ѣда, обѣдъ. Ман. буда.

бада сіρé. D⁴. столъ (букв. обѣденный).

бада угéіло. D¹. голодать, нѣтъ пищи.

bадá. D²., béда. D³. мы. Монг. біде.

басé. D³. опять, еще. Монг. баса.

банахá. D⁶. благодарю. Ман. баніха — благодарность.

бандéн (кит.) -сіρэ́. D². большой столъ.

bаннáза. D³. нашъ. Монг. біден-у, біденеі.

балаі-тазу́. D⁶. кунжутъ, кунжутное масло (су-ю). Это, очевидно, переводъ кит. слова: су (Ман. балаі)-ю (тазу́, Монг. тосун масло).

бáлза. D⁴. земля (полъ въ фанзѣ).

барáн. D². правый. Монг. барӱн.

барáн болзóн (болосáн). D². больше. Ср. Монг. гарун — больше.

бардазі. D³. (-беі) окончиться. Монг. баракдаху.

баркáн. D². богъ (Монг. бурхан).

баргéзі узі́. D². беречь. Ман. барґамбі, Монг. ӱзекӱ.

багілцібéі. D³. буйствовать. См. отрывки (VI).

бэзіbe. D². блевать. Монг. бӧлцісӱн рвота.

бэбэобéі. D². баюкать.

béда. D³. мы. См. báда.

бéде. D². внѣ, вонъ.

бедеребéі. D³. возвращаться. Ман. бедерембі.

бендуру́. D². завтра.

бендуру́ бі елéге баіцібé. D². завтра я явлюсь по начальству.

белебесу́н ху́. D². вдова. Монг. белбесӱн.

белебесу́н саобé. D². вдовствовать. Монг. сагуху, сӱху сидѣть.

бі. D¹. D². D³. я (Ман.=Монг.).

Единственное число.

И. бі D³. я.

Р. (*мінíbе D³, мінí D³ мой, т. е., = меня).

_____

*) По D³. родительнаго падежа нѣтъ, но мы знаемъ, что въ этихъ языкахъ притяжательныя мѣстоименія замѣняются родит. падежомъ, ergo притяж. мѣстоименіе = род. п.

3*

Д. Т. намáда.
В. намаjý (намáі, отр. II).
П. нáмасý.

Множественное число.

И. ᾿бéда D³., ᾿бáда D². мы.
Р. ᾿баннáҕа.
Д. Т.᾿бедендé D³., ᾿бадендé. D².
В. ᾿бедені.
П. ᾿беданáсу.

бііхе. D¹. гордый. Монг. бі jехе (кит. цзы-да 自 大).

бітеҕé. D²., бітíҕе. D⁴., біткé. D⁵. книга. Ман. бітхэ.

бітеҕé хафáн. D². гражданская должность, -ій чиновникъ.

бісін-ку. D³. другой человѣкъ. Мон. бусу (біші) кӳмӳн (кӳн).

бігé. D⁹. былъ. Ман. біхе.

біҥ. D². лепешка (кит. 餅).

бызе. D⁶. поясъ. См. пӳза.

(цакá) боалҕáбе. D². выгружать (вещи). Монг. багулгаху.

бодá ідебé. D⁴. ѣсть. См. бадá.

Бодíн хутýн. D¹. столица (Пекинъ). Монг. хотон — городъ.

болóн. D². прѣсный. Ман. болго чистый (постное кушанье), уменьшит. болгокон, болокон.

баjін болзáн. D². богатѣть. Монг. болоксан. Баjін см. выше.

бóрціхе (бóрціх). D¹. горохъ. Монг. бурцак.

бóҕоні. D². низкій. Монг. богоні.

Бóзін. D⁴. Пекинъ.

бу усуꙣзí. D⁴. не говори. Бу — Монг., усуꙣзí см. выше.

(áула доргідá) буобéі. D². спускаться (съ горы). Монг. багуху.

будýн. D¹. D². грубый (Монг.). будýн-ху. D². невѣжа (Монг.).

бýзу. D⁶. шея (кит. бó-цза 脖 子).

бундурý. D⁶. завтра. См. бендурý.

бурí. См. ердыртéн.

бурхáн. D⁸. богъ (Монг.).

(бі) бáіта бі. D². я имѣю дѣло (Ман.).

бáіта барсáн. D². агентъ. Монг. баріксан — взявшій.

бáіталасí уҕéі. D². безполезный. Отъ Ман. баіталамбі съ Монг. окончаніемъ.

бі ордó елéге бáіса. D². я первый сдѣлалъ визитъ. Монг. уріда, Ман. елхе баімбі.

баохéза (кит. 寶 盒 子) необé. D². банкометъ. Монг. негеку, Ман. неімбі — открыть.

беі¹). D². есть. Монг. буі, Ман. бі.

(кӳі) фанчáбе. D². разсердить (человѣка). Ман. фанчамбі сержусь.

фі. D². кисть писчая (Ман.).

фологó. D⁹. мѣшокъ. Ман. фулху.

фӳжен нáінаі (кит.). D². барыня.

Вáте. См. петкунýр вáте.

(нáран) ванаҥóкуꙣ. D². западъ. См. нáра уанобéі боꙗ.

вантебéі. D²., вантыбáі. D⁴. спать. Монг. унтаху.

вардені бáіта. D². (Монг. ерден(-у), древній, Ман. бáіта дѣло) анекдотъ (кит. гу-ши-ръ 故 事 兒).

вáхала. D⁶. рубашка. Ср. Ман. гахарí — рубаха.

ваҥ-фá (кит. 王 法 царскіе законы) уҕéі. D². беззаконникъ.

вазірó, вазірá. D⁴. войди.

вынсерé. D¹. спать. См. вантебéі. Серé — по образцу Ман. глаголовъ, образованныхъ изъ междометій?

вáіꙗа. D¹. горькій.

ваіꙗáн. D². писарь (Ман. съ кит.).

вáіре. D². близко. Монг. оіра.

вéізу. D⁶. береза.

Wакáр. D². короткій. Монг. охор, калм. ахар.

Мадáҕá. D². барышъ. Ман. мадаган.

мадíн. См. нéкума ін мадíн.

машáоза. D⁴. поварёшка (кит. 馬 杓 子).

мантóу. D⁶. булка (кит. 饅 頭).

---

1) Почти бі.

ма́рда. D². барсъ.

ма́ҥа. D². мясо. Мон. міха, маха.

ма́ҥала. D²., ма́хала. D⁴. D⁶. шапка (Ман. = Монг.).

ма́нга. D². богатырь (Ман.).

ма́нга. D²., ма́нҥа. D⁴. тысяча. Ман. = Монг. мінган.

ма́нҥа җаҥа́. D⁴. тысяча чоховъ, связка чоховъ (кит. и-дяо-цянь).

мангі́л. D⁶. лобъ. Монг. маҥнаі, маҥлаі.

(бі) метте́. D². (я) знаю. Монг. меден́е (отъ медекӱ).

меден́е. D⁶. знаю, знаешь.

медекӱ уге́і. D⁶. не знаю (Монг.).

бітеге́ ӱлу медуҥӱ. D². безграмотный. Ман. бітхе, Монг. улу медекӱ.

(мурі́) мерде́н. D². берегъ рѣки.

морі́ міна́. D⁴., мо́рі міна́. D⁵. плеть. Морі́ см. ниже; міна́ плеть (Монг.).

не́ге міҥмі́ҥ. D¹. тысяча. Ср. міҥган.

мojáp каллірта́. D². безвыходный. Монг. харіл угеі невозвратный.

мojó. D³. вин. пад. отъ му, мао дурной.

мо́буpі. D¹. полотно.

мо́до. D². D⁴. дерево, бревно (D²). Монг. модон.

не́ке мо́до. D². бревно.

мо́ду. D⁶. дрова.

моні́. D¹. мы. Ман. нашъ (род. пад. мн. ч.).

мо́рі. D².D⁶.,мо́pін. D⁴. лошадь (Ман. = Монг.).

морківе́і. D³. возвращаться, возвращеніе. Ман. марімбі.

му. D⁶., мао D¹. худой. Монг. магу, мӯ. Ср. мojó. D³. (стр. 15, отр. XII).

мутӱ. D⁵. ведро, бадья. Кит. му-туҥ
木桶

муpí. D²., мурі́. D²., муре. D⁴., муру. D²., D⁴., D⁶. рѣка. Монг. мӱрен.

муpі мерде́н. D². берегъ рѣки.

мӱрі дере́н. D². верховье рѣки. Мон. дӗре.

муре едел́бе́. D⁴. переправиться черезъ рѣку.

му́ру. D⁴. плечо (Монг.).

мурҥубе́і. D². кланяться (въ землю, кит. кэ-тоу). Монг. мӱргӱкӱ.

мурҥуде́р укӱру. D².бодливый быкъ. Мон. мӱргӱлдеку бодаться.

му́нго. D⁴. серебро. Монг. мӱнгӱ(н).

мучу́рту. D². виноградъ. Ман. мучу. Ср. Мк. mучykta (CA.) виноградъ.

маіма́ні ге́сен. D². банкрутиться. Ман. маіман — торговля отъ кит. маі-маі; ср. Ман. гесеҫембі рвется, обрывается; Мон. кесек кусокъ, обломокъ.

ма́іза. D². пшеница (кит.).

мао см. му.

ма́о о́мо. D¹. отрава. Монг. магу дурной, ем — лекарство.

мао кӯ. D¹. грабитель (букв. злой человѣкъ).

ма́очан. D⁶., ма́оца́н. D⁴., ма́оцін. D². ружье. Ман. ма́очан отъ кит. няоцянъ.

ме́ізу у́туме. D⁶. бѣлый (букв. пшеничный?) хлѣбъ.

ме́іза. D⁵. войско.

Та. D². D³. вы (Монг.).

таа́ҥу. D². пять. См. та́бу.

та́бі. D¹. D²., та́ібі. D⁴. пятьдесятъ. Монг. табі.

та́бу. D¹., та́ван. D⁴. пять. Монг. табу(н).

(терге́) та́са. D¹. отпрягать телѣгу.

тасе́н. см. некці а́мо тасе́н уҥе́і.

та́ні. D³. вашъ. Монг. танаі.

таҥде́. D¹. вы (дат. п. вм. имен.?).

(ҵаҥаҥ) талебе́. D². выдавать провіантъ. Монг. талбіху.

та́лҕі см. сана́ та́лҕі со́н(о)су. Мон. талбіҵу (-ці) положивши, помѣстивши.

тара́лі. D². двоюродные по матери братья. Ман. тара — двоюродный съ отцовой (иногда и съ матерней) стороны.

таре́ ге́рі. D⁵. балаганъ (мазанка) для лѣтняго жилья земледѣльцевъ. Монг. тарíja, тара́ (пашня); гер (домъ).

тарты́га́. D⁴. кисетъ. Ср. сол. хап-ту́рҕа и др.

суанпы́н (кит.) тарка́зі у́lесі-ада́н. D². безразсчетный. [Мон. таркаху (таркагаху).] Букв. неумѣющій (не могущій) пользоваться счетами (кит. суань-па́нь 算 盤).

таркыбе́. См. шенца́ң таркыбе́.

тарҕу́н. D². брюханъ. Ман. тархун, Монг. таргун — жирный.

така́і. D². временно. Ман. така.

такараба́бе́і. D³. посылать, (бі) таку-ра́бе́і. D². употребляю. Ман. таку-рамбі.

та́ңгун ʼбе. D⁴. 5-ая луна. Монг. табу, ср. сол. тунга́; Ман. ʼба.

те́буке. D². влагалище. Ман. тебуку.

темшелцебе́і. D³. спорить другъ съ другомъ, оспаривать другъ у друга. Мон. темецелцеку; Ман. темшембі.

темчеlзі уҕе́і у́лу ба́італан. D². безспорный (букв. о которомъ совершенно не нужно спорить).

тѣза. D⁴. билетъ, бумажныя деньги (кит. тѣ-цза 帖 子).

тезе́. D³. ихъ. Ман. тесеі.

тенде́. D². тамъ (Монг.).

те́ре. D³. тотъ (Ман. = Монг.), тере́. D¹. D². онъ, они (D¹.).

Единственное число.

И.	те́ре D³. тотъ	
Р.	нѣтъ¹)	
Д. Т.	теры́нде́	
В.	тереjу́	
П.	тере́су D². } тере́се D³. }	

Множественное число.

И.	терені D³. (sic) тѣ	
Р.	нѣтъ¹)	

1) По D³. замѣняется имен. падежомъ. См. однако теры́ҕе.

Д. Т. тедынду́
В. тедынсоло́і
П. тедынсоло́со

Единственное число.

И.	(нѣтъ) D³. онъ¹)	
Р.	теры́ҕе	
Д. Т.	теры́нде	
В.	тереjу́	
П.	тересу́	

Множественное число.

И.	(нѣтъ) D³. они	
Р.	тезе́ (sic)	
Д. Т.	теденде́	
В.	тедені²)	
П.	теденесе	

тере́ асо́бе. D². онъ спрашиваетъ. Мон. асагуху и др.

те́ре (sic) іцісе́н. D². онъ ушелъ (Монг. ічіксен).

тере́ усуlзібе́. D². онъ скажетъ.

тере́ газі́р (Монг. газар). D². тамъ, въ той мѣстности.

терені́. D³. они (ихъ?³)

теребте́і (Монг. керекте́і?) пу́за. D⁴. мѣшокъ.

терегу́ле, тереҕу́ll. D²., тыргу́ll. D⁶. дорога.

терегу́ле укоці́у хафа́н. D². про-вожатый — чиновникъ (кит. ху-сунъ-гуань). См. укуці́бе.

терегу́ле jaубе́. D². ѣхать по до-рогѣ.

1) Во фразахъ вездѣ замѣняется указа-тельнымъ мѣстоименіемъ тере́ тотъ (отъ котораго и все ед. число).

2) Параллельная форма едені D³. отъ ене́ этотъ.

3) Это по его словамъ соотвѣтствуетъ Ман. тесе, а родит. пад. (Ман. тесеі) нѣтъ въ дах. яз. у этихъ мѣстоименій.

тереҕу́л jауҕу пао. D². подорожная (букв. свидѣтельство о про-
ѣздъ по дорогѣ; кит. лу-пяо).

тереҕу́ле jаре́ҕу. D². вожакъ
(букв. человѣкъ ведущій по до-
рогѣ). Ман. jарумбі.

те́ріҕе. D⁴., терыге́. D².D⁶., терыҕе.
D². телѣга. Монг. терге(н).

терыҕе. D³. его. Мон. тереі.

терыҕе геду́ҕу кутулу́. D². возчикъ. Ср. Монг. келіку́ везти съ
собой; Ман. кутуле стремянный,
слуга.

терсу́лта. D². бедро.

тенге́рі. D². небо, тенгері. D⁷. богъ.
Монг. теҥгрі, теҥгері.

тенге́р дуаріҕі. D². вселенная
(кит. тянь-ся, букв. поднебес-
ная). Монг. дооракі находящійся
внизу.

Тенгы́р Газі́р оуҕіҕу ҵукту́. D².
алтарь Неба и земли. Ман. ве-
чембі — приносить жертву, ҵук-
техен — храмъ.

теҵебе́і. D². питать. Монг. теҵігеку́,
теҵіjеку́.

тінза. D². бесѣдка (кит. 亭子).

тыргу́л. D⁶. дорога. См. терегу́ле.

тōтірда́ (туатірда́). D². внутрь.
Монг. дотокші.

тōтірда́ (туатірда́) татабе́. D².
вдыхать. Монг. дотокші татаху.

тōтірда́ (туатірда́) тулкібе́. D².
вдвигать. Мон. ту́лкіку́ — тол-
кать, двигать.

тотірда́ (туатірда́) шорó(-бе).
D². втащи. Монг. шіреку́, чірку́
— тащить.

тóсо. D². масло. Монг. тусун. Ср.
токсó.

тошáн (ср. тушáн) алібе́. D². вступить въ (букв. принять) должность.
Ман. тушан алімбі.

тон уҕéі. D². безчисленный. Ман.
тон, Монг. тога, тō — счетъ.

тондó. D². безпритворный. Ман. тондо.

толі́. D³. зеркало металлическое на
одеждѣ шамана (Ман. = Монг.).

толомá. D⁶. ведро¹). Монг. тулум,
Ман. тулума кожанный мѣшокъ.

толде́. D³. для. ради. Монг. тулада.

толдіх. D². колѣно. См. туарчіга.

тороҕó. D². атлáсъ. Отъ кит. дуань
緞, какъ изъ кит. дао образовалось
Ман. доро, изъ тао — торо? Монг.
торгар, торго.

торҕó. D¹. голова. Монг. тологаі(-гоі).

тóрчі. D⁴. пуговица. Монг. тобчі.

токсó. D⁴. масло. См. тосó.

тогілцібеі (чогілцібеі? см. стр. 8) D³.
шумѣть, буянить. Монг. ҵокілцаху
биться другъ съ другомъ.

тоҳорóл (тоорóл). D². аистъ. Монг.
тогороо журавль.

т'уáда. D⁷. дрофа, драхва. Ман. тодо.

туатірда́. См. тōтірда́.

туарчіга. D³. колѣно. Ср. Ман. тобҕа.

ту́мо. D². D⁴. десять тысячъ. Монг.
ту́ме, Ман. тумен.

ту́ду. D⁴. D⁶. картофель. Кит. ту́-доу.

ту́сун. D². кислый.

тушáн вакылабе́. D². выключать со
службы. Ман. вакаламбі.

тун. D⁴. роща, туҥ. D⁶. лѣсъ.

ту́нші (кит. 通事) гурукó. D⁴. переводчикъ. Монг. гуру учитель.

тулердесе́н отъ тулердебе́. D³. быть
сожжену, сгорѣть. Монг. ту́леку́,
ту́ліку́ — жечь.

тулкібе́. См. тōтірда.

турібе́. D². арендовать. Ман. турімбі.
См. турмібе́.

(теріҕе) туругундеобáі. D⁴. нанимать телѣгу. См. слѣд. слово.

туруҕу́н терыҕе. D². наемная телѣга. Ман. турі́ген наемная плата.

турмібе́. D². нанимать. См. турібе́.

ту́нку. D². барабанъ, бубенъ. Ман.
тункен; Монг. ду́нгур шаманскій
бубенъ.

тáібі. D⁴. пятьдесятъ. См. табі́.

---

1) Мóдо тулумá. D². бадья.

тáіһу (тáіу) D². балка. Монг. = Ман. таібу.

тáун хорó. D². пять пальцевъ. Монг. табун хуругун.

таодебé. D². возвращать. Ман. тоодамбí.

Даі́. снова, см. ердезí дасазí ӊібе. Монг. дахін.

дамагá. D⁶. табакъ. См. дáнӡа. Монг. тамахі. Ман. дамбаг̄у.

дасазí (дасабé). D³. исправлять (Ман. дасамбí).

дасу́ӊ. D². сладкій.

ӊан. кит. 店 дянь гостинница.

ӊáнда аабé. D². остановиться въ гостинницѣ. Монг. аху быть, находиться.

ӊан-герí. D¹. D⁵. гостинница. Мон. гер домъ.

ӊанлебé. D². арендовать. Отъ кит. дянь 佃 (аренда).

данӡáда (кит.) éре. D⁴. мужъ. Монг. ére мущина.

ӊáлá. D². D⁴., ӊáра. D¹. семьдесятъ. Монг. дала.

ӊалéі мердéн. D². взморье. Монг. далаі море. См. подъ мерден.

ӊáлбаӊа. D⁶. прикладъ (у ружья). Ман. далба.

ӊáра. D¹. семьдесятъ. См. дала.

ӊáрма. D²., ӊарума. D⁴. поясница. Ман. дарама.

ӊáрзі ӊурукудебéі. D². вздрагивать.

ӊаӊу́р кéнке. D⁴. дыня. Даӊу́р дахуръ, дахурскій; Ман. хеӊке общее названіе тыквенныхъ растеній.

ӊáӊза. D². журналъ (кит. 檔子).

ӊангíн. D⁶. чиновникъ. Ман. цаӊгін — родъ штабъ-офицера.

дембелé куї-танебé. D². вклепываться. Ман. дембеі, куї — человѣка; танебé — монг. теӊу́ку заблуждаться¹).

---

1) Перевелъ дѣйствительнымъ залогомъ вмѣсто средняго?

дембéл дембéл (дембéіӏе дембéіӏе) наоӏебéі. D². безпутничать. Отъ кит. нао 閙.

дéсо, D²., дéзу. D⁶. веревка. Монг. дēсун.

дéлí. D⁶. шуба. Монг. дегел, дёл.

деӏó. D⁶. (Монг. ӊоӏó). поводья.

дéре. D². верхъ. Монг. дёре. См. дерíӊе.

дéре угéлі. D¹. голый (букв. безъ верха).

дéрезу. D⁴. рогожка. Монг. дересун степной ковыль.

дерéн — Монг. дёре верхній. См. мурí дерéн.

дерібá. D⁴., дерыбó. D². подушка. Монг. дере.

дерíӊе. D². верхъ. Ман. дергі, Монг. дегере, дёре.

дерыбó. D². подушка. См. дерібá.

дéза. D⁶. тарелка (кит., см. стр. 26).

ӊептеӏé. D⁶. книга. Ман. дебтеӏін.

дínза. D². D⁴. шарикъ на шапкѣ (чиновниковъ) (кит. 頂子).

ӊіліту́. D². áтласъ (кит. 地理圖).

дотóн асíребé. D². въ мутной водѣ рыбу ловить¹). Асíребé — Монг. ашіклаху получать выгоду; дотóн — Монг. дотона, дотоно.

дотéрíӊі. D². внутри. Монг. дотора(кі).

дотóр ердéму ӊíге. D². великодушный. Монг. дотора, ердем (Ман. ердему) добродѣтель; јеке великій.

доӏó. D¹. ²). D². D⁴. семь (Монг.).

доӏó хотó. D³. Большая Медвѣдица (Монг. доӏó(н) одó(н) «семь звѣздъ»).

дорí мáӊала. D². шапка съ шарикомъ.

дóро јóсо (Ман., сх. Монг.) уӊéі. D². безчинный.

дорóн. D². печать. Ман. дорон.

дōргідá. D². внизъ. (См. слѣд.). Монг. дōші внизъ, дōро внизу.

---

1) По кит. 暗中取利.
2) Отчасти произносилъ какъ даолó.

дорҕідá десібé (десí, -сéн). D². вдавить (вдави, вдавилъ). Ман. доргі
внутри. Да — част. мѣстн. пад.

ду. D¹. переправляться (кит. 渡).

дуара. D². ниже, внизу. — Монг.
дōро (доора); низъ.

дуáнde хорó. D⁴., дуандíҕе хорó. D².
3-ій (средній) палецъ. Монг. дун-
дакі, хуругу(н).

дуарíҕі (почти дōрíҕі). D². внизу.
Монг. дооракі.

дуаргідá. D². внизъ. См. доргідá.

дуáнга. D²., дуáнҕа. D⁴., дуáнха. D⁶.
арбузъ. Ман. дунган.

дуíн̇ бе. D⁴. 4-ая луна. Ман. дуін ба.

дузé. D⁶. стѣна.

дýн̇dере. D¹. половина. Монг. дум-
дагур (= дундӯр).

дулэ́со. D². ушелъ. Ман. дулембі —
проходить.

дурубé. D². продавать. Ср. Ман.
турімбі — нанимать.

дурýбо. D². четыре. См. дурба.

дурéлеге. D⁶. стремя. Монг. дōрö
(дӯрӯге).

дурулдебé. D². покупать. См. дурубé.

дурба. D¹., дурбэ́. D⁴. четыре. Монг.
дӯрбе(н).

дурбы́н Форҕóн. D². 4 времени
года. Ман. форгон.

дýрку. D². вполнѣ. Монг. дӯрен (дӯ-
гӯрен).

дунҙá лінлебé. D². агентъ. Отъ кит.
линъ-дунъ-ды 領 東 的.

дýці. D¹. D². D⁴. сорокъ. Монг. дӯчін.

дáіре. D⁴. трубка. Отъ кит. дай —
трубка (янь-дай).

деідé. D². вверхъ. Ман. ден высокій,
высоко; Монг. дēші вверхъ.

дéіра. D⁶. трубка. См. дáіре.

(біꙋік) даутбé. D⁴. читать (книгу).
Монг. дагудаху.

деуркул. см. нембу́з деуркул.

доу. D². младшій братъ. Ман. доу,
Монг. дӯ.

Саібé. D². охранять. См. саҕіҕý. Монг.
сакіху.

самáн. D⁶. шаманъ (Ман.).

самáсҕі. D³. шаманское платье (ср.
Мк. samäšik (М.)); поясъ шамана
съ побрякушками (кит. яо-ли-ръ).

са-тáн. D⁶. сахаръ. Кит. ша-тáн 沙
糖.

санá. D². Монг. санā (санага) мысль.
санá тáҙі сóн(о)су. D². вслушиваться.

санабé. D². думать. Монг. санаху.

сан̇. D¹. гора. Кит. шань (по мѣстн.
сань.

сáн̇-сéн. D⁴. учитель. Кит. сянь-шэнъ
(сэнъ 先 生).

сан̇гучý. D⁶. D⁸. другъ. Ман. саін
гучу.

сáра (Монг.). D¹. D⁴., сарóро. D⁴.
луна.

сарóро гаціррзáн. D⁴. луна взошла. Монг. гаруксан.

сáра кузí. D⁴. комодъ (кит. хуанъ-
чжу-сянъ). Монг. шіра, шара желтый. Кузí см. подъ к.

сáрпо. D⁴. куайцзы, палочки для ѣды.
Ман. сабка, Монг. серē. См. стр. 28.

сарметó. D⁴., сармíлт. D². брови.
Ср. сол. сармуктó.

сарды: см. неīгендé сарды болó.....
Ман. сакда — старый.

сáрчáізан. D². блѣдный. Монг. чіра
чаіксан.

сáҕала. D²., саҕалá. D⁴., сахалá. D⁶.
борода, усы (D². D⁴.). Монг. сахал.

саҕіҕý. D⁸ охраняющій. Мон. сакіху.
См. саібé.

сан̇. D¹. глотка (кит. 顙).

сéФу. D². учитель (Ман.).

сен. D⁶. хорошій. Монг. = Ман.
саін.

селыҕéбе (повел. селыҕé). D². бу-
дить, разбудить. Мон. сергегекӯ
ободрить, привести въ чувство.

серкí. D². шаманская шапка.

сітáбе. D². (Монг. шітаху горѣть, шітагаху зажечь) воскурить.

сі. D³. ты (Ман.).

Единственное число.

И. Сі. D³.
Р. шамáі
Д. Т. шамáда
В. шамајý (шамéі отр. IV).
П. шáмасý.

Множественное число.

И. та D³.
Р. тáні
Д. Т. тáнда
В. тáніјý
П. тáнаhасы́.

сідéн бáіта. D². казенная бумага, казенное дѣло. Ман. сіден-і баіта.

сідéн бітегé кіібé. D². писать казенную бумагу. Ман. бітхе, Монг. кіку̌ дѣлать.

сісы́ге. D⁴. войлокъ. Ман. сісхе — постилка.

сíнкéн. D². новый. Монг. шіне. Кит. синь 新.

сíле. D². бульонъ (Ман.).

сірáс. D¹. нитка. Ман. сірге.

сірэ́. D². столъ. См. шірé.

сíгуа. D⁵. арбузъ (кит. 西 瓜).

сіхáнінге. D². твой. Ман. сінінге.

сíза (кит. 戲子) наdабéі. D⁵. актеръ. Монг. нагадху — играть.

сіры́т. D². акація.

сырé. D³. трезубецъ шамана. Монг. сереге, серѐ.

соорíн саобéі. D². взойти на престолъ. Ман. соорін тронъ, Мон. сагуху, сȳху сидѣть.

собургá. D². ступа буддійская (Монг.).

сóму. D⁶. лукъ (sic!). Монг. суму стрѣла.

сóн(о)су. D². Монг. соносху слушать. бі сононсан. D⁴. я слышалъ.

соленбóі. D². лѣвый (Монг.).

соробéі. D³. учиться. Монг. сурху.

усу̌нбу соробéі. D². учиться языку. Монг. усук буква.

сортосóн. D³. (отъ сортобéі. Монг. соктаху, соктоху; Ман. соктомбі) пьяный, напился.

сордóл. D². ученіе. Мон. суртал, суртагул.

сонбу̌р. D². безглазый, слѣпой. Монг. сохор.

суанпáн (кит.) бітегé (Ман.). D². ариѳметика.

суіткó. D². мизинецъ. Ср. Монг. шігезеі хуругун, еще ср. сол. ціміткí, чоідогó.

сусу мóдо. D². бамбукъ. Сусу — Ман. чусе — кит. чжу-цзы бамбукъ, мóдо (Монг.) дерево.

суні. D⁶. ночь (Монг.).

сýні болзáн. D⁴. стемнѣло (Монг. болоксан — сдѣлалась ночь).

сунодэ́. D². вечеромъ. Мон. сунідур (ду) ночью.

сунксáнда. D⁶. гребенка. Монг. сам, шігу̌р.

суркý. D². багоръ.

сугý. D⁶. топоръ. Ман.=Монг. сухе.

сáібі. D⁵. башмаки. Ман. сабо отъ кит. сѣ 鞋.

саісá. D². благородный (человѣкъ) (Ман.).

саін éре. D². молодецъ (Монг., букв. хорошій мущина).

саін санáтеі. D². доброе сердце (имѣющій) (Монг.).

саін кубурí. D¹. гнѣвливый. См. кубурí.

саобéі. D². сидѣть, сѣсть. См. соорíн саобéі.

сáу (сáо). D⁴. садись.

тéріге сáубе јаубéі. D⁴. (ѣхать букв. сидя) въ телѣгѣ.

саo-зéе (кит. 小姐) уhíн. D². барышня.

Луáці¹) ша. D². батистъ (кит.).

шабурá (шабрá). D¹., шáура. D⁶. грязь. Монг. шібар (шабар) грязь, глина. Ср. Мк. siwar (М.) болото.

¹) Русскій.

шама́i. D³. твой. См. сi.

бi шама́i санабе́. D². я думаю о тебѣ.

бi шама́да ца́ja. D². я тебѣ скажу.

шадбе́i. D³. мочь. Мон. чiдаху, чадаху.

шаделе́. D³. сила, способность. Монг. чiдал.

ша́ра. D⁶. желтый. Монг. шiра.

шенца́н (кит.) таркыбе́. D². восторжествовать. Мон. таркаху, таркагаху.

шiла́зу. D⁶. нитка. См. сiра́с.

шiлле́. D⁶. полъ. Монг. шiроi—земля.

шiре́. D⁶. столъ. Монг. шiрѣ.

шiге. D⁶. большой. См. цiге.

шоро́. См. тōтiрда́ шоробе́.

шōрз̌у вазíре (-рсе́н). D². вводить.

шоцо́. D². беркутъ. Монг. шоцхор.

ша́о-jе́. D². баричъ (кит. 少 爺).

шао-бiц (кит.) уты́м. D⁴. лепешки съ сахаромъ (кит. шао-бинъ).

ша́ура. D⁶. грязь. См. шабура́.

На́i. D². (См. наijе́, на́ije) восемьдесятъ. Монг. наjа́.

н̇ама́н. D⁴. ямынь, канцелярія, присутственное мѣсто (съ кит.

нама́нда (Монг.) беi. D⁶. у меня есть.

мунгу́iн намы́н. D². казначейство.

да́мзе (да́нзе) тал̇у нама́. D². архивъ. Ман. намун.

н̇амарзí. D³. всякій. Монг. jамбар-чу (jамар-чi).

намуру́. D². осень. Монг. намур.

на́да аубе́i. D⁶. дай (мнѣ), возьми. Ср. Монг. у̇кку̇, абху.

на́дан̇ бе. D⁴. 7-ая луна. Ман. надан ба.

н̇а́дыма. D⁴. D⁶. лицо.

зiз̌а́ на́дуз̌у. D². азартная игра (букв. на деньги). Монг. нагадху—играть.

на́ра. D¹. D⁴. солнце (Монг.).

наре́м. D². пшено (кит. сло-ми-цза). Монг. нарам попутникъ (растеніе) plantago major.

нарíн. D¹. нѣжный, D². тонкій, узкій (Монг.).

на̇з̌у́н усугу́ гуру́ бiсijá. D⁴. понимаешь ли? (см. 29 фр.)

назíр. D². лѣто.

неiре́ уз̌е́i уантазí ада́н. D². безсонницей страдать, (Монг. наiр согласіе, удовольствіе), букв. отъ безпокойства не быть въ состоянíи спать.

неiге́н. D². безпристрастный. Монг. неiген.

неiгенде́ сарды́ боло́ уз̌е́i у́лу меде́. D². безсмертный (никогда не знающій смерти и старости). Монг. нiгенде — однажды, сарды — Ман. сакда (старикъ), боло уз̌еi — Монг. болху, угеi; улу медé — Монг.

не́ме. D². стрѣла. Монг. намун, нумун лукъ.

нембузу́. D⁶. крыша.

нембу́з деуркуj̇л. D². багажъ.

н̇е́ту. D¹. мокрый. Монг. ноiтан.

ненéн. См. курб ненéн.

нелерз̌а́н. D². въ то время.

не́ре (нере́) уз̌е́i. D². безъимянный (Монг.).

нере́ уз̌е́i хоро́. D². безъимянный палецъ.

нерíгу о́нцi. D⁴. дорожный ножикъ (кит. ху-чжао-дао 虎 爪 刀¹).

пе́ке. D². D⁴. одинъ, Монг. нiге(н).

не́ке теры́з̌е. D². возъ.

не́кума-iн-мадíн. D². артель.

нéк-сунi лантаба́i. D⁴. переночевать. Монг. нiге(н), су́нi, унтаху (букв. проспать одну ночь).

некцí а́мо тасéн уз̌е́i. D². безупречный. Монг. нiге-чу(чi) — хотя бы одинъ; Монг. таш̌іjа (таш̌а), Ман. таш̌ан ложь, ошибка; а́мо — Монг. аму крупа (отсюда зерно? ни на одно зерно = ни малѣйшей).

нéге. D¹. D². одинъ. См. неке.

¹) Въ ножнахъ, съ палочками для ѣды, прикрѣпляется къ поясу.

4

нíде. D². D⁴., н̇у́ду. D⁶. глаза. Монг. нідӯн, н̇ӯдӯн.

не́ге нíде. D². одинъ глазъ.

нíсі. D⁵. бить. Монг. нíселку давить, ударять.

нíндӯр гáрі. D². одна рука.

нíнгу̇н̇ 'бе. D⁴. 6-ая луна. Монг. нін̇гун̇ 'ба.

но. D². мальчикъ. Монг. ногон, нігон.

ноíн. D⁵., нойóн D². D⁴. баринъ, господинъ, чиновникъ.

ноíн-ку. D¹. господинъ. Ку — человѣкъ (Монг.).

ціӟа̀ ноӟа̀. D⁴. капуста. Монг. цаган ногō (нугуга).

нóӟо. D². D⁴. собака. Монг. нохаі, нохоі. См. нуӟо́.

н̇у́ду. D⁶. глаза. См. нíде.

ну́ру угéі. D². безбрачный. Монг. н̇ӯку̇р другъ; супругъ, мужъ.

нуӟо́. D⁸. собака. См. нóӟо.

нуӟу́. D⁶. дуло у ружья (Ман.?).

нáіје. D⁴., наіјé. D¹. восемьдесятъ. См. наí.

нáіма. D¹. D². D⁴. восемь (Монг.).

нáузу. D⁶. утка. Монг. ногосу(н).

нáура. D⁶. озеро. Монг. нагур (нӯр).

Лаба ху́лубе. D². трубить въ трубу. Лаба — кит. 喇叭, ху́лубе — Ман. хуламбí.

латáі. D⁴. подсвѣчникъ (кит. 蠟臺).

лантабáі. D⁴. спать. См. уантабéі.

л̇ансíн (кит. 良心) уѳéі. D². безсовѣстный.

лӭке. D². брусокъ (Ман.), точильный камень.

лонкó. D². банка (Ман.).

лу. D⁶. бочка (кит.).

луáці му́нгу зіӟа̀. D². русскія серебряныя деньги.

лóуза. D². башня (кит. 樓子).

Катá. D². D⁴. D⁶. соль. Ср. Мк. katagan (M.), kata соль.

касó. D². D⁴. желѣзо.

ка́на. D⁴. трава.

кантачíнкі. D⁶. коротенькая рубаха. Кит. хань-та-цза.

каллíртá. См. мојáр каллíртá.

ка́ра. D⁶. черный. Монг. хара.

ка́ра у́туме. D⁶. черный хлѣбъ.

каракӯзі ердебé. D². выкалывать. Ср. Монг. хатхуху колоть; Монг. ебдекӯ — разрушать.

каró. D². караулъ. Монг. харӯл (харагул).

каróса саоӟа́ӟу чуӟа́. D². гарнизонъ.

карӯ (карáу). D¹. гусь. Монг. галӯ. Ср. Мк. karaw (M.) журавль.

карукӯ. D⁶. медвѣдь. Монг. харагöрöсӯн.

картазá. D⁴., картыіс. D². доска. Монг. хабтасу́(н).

какарá. D⁶., каӟарá. D⁴. курица.

кедé. D⁷. сколько? Монг. кеду, кедуі, кедун.

кéлі. D². D⁴. брюхо, животъ. Ман. хеѳелі.

кéлі ӟіге. D². брюханъ, -тый.

кéлі чаттá. D⁴. сытъ, наѣлся. Монг. цатху быть сытымъ.

керé. D³. какимъ образомъ? Ср. Монг. керкіцу (вторая часть отъ глагола кікӯ).

керí (келí). D¹. говорить. Монг. келекӯ.

хотóн керыіме D³. амбразура (?стѣна). Монг. керем — стѣна.

керӟé. D⁴. огородъ.

кéке. D⁶., кекé. D²., кӭкэ. D⁴. кошка. Ман. кесіке.

кéку. D².D⁶., кóуке. D⁴. сынъ. Монг. ху̇бу́н, ху̇.

кекурé. D³. дѣти.

Единственное число.

И.	кéку D³. сынъ	᠊ᠺᡝᡴᡠ
Р.	кекуíге	᠊ᠺᡝᡴᡠᡳᡤᡝ
Д. Т.	кекудé	᠊ᠺᡝᡴᡠᡩᡝ
В.	кекумолó	᠊ᠺᡝᡴᡠᠮᠣᠯᠣ
П.	кекóсе	᠊ᠺᡝᡴᠣᠰᡝ

Множественное число.

И. кекоре́ (кекуре́)
Р. кекореје́
Д. Т. кекурсо̀лда́
В. кекурсоло́
П. кекурсо̀лде́

ке́нке. D^4. огуречъ. См. кынке́. Ман. хенке — тыквенное растеніе.

кі́беі. D^3., дѣепр. кі́зі. D^3. дѣлать. Монг. кіку́.
  бі́чік кїбеі. D^4. }писать. Монг. бі-
  бі́тіхе́ кїбеі. D^6. }чік, Ман. бітхе.

кі́мынбе́. D^2. враждовать. Ман. кі-мун — вражда.

кі́мынте́і. D^2. враждебный. Ман. кі-мун съ окончаніемъ монгольскихъ прилагательныхъ.

кіру́зі алібе́і. D^2. безропотный, тер-пѣливый (глаголъ?). Ман. кірумбі терплю, алімбі принимаю.

кынке́. D^4. огуречъ. См. ке́нке.

коара́н ге́рі. D^2. лагерь. Ман. куа-ран — лагерь, Монг. гер домъ.

ко́кіртакебе́. D^2. ватажиться. По-добно Ман. хокіламбі отъ кит. хо-цзі (хогі) — товарищъ, артель-щикъ[1]?

кочо́ро. D^2. D^4., гочо́ро. D^5., кучу́р. D^6. сапоги. Ср. Монг. гутул, Ман. гулха.

ку. D^6. человѣкъ (Монг.).
  ку-те́і. D^3. съ человѣкомъ[2]).

ку́ї орібе́. D^2. звать (человѣка). Монг. оріху.
  ку́де сана̀ ѡаллага́бе. D^2. вну-шать [человѣку. Ср. Монг. оро-гулху, сана олху (олгаху)].

---

1) Съ глаг. кібе́ (Монг. кіку́), та = да въ нарѣчіяхъ.

2) Соотвѣтствуетъ монгольскому сое-динительному падежу съ луга, лугэ. Въ дахурскомъ языкѣ это окончаніе теі упо-требляется преимущественно (какъ и въ

куалі́мпо. D^2. овесъ.

ку́бу улаꙗі́н. D^2. безстрашный.

кубурі́. D^1. гнѣваться. Ср. Монг. урін гнѣвъ; ср. ку́бу.

ку́ма. D^6. родъ шемизетки (у знамен-ныхъ).

кута́ра зіреꙗе́і саін. D^2. третьесте-пенный. Монг. гутагар — третій, въ третьихъ.

кутулу́. D^2. слуга. Ман. кутуле. См. терьꙗе гелу́ꙗу кутулу́.

ку́лі. D^2. D^6. нога, D^4. ступня. Монг. кӱл — нога.

курі́. D^6. синій. Монг. куке.

куро́ нене́н. D^2. курица.

куруме́лто. D^4. нога до колѣнъ. Ср. кулі нога.

куꙗу́н D^2. вата. Ман. кубун, Монг. кубуꙗ.

куꙗба́і (кит. 空白) дорабе́і. D^2. бланка. Отъ Ман. дорон печать.

кучу́н-ку. D^2. батракъ. Монг. хӱ-цꙗн — сила, кӱ — человѣкъ.

кучу́р. D^6. сапоги. См. кочо́ро.

кучура́се. D^3. услов. накл. отъ кучу-ребе́ усиливаться, дѣлаться тяже-лой (болѣзнь). Монг. кучірдеку.

венꙑу́(кит.)куціу-ху́. D^2. курьеръ[1]). Куціу вм. укоціу, см. укуцібе́ (= кит. сунъ). Ху человѣкъ.

(бі ангаді) куцірза́. D^2. (я) прибылъ (сюда). Монг. кӱркӱ.

куцу́. D^2. шея. Монг. кузꙗн.

ку́зі. D^4. ящикъ. Кит. гуй-цзы 櫃子.

ку́зі сіта́бе. D^2. воскурить ѳиміамъ. Монг. кӱці курит. свѣчка, шітаху горѣть, шітагаху зажечь.

коіма́лі. D^2. безразсудный. Ман. хит-рый.

коіма́лі усулзібе́. D^2. безразсудно говорить.

монгольскомъ) для образованія именъ при-лагательныхъ.

1) Кит. сунъ-вэнь-шу-ды 送文書的.

куі іребеіjá. D⁴. вернуться домой. Кит. хуй вернуться, Монг. ірекӱ придти

каоцін. D². старый. Монг. х(аг)учін.

каоцін уребӯр (урубӯр) чоӊá. D². ветеранъ. Ман. уребуре чооха.

геге́н ка́улан. D². блѣдно-голубой. Отъ кит. кянь-лань(?).

каучін. D⁶. старый. См. каоцін.

ко́уке. D⁴. сынъ. См. ке́ку.

Габсіján. D². авангардъ. Ман. габсіхан.

ѓа́мын. D². станція. Ман. ѓа́мун.

ѓа́мын терыге́. D². почтовая телѣга.

ѓа́мун-ху. D². почтовый, приписанный къ станціи.

ѓа́да, ѓа́ды. D⁶. ворота. Монг. гадӑ наружу, внѣ; ӱден, егӱден — двери.

ѓа́де. D⁴. рука. См. ѓа́рі.

ѓа́ды см. ѓа́да.

гасу́н. D². терпкій. Монг. гашӱн горькій.

ѓа́лі. D². огонь. Монг. гал.

галі-і́ӊ, ѓа́лі мо́со. D². мельница паровая (кит. хо-мо́ 火 磨). Iӊ — Монг. мельница.

галу́. D⁶. гусь (Монг.).

на́ра гараӊо́кул. D². востокъ. Монг. гарху. См. гархо́ін.

гаре́ хуру́. D⁶. ладонь (букв. пальцы руки).

ѓа́рі. D². D⁶. рука. Монг. гар.

ѓа́рі ку́лі сіребу́се ауде́бе́. D². боль въ сухожиліяхъ (рукъ и ногъ). Монг. шірбу́сӱн сухая жила.

гардыку́ оӊде́. D². безденежье. Переводъ кит. выраженія шоу-фа 手 乏 (въ рукахъ не имѣть) — нуждаться.

на́ра гархо́ін боі́. D². востокъ (страна восхода солнца).

ѓа́га. D⁶., ѓа́ӊа. D². ⎱ свинья. Монг. ѓа́ха. D¹., ѓа́іха. D⁴. ⎰ гахаі.

на́ра гаці́рзан. D⁴. солнце взошло. Монг. гаруксан.

гаці́р. D⁶., гаѕі́р. D². земля. Монг. газар.

гаці́ре пі́ӊ (кит. 平). D². равнина.

газі́ре іру́. D¹. далекій.

ѓетуку́н. D². внятно, ясно. Ман. гетукен.

бі геткӱн болодо́. D². я понялъ (букв. мнѣ сдѣлалось ясно).

геді́ге. D⁴. коса. См. гыці́га. Ср. Мк. gadykän (M.), gödykän (M.) коса.

геса́н. D⁴. дверь. См. ге́шан.

гензо́ озо. D⁴. холодная вода.

бенца́н (кит. капиталъ) ге́сен. D². банкрутиться. Монг. гегекӱ терять.

ге́шан. D²., геса́н. D⁴. дверь. Кит. гэ-шань. (См. стр. 32).

те́ріӊе гелеку́. D⁴. ⎱ тѣрыӊе гелу́ѕу кутулу́. D². ⎰ извозщикъ, возчикъ. Ср. Монг. келікӱ — везти съ собой.

гере́н горроко́ (ху). D². безумный (человѣкъ).

ге́рі. D⁴., гері́. D⁶. домъ. Монг. гер.

геге́н. D². ясный, свѣтлый (Монг.). геге́н удӯр. D². ясный день (Монг.) геге́н тенгері́. D². ясное небо (Монг.).

гі́ӊ. D². безмѣнъ (кит. 斤 фунтъ).

гыці́га. D⁶. коса. Монг. геӊіге — коса (изъ волосъ).

горібі́де. D³. Созвѣздіе «Три звѣзды» (Орла).

гочо́ро. D⁵. сапоги. См. кочо́ро.

го́ці. D¹. D²., гу́ці. D⁴. тридцать. Монг. гучін.

гу. D⁴. стекло. Ман. ѓу нефритъ. гу ло́нко. D⁴. бутылка.

гуá-ма́н. D². вермишель (кит.).

гуá́ла(-бе). D². (отъ кит. гуань) завѣдывать, входить во что.

гуа́нза. D⁶. бревно (съ кит.).

гуа́рба¹). D². D⁴., гу́рба. D¹. три. Монг. гурба(н).

¹) D³. (отр. VIII) гуарбе́н.

гурӯн. D². государство. Ман. гурун.

гӯрба. D¹. три. См. гуа́рба.

гўба́н. D². Монг. гуіхун мелкій.

гӯн̣фу бі̆ге уб̆е́і. D². вскорѣ. Кит. гу́нъ-фу свободное время.

гу́ці. D⁴. тридцать. См. го́ці.

гуиэ̣̄. D². брюхо. Ср. сол. гуде́, гудеге́. Монг. гедесӯн.

га́іха. D⁴. свинья. См. га́га.

го́іб̆еі, гу́іб̆еі. D². просить. Монг. гуіху, гу́јуху.

гуіве́іні. D³. прошеніе (то, что просится).

гу́ізі. D². бѣгомъ (дѣепр.). Монг. гӯіхӯ.

гу́ізі іребе́. D². прибѣжать (бѣгомъ придти).

га́олі. D². D⁴. мѣдь. Монг. гаолі, гӯлі.

б̆а́рба. D¹. десять. Монг. арбан.

б̆арбе́. D². выходить. Монг. гарху. а́ула б̆арбе́. D². всходить на гору.

б̆азіребе́. D³., б̆азірбе́. D². вернуться. Монг. харіху.

б̆еры̆ге. D². большой палецъ. Монг. хуругу(н) палецъ?

б̆іб̆е. D². Монг. кікӯ дѣлать.

б̆іге. D². большой. Монг. јеке, јехе.

б̆іге ішке́н. D². величина (перев. кит. да-сяо).

б̆іге пао. D². пушка (кит. да-пао).

б̆іге шуаі. D². вождь (кит. юань-шуай).

б̆іге гуц-дуа́н торо̆б̆о́. D². дворцовый атла́съ (кит. да-гунъ-дуань 大 貢 緞).

б̆іге ху. D². большой, великій человѣкъ (но не генералъ — кит. да-жень, которому соотв. амбан).

б̆іге хуі-ся́ц. D². анисъ (кит. да-хуй-сянъ).

б̆іцціве́і у́лу-меде́н. D². безстыдный (букв. незнающій стыда). Монг. ічіхў, ічехў стыдиться.

б̆унду́р. D². высокій, высотою. Монг. ўндўр.

Хава́н. D⁶., хаве́ хафа́н. D². офицеръ, хавӣн. D⁴. чиновникъ. Ман. хафан.

хама́р D²., хамуру́ (хамару́). D⁴., хамы̆р. D². носъ. Монг. хамар.

ха́да. D². большая гора (Монг.).

хада́ла. D². D⁶. узда. Ман. хадала, Монг. хацзāр.

хадазі́ ванагáбе. D². (прош. вр. ванагáсан) валить (вѣтромъ). Монг. упагáху свалить. Ср. Монг. хадуху скосить.

хасо́ (-бе́). D³. спроси (-ть). Монг. асаху, асхаху.

ха́на. D². гдѣ (Монг.), откуда (Монг. ханāса).

ханта́цінці. D⁴. рубашка. Кит. ханьтāр, Монг. цамца.

(э̆кі) ханда́бе. D². брить (голову).

ханйдагá. D⁶. сохатый, лось. Ман. кандахан, Монг. хандагаі.

ха́лага, ха́лаб̆а. D². ворота (Монг.).

халóн бзо. D⁴. горячая вода. Монг. халӯн, усун.

хару́н неге́. D¹. одиннадцать. См. слѣд.

ха́рба. D². D⁴. десять. См. б̆а́рба.

ха́рбан неке́. D⁴. }
харбы̆н неке. D². } одиннадцать.

харбы̆н та́б̆у. D². пятнадцать.

харбóбо. D². вполнѣ (кит. ши́-чэнъ 十 成). Монг. арбагула?

харсы̆н уту́мо, ха́рсын у́тум. D³. лепешки (го-ку́й по кит.), блины (кит. бінъ).

хаб̆у́ра. D². весна. Монг. хабур.

хаб̆у́ру еду́ро. D³. весенній день. Монг. хабур-уп едӯр.

хеде́н б̆азі́р. D². сколько верстъ? Монг. кеду(н), газар.

хеле́б̆е. D². багровый. См. ха́ра хелы̆б̆е бóчо. Монг. еліген (ўнге).

хелы̆х. D². печень. Монг. ілген, еліге(н).

ха́ра хелы̆б̆е бóчо (Ман.). D². бурый (цвѣтъ — бочо). Монг. хара черный, Монг. еліген (ўнге) темнокоричневый.

хелу́н. D². горькій (жгучій? отъ халóн, Монг. халӯн).

херегéчі. D⁴. родъ жилета (кит. кань-
дя́нь-цза).

хéрі. D¹. двадцать. См. хорí.

хéриге. D⁴. большой палецъ. См. ӈе-
рыге.

херзі́. D³. какимъ образомъ? Монг.
керкіцу. См. керé.

хекí. D⁶. голова. См. óкі.

хілá. D². блюдо.

хíге. D². большой. См. ӈіге.

хоірá. D¹., хоірó. D⁴., хоjýр. D². два.
Монг. хоjар, хоjур.

хóбі. D². влагалище. Монг. хубіӈ
урна, кувшинъ.

хотóн. D². городъ (Монг.). См. хутýӈ.

Хотó. D³. звѣзда. Монг. одон.

хóло. D². далеко (Монг.).

холóбе. D². воровать. Монг. хула-
гаху, Ман. хулхамбі.

хорí. D²., хóрін. D⁴., хéрі. D¹. двадцать. Монг. хорí(н).

хорó. D². D⁴. палецъ (D⁴. еще указательный палецъ). Монг. хуругу.

хорогубé (прош. вр. хорогусáн). D².
бѣгать. Монг. оргоху.

хорогудáр ху. D². бѣглецъ. Монг.
оргодбл.

хóні. D². D⁴. баранъ, овца. Монг.
хоні, Ман. хоніп.

хон, хуáн. D³. годъ. Монг. он.

хуáла. D². D⁴. канъ. Монг. кулаӈ
дымникъ, камінъ; Ман. хулан дымовая труба.

хуалáӈа. D². воръ. Монг. хулагаічі.

хуалíмбо. D⁶. овесъ. См. куалímпо.

хуáра варбéі. D⁴. идетъ дождь. Монг.
борога (боро) оромуі.

хуáрага. D⁶. рѣчка. См. хурага¹).

хуаіjандá. D³. назадъ. Монг. хоіна
(-кші, кшіда).

хуáіна. D². заднíй; послѣ, сзади; сѣверъ. Монг. хоіна.

1) D³. (отр. VIII) даже хуаргé.

бі хуáіна jауіjá. D². я поѣду
сзади.

хуáін боí. D³. сѣверъ.

хуаінасы́. D³. послѣ, послѣ того
какъ. Монг. хоінакші.

ху-баіты́ у́лу-медé. D². безпамятный
(букв. незнающій человѣческихъ
дѣлъ). Монг. ху человѣкъ, у́лу не,
медеку знать; Ман. баіта дѣло.

хутýӈ. D¹. городъ. См. хотон.

худá угéі. D². безцѣнный. Ман. худа
цѣна.

хýзу. D⁴. волосы. Монг. у́сун.

хуӈту́ру. D³. (барабанъ), бубенъ шаманскій. Ср. сол. уӈтý.

хýнду. D². тяжелый. Монг. ку́нду́.

хýнзу. D². зола. Монг. у́несу́(н).

хулá. D⁶. красный. Монг. улáн.

хýлубе. См. лáба хýлубе.

хуа́лдубé(-сéн). D². замерзать. Монг.
ку́лту́ку́ мерзнуть.

хýлзі ӈарӈáбе. D². выдувать.

хурага. D³., хуáрага. D⁶. рѣка, рѣчка.
Монг. гуруха, гуріхун.

хурý. D⁶. палецъ. См. хорó.

хýӈко. D⁴. платокъ. Ман. Функу —
кусокъ холста.

хýӈген. D². легкій. Монг. ку́ӈген
легкій.

хуцíн. D¹. давній. Монг. хӯчін.

хаідá. D². куда. Монг. хаіші.

хýіза. D². мусульманинъ (съ кит.).

хао мутубéі. D¹. переводчикъ. Кит.
хао хорошо, Ман. мутембі — мочь.

хáоле. D². греча.

хаоцín бурí. D². ветошка. См. хуцín.

хоудý. D². глупый. Кит. ху́-ду 糊塗.

Ча чáчока. D⁴. чайная чашка. См.
чáчуку.

чáза. D²., чáзу. D⁶. бумага. Монг.
цасун.

чáлба. D². береза. Ман. чалфа береста. Ср. сол. чалбáн.

чагáн jамá. D¹. осина. Чагáн бѣлый
(Монг. = Ман.).

чáчуку D²., чáчуху. D⁶. чашка.

чéза. D². реестръ (съ кит.).

чiкí. D⁶. уши. Монг. чiкiн. См. цiкí.

чiгáн. D⁶. бѣлый. См. чагáи.

чооӄéи áӄура цáка. D². вооруженіе. Ман. чоохаи агура цака.

чосé. D³. кровь. Монг. чусун (цасун).

чосотéи wáзi. D². багровыя (букв. кровавыя) пятна.

чосу́и бáита. D². частное дѣло. Ман. цiсуи баита.

чолó. D⁶. камень. Монг. чiлун. Ср. сол. цолó.

чоӈ. D². барка. Кит. чуань 船.

чонку́. D⁶. окно. См. чóнху.

чонку́ӈ. D³. красная тушь (киноварь) для печатей. Ман. цiнухун, Монг. шiнку.

чóнху. D⁴. окно. Кит. чуáнь-ху (стр. 33).

чуагé аӄу́р ӄíу газáр. D². арсеналъ. См. чооӄéи áӄура цáка; ӄíу = Монг. хiху́ дѣлать.

чуаӄé-ху. D³. знаменный. Ман. чоохаи (йалма =) Монг. ху человѣкъ.

чуӄá, D³. армія. Ман. чооха. морíн чуӄá. D². конница.

чу́за. D⁴. поваръ (кит.). См. чу́за.

чу́цi. D⁶. долото. Монг. цуце.

чу́за. D⁶. поваръ, стряпка (кит. 厨 子). См. чу́за.

чаi. D². чай. См. цаi.

чуí-ды́ӈ. D⁶. спички (кит. цюй-дэн, чуй-дэнъ). См. подъ цуi-ды́ӈ.

чаохерхá. D¹. гроза. Монг. цахiлган — молнія.

Цáйцi. D⁴. халатъ. Монг. цамца рубаха.

цаху́. D⁴. чайникъ (кит., стр. 33 чаку́).

цаӈ. D⁹. амбаръ (кит. 倉).

цаӈ гéрi. D⁵. амбаръ. Монг. гер — домъ.

нéге цаӈ. D¹. десять тысячъ.

цéйцi. D². халатъ. См. цáйцi.

цi. D¹. ты. Монг. чi.

бi у́ле-цiмбí. D². я не пойду. Ман. зiмбí.

цiфы́н. D². акцизъ. Ман. цiфун отъ кит. чоу-фынъ.

цiрлiде. См. аларцiцi цiрлiде . . . . .

цiке. D⁴., цiкi. D². уши. См. чiкi.

цiӄá см. цiӄá ноӄá. Цiӄá бѣлый. См. чагáн.

цiнкерi. D¹. голубой. Монг. чiӈгiр свѣтлолазуревый.

цуй. D². дюймъ (кит. 寸).

цаi у̃обé. D⁴. пить чай. Монг. цаi у̃ху.

цуí-ды́ӈ D⁴., цуi-дэ́ӈ. D². спички (кит. цюй-дэнъ-эрлъ 取燈兒).

Цáлага. D⁶. болото.

цалкó. D². лѣнивый. Монг. залiхаи, залхагу.

цакóн гóса. D². восемь знаменъ. Ман. цакун гуса.

цаксулé ӄарӄáбе. D³. вывозить. Ман. цака — вещи, Монг. гаргаху.

цаӄá. D⁴. чохъ. Ман. зiха.

цáхуй бе. D⁴. 8-ая луна. Ман. цакун ба.

цангуiдé. D⁴. купецъ. Кит. чжанъгуй-ды.

цíвi. D⁶. лодка. См. зéбе.

цу. D⁶. иголка. Монг. зу̃.

цу̃ уорí оiрдебé. D². швейная машина (букв. иголка сама шьетъ).

цуáй бе. D⁴. 10-ая луна. Ман. цуан ба.

цу́ру. D². козуля, D⁶. гуранъ.

нéге цу́ру (цу́ру). D¹. отрядъ (кит. дуй).

цуру́ (Ман.) гáрi. D². обѣ руки. Монг. гар.

цуру́ӄу, зуру́ӄу. D³. сердце. Монг. цiрухен.

цуӈ. D⁶. рѣчка.

цаi зíрӄе. D². второстепенный. Ман. цаi церги.

цаiлзi. D². дѣпр., Монг. заiлаху удаляться.

цао. D². D⁴., нѐге цао. D¹. сто, сотня. Монг. загун, зӯ.

(Сі joxi) ӡабé. D². ты что дѣлаешь? Монг. jахін какъ?, jакіху что дѣлать?

ӡанцібéі. D³. быть. Монг. ӡанчіху.

ӡанцізі ӊарӊабе. D². выгораживать (перев. кит. дá-чу 打出).

ӡáра. D¹. D². D⁴. шестьдесятъ. Монг. цара.

ӡáрна. D¹. учить. Кит. цзяо, Монг. ӡакіхӯ (?).

ӡа-хó (кит.) цáка (Ман.). D². бакалейные товары.

ӡéбе D⁴., ӡéбі. D⁵. лодка. Монг. забі, Ман. цаjа берестяная лодка.

ӡéбе еделгébаі. D⁴. перевозъ.

ӡін-ші (кит. 進士) олобé. D². выдержать экзаменъ на цзинь-ши (доктора). Монг. олху — получить.

ӡін-шén (кит.) бітеӊé. D². адресъ-календарь. Ман. бітхе книга.

ӡірі. D¹. годъ. Монг. ціл.

ӡірӊе. D². степень, чинъ. Ман. чжергі, Монг. ӡерге.

ӡірӊó. D². D⁴. шесть. Монг ӡургä. См. ӂурӊó.

ӡіӊá улаӊӯ. D³. безвозмездно. Ман. ӡіха — чохъ, мѣдная монета.

ӡíӡы. D⁶. курокъ у ружья (кит. 機子).

ӂӯо бе. D⁴. 2-ая луна. Ман. цӯо ́ба.

ӂурібé. D². указывать. Ман. цорімбі. ку ӂурібé. D². указывать человѣка.

ӂурӯӊу. D². сердце. См. цуруӊу.

ӂурӯӊу ӊіге. D². безстрашный (кит. дань-цзы-ды 胆子大), букв. съ большимъ сердцемъ.

ӂурӊó. D¹. шесть. См. ӡірӊó.

ӂуіза (кит.) тадó ӊазір. D². азартная игра, Монг. талбіху ставить.

заор-тáн. D². баня (кит. 澡堂).

III.

УКАЗАТЕЛЬ ДАХУРСКО-СОЛОНСКИХЪ СЛОВЪ

ПО ИХЪ РУССКИМЪ ЗНАЧЕНІЯМЪ¹).

Авангардъ. Габсіján. D².

агентъ. Баіга барсáн. D². Дуӊӡа лінлебé. D².

адресъ-календарь. Зін-шéн бітеӊé. D².

азартная игра. Зіӊá нáдуӊу (ӊазір). D². ӂуіза тадó ӊазір. D².

аистъ. Тоорóл (Тоӊорóл). D².

акація. Сірыт. D².

актеръ. Сíӡа надабéі. D⁵.

---

1) То, что не всякое русское слово имѣетъ въ этомъ спискѣ соотвѣтствующія и солонское и дахурское слова, объясняется тѣмъ, что собираніе словъ всетаки носило случайный характеръ: благодаря знанію однимъ дахуромъ китайскаго письменнаго языка я могъ переводить слова, помѣщенныя въ словарѣ Попова, на дахурскій языкъ, а солоны часто отзывались запамятованіемъ или незнаніемъ солонскаго слова, или упорно предлагали вмѣсто солонскаго слова дахурское, которое я поэтому и не записывалъ. Основной списокъ русскихъ словъ для записыванія соотвѣтствующихъ имъ солонскихъ и дахурскихъ словъ у меня былъ, конечно, составленъ, но онъ не могъ быть великъ уже потому, что спрашиваемые старались какъ можно скорѣе отдѣлаться отъ сообщенія словъ.

акцизъ. Ціфыін. D².

алтарь неба и земли. Тенгыір Газір оуці̯у цукту́. D².

амбаръ. Цаӈ. D². Цаӈ гéрі. D⁵.

амбразура(?). Хотóн керыіме. D².

р. Амуръ. Шіркэ̂л. S¹⁰.

анекдотъ. Вардепі ба́іта. D².

анисъ. ᚻіге хуі-ша́ӈ. D².

аппетитъ. Сана́да ја̄мур̯у̯ула ца́ка іӟеіја́. D².

аптека. Эмыі пусыіе. D².

арбузъ. Дуа́нга. D². Дуа́нꙅа. D⁴. Ду-а́нха. D⁶. Сі гуа. D⁵.

арестантъ. У́ʼіліӈге. D².

ариометика. Суӓппа́п бітегé. D².

армія. Чуꙅа́. D². Чоꙅа́. S⁹.

арсеналъ. Чуагé аꙅу́р ꙅі̯у̯ газа́р. D².

артель. Нéкума-ін-маді́н. D².

артиллерія. Пао-куара́н. D².

архивъ. Да́мзе (Да́нзе) та̄лу́ нама́. D².

а́тласъ. Діліту́. D².

атла́съ. Торо̯о́. D².

дворцовый атла́съ. ᚻіге гуӈ-дуа́п торо̯о́. D².

атмосфера (воздухъ). А́ʼура. D².

ахать. Аја́ некда́у. D².

ахъ. Ара́. D².

Баба (см. женщина). Ему̯у̯н-ху. D².

бабка (повивальная). Таіта́і етéᚻу (етéу). D².

багажъ. Нембу́з деуркӯл. D².

багоръ. Сурку́. D².

багровый. Хелé̯е. D².

багровыя пятна. Чосотéі ва́зі. D².

бадья. Мо́до тулума́. D². Толма́. S⁵.

бакалейные товары. За-хó ца́ка. D².

бакенбарды. Ку́ше. S¹¹.

балаганъ. А́ʼнга. D².

балаганъ для земледѣльцевъ. Таре́ гéрі. D⁵.

балка (у крыши). Та́іᚻу. D². Таібо́. S⁵.

балясничать. Усу̯у̯ бар̇зі̇ на́далꙅі. D².

бамбукъ. Су́су мо́до. D².

банка. Лонко́. D².

банкоментъ (-ничать?). Бао хéза

необе́. D².

банкрутиться. Бенꙅа́н (Маіма́ні) гé-сен. D².

баня. Заор-та́ӈ. D².

барабанъ. Ту́нку. D². Іпці таіде́. D⁵. S⁷. Кунíн. S¹⁰. S¹¹. [Хонí¹)].

баранъ. Хóні. D². D⁴. S¹. S⁶. Хонí. S⁴.

баринъ. Нојóн. D². Ноíн. D⁵.

баричъ. Шао-јé. D².

барка. Чоӈ. D².

барсъ. Ма́рда. D².

барыня. Фу́жен на́іnaі. D².

барышня. Чао-ꙅé уᚻíн. D².

барышъ. Мада̯а́. D².

бастіонъ. Паота́і. D².

батистъ. Луа́ці²) ша. D².

батогъ. Па́іза. D².

батракъ. Кучу́н-ку. D².

башмаки. Са́ібі. D⁵. Са́ві. S⁴.

башня. Ло́уза. D².

баюкать. Бэбэобéі. D².

бедра. Терсу́лта. D².

безвозмездно. Зіꙅа́ улаꙅу́. D².

безвредный. Јарꙅасу́н (Аꙅірсыін, Ер-десыін) уᚻéі (уwéі). D². Ја́ра ача́ ју́ре. S⁹.

безвыходный. Моја́р каллірта́. D².

безграмотный. Бітегé у́лу медуꙅу́. D².

бездарный. Ердéм уwéі (уᚻéі). D². Ердéму а́чі. S⁹.

безденежье. Зіꙅа́ уᚻéі аꙅа́са, гар-дыку́ оӈдé. D².

безделица. Оју́нго уᚻéі. D². Іцíкен ба́іта. D². Нічуку́н ба́іта. S⁹.

безжалостный (человѣкъ). Уннако́ танімóк (ку). D².

беззаконникъ. Ваӈ-фа́ уᚻéі. D².

беззаконничаю. Бі не уеілтéбе. D².

беззаконничать (повел. накл.). Уеіле-тé. D².

1) Значеніе этихъ скобокъ и знака * объяснено въ концѣ введенія.

2) Луа́ці значитъ русскій. Русскихъ на Амурѣ китайцы прежде звали Ло́ча, теперь зовутъ Ла́о-цянь.

4*

безъимянный. Нѐре (нерѐ) уӊѐі. D².
безъимянный палецъ. Нерѐ уӊѐі хорó. D². Герібѐ áці онӽá. S³.
безмѣнъ. Гіӊ. D².
безоблачный. Аулѐн угѐі. D². Тукшí áчі. S⁹.
безпамятный. Ху-баітьі у́лу-медѐ. D².
безпокойный. Елеӽѐ уӽѐі. D². Амьі-ла áчі. S⁹.
безпокоиться. Іу́ саná ӄоӽубѐі. D².
безполезный. Бáіталасí уӊѐі. D². Баіталарáчі. S⁹.
безпристрастный. Неігѐн. D².
безпритворный. Тондó. D². S⁹.
безпутничать. Дембѐӆ дембѐӆ (Дем-бѐіӆе дембѐіӆе) наолебѐі. D².
безразсудный. Коімáлі. D². Коі-мáлі. S⁹.
безразсудно говорить. Коімáлі усуӆӟібѐ. D². Коімáлі уӆгучáнен. S⁹.
безразсчетный. Суанпьін таркáӟі уӆесí-адáн. D².
безсильный. Ердѐм укýці уӊѐі. D².
безсмертный. Неігендѐ сардьі болó уӊѐі у́лу-медѐ. D².
безсовѣстный. Лансíн уӊѐі. D².
безсонницей страдать. Неірѐ уӊѐі уантаӟí адáн. D².
безспорный. Темчеӆӟí уӊѐі у́лу бáі-талан. D².
безстрашный. Кýбу улаӽíн. D². ӽу-рýӽу ӽíге. D².
безстыдный. Ӄіцціѳѐі у́лу-медѐн. D².
безумный (человѣкъ). Герѐн горро-кó (ху). D².
безупречный. Некцí áмо таcѐн уӊѐі. D².
безчисленный. Тон уӽѐі. D².
безчинный. Дóро јóco уӽѐі. D².
безцѣнный. Худá угѐі. D².
берегъ рѣки. Мурí мердѐн. D². [Му-рí хѐші].
береза. Вѐізу. D⁶. Чáлба. D². Чал-бáн. S¹⁰. Талѐ (Тал). S⁴.
береза черная. Тебгурáн. S¹⁰.

береста. Талý. S¹⁰. [Талá монí, токтá монí].
берестовые бураки. Тáла мунѐке. S³.
беречь. Баргѐӟі уӟí (-бѐ). D².
бери. А́рці. D². Нáда аубѐі (?дай?). D⁶. Барí. S⁷. Гахáӆ. S¹⁰.
беркутъ. Шоӽó. D². Јіӊ. D⁵.
бесѣдка. Тíнза. D².
билетъ (денежный). Тѐза. *D².
бить. ӟанцібѐі. D³. Нісі. D⁵. Мук-дахáн. S⁸.
бить челомъ (кит. кэ-тоу). Муруӽу-бѐі. D².
благодарю. Баӊахá. D⁶. Алеӵáу. S¹⁰.
благородный. Саісá. D².
бланка. Куӊ-бáі дорабѐі. D².
блевать. Бээӆӟібѐ. D².
близко. Вáіре. D². Даӽахý. S¹⁰.
блинъ. Хáрсын ýтум. D².
блоха. Ӵурá. S¹¹.
блюдечко. Ішікен ӆѐза. D².
блюдо. Хіӆá. D².
блюсти. Уӟíӟі саібѐ. D².
блѣдноголубой. Гегѐн каулáн. D².
блѣдный. Ӣарчáізан. D².
богатѣть (прош. вр.). Бајíн бол-зáн. D².
богатый. Бајíн. D².
богъ (бурханъ). Бурхáн. D⁸. Буркáн. S¹¹. Баркáн. D². S⁶. Аӊдýӷ бурхáн. S⁴. Еӊдурí. D⁷. S⁹. Тенгерí D⁷. Се-вукí. S¹⁰. [Бурӽáн.]
бодливый быкъ. Мурӽудѐр укýру. D².
божественный. Еӊдýріӊге. S⁹.
бокалъ. Арӽí чомó. D².
болото. Цáлага. D⁶.
боль. Ауре. D².
боль подъ ложечкой. Арчó аудебѐ. D².
 » въ сухожиліяхъ. Гáрі кýлі сі-ребýсе аудебѐ. D².
 » въ сочленіяхъ. Јаcѐ у́і аудебѐ. D².

больно (маньчж. німекулехе). Аутте́. D².

больной (человѣкъ). Аурты́ ху. D².

больше, бо́льшій. Бара́н болза́н (бо-лоса́н). D².

большой. Хі́ге. D². Ҕі́ге. D². Шіге. D⁶.

болѣзнь. Ау́ре. D².

болѣть. Аудебе́. D². D⁶.

заболѣлъ. Аурте́. D².

борода. Сахала́. D⁶. S⁷. Саҕала́. D⁴. S². S³. S⁵. Саха́р. S¹. Гурҕакта́. S¹⁰. S¹¹.

бочка. Лу. D⁶.

бояться. Ҳалари́н. S⁹. Нееѣре́не. S⁵.

браниться. Wа́лдерен. S¹⁰. Еіде́-ту-ра́ні. S¹¹.

браслетъ (мѣдный). Ділапту́н. S¹¹.

брать. Арці́бе́. D².

братъ младшій. До́у. D². S¹. S³. Дӯ*. S². S⁷. Неку́н. S³. S¹¹. Неҕу́н. S¹¹. Неҕу́. S⁴. Нукі́н. S⁶. Čao-ха́і. S¹⁰.

— старшій. Ака́. D². D⁴. S². S⁸. S¹¹. Аҕа́. D⁴. Аха́.* S¹.S⁴. Ака́і.S¹⁰. Акі́н. S³. S⁶. Аху́й. S⁷.

братья двоюродные по матери. Тара́лі. D².

бревно. (Не́ке) мо́до. D². Гуа́нза. D⁶.

брить голову. Э́кі ханда́бе. D². Хан-на́ран. S¹⁰.

брови. Сармі́лт. D². Сармето́. D⁴. Са́ремікте. S³. Сармукто́. S⁸.

бродъ. О́со гуҕа́н газі́р. D².

брусокъ. Лэ́ке. D².

брюханъ, брюхатый. Кélі ҕі́ге. D². Тарҕу́н. D².

брюхо. Ке́лі. D². D⁴. S⁶. Гуҕэ́. D². Гуде́. S⁴. Гудеҕе́. S¹⁰.

брызгать. Пуцці́бе́. D².

бубенъ шаманскій. Хунту́ру. D³. У̂нту́ (Унту́н). S⁵.

буда́ (ѣда, каша). Ҳакты́. S³. S⁴. S⁸. З̆а́кта. S¹⁰., ҕа́кты. S¹¹.

булка. Ма̂нто́у. D⁶.

булочникъ. Уту́м ҕі́ҕу ху. D².

бульонъ. Сі́ле. D².

бумага. Ча́за. D².S⁶. Ча́зу. D⁶. Ча́чун. S¹¹. Ча́шун. S¹⁰. Цасу́н. S⁴. [Ча́са].

бурый. Ха́ра ҕелҕе бо́чо. D².

бутылка. Гу ло́нко. D⁴.

буянить. Тогілці́бе́і ¹). D³. Багілці́бе́і. D³.

бѣглый, бѣглецъ. Хорогуда́р ху. D². Уктылене́. S⁹. Чачача́ бэ́je. S⁹.

бѣгомъ. Гу́ізі. D².

— придти. Гу́ізі іребе́. D².

бѣлый. Чіга́н. D⁶. Чіҕа́н. S⁸. Чіҕа́. S². Багдарі́н. S¹⁰. Богдарі́н. S¹¹. Гіл-тері́н. S⁴. [Ціҕа́н.]

— хлѣбъ. Ме́ізу у́туме. D⁶.

быкъ. Уку́ру. D². D⁴. D⁶. S². Уку́ру́. S¹. Уку́р. D⁸. У̂ҕу́р.* S⁴. Іха́й. S¹¹. Іха́н.S⁷. Акта́. S¹⁰. Ерегы́л. D². S⁶.

былъ. Бі́ге. D⁹.

Валенки. Ало́ці. S⁹.

валить (вѣтромъ). Хадазі́ ванага́бе (-га́сан пр. вр.). D².

вата. Куҕу́н. D².

ватажиться. Ко́кіртакебе́. D².

вверхъ. Деіде́. D².

— идти. Гороло́ генере́н. S¹⁰.

вводить. Аці́рзі вазі́ре (-бе). D². Шо́рҕу вазі́ре (-рсе́н прош. вр.). D².

вдавить. Дорҕіда́ десібе́ (десі́, -се́н). D².

вдвигать. Туаті́рда́ (То̄ті́рда́) тулкі́-бе́. D².

вдова. Белебесу́н ху́. D².

вдовствовать. Белебесу́н саобе́. D².

вдыхать. Туаті́рда́ (То̄ті́рда) татабе́ (тата́, -са́н). D².

ведро (см. бадья). Муту́. D⁵. Мо́до тулума́. D². Толома́. D⁶. Толма́. S⁵.

великій человѣкъ. Ҕі́ге ху. D².

великодушный. Дото́р ерде́му ҕі́ге. D².

величина. Ҕі́ге шіке́н. D².

верблюдъ. Темуҕе́. S⁴. [Темо́.]

веревка. Де́со.* D². Де́зу. D⁶. Орку́н. S⁸. S¹⁰. Орху́н. S⁵. Урку́н. S⁴. Ур-ху́н. S¹¹.

_____

¹) Чогілці́бе́і?

вермишель. Гуа-ма́й. D².

вернуться (см. возвращаться) домой. Ку́i iребе́iја́. D⁴. Цула́н енуре́н. S⁸.

верхній (см. верхъ). Угіло́. S⁴.

верховой. Мо́рі оносо́н. D².

верховая лошадь. Убі́рі мо́рін. S⁹.

верховье рѣки. Му́рі дере́н. D².

верхъ (см. верхній). Де́ре.* D². Де-рі̄ɥе. D². Убі̄лё́. S⁹.

верёя. Ауды́ ду́р. D².

весенній день. Хабу́ру еду́ро. D².

весна. Хабу́ра. D².

ветеранъ. Каоці́н уребу́р (урубу́р) чоба́. D².

ветошка. Хаоці́н бурі́. D². Ердырте́н (Ередырте́н) бурі́. D².

вечеромъ. Сун-дɔ́. D².

къ вечеру. Орооко́н. D².

вещи таскать (изъ телѣги). Ку́di менеуке́i. S¹⁰.

вздрагивать. Да́рзі су̀рукудебе́i. D².

взморье. Дале́i мерде́н. D².

взойти на престолъ. Соорі́н саобе́. D².

видѣть. Узібе́ (-сён). D².

визжать. Орібе́. D².

я первый сдѣлалъ визитъ. Бі ордо́ еле́ге ба́iса. D².

виноградъ. Мучу́рту. D².

вкапывать. Балабе́i. D².

вклепываться. Дембеле́ куi-тане́ (-бе́). D².

влагалище. Хо́бі. D². Те́буке. D².

внизу. Дуарі́бі(Дɔ̄рі́бі). D². Дуа́ра. D².

внизъ. Дуаргіда́ (Дɔ̄ргіда́). D².

внимательнымъ быть. Гінгуле́рен. S⁹.

внукъ. Но о́моло. D². Омоле́. S⁴. [Омоло́.]

внучка. Уін омоло́. D². Омоле́ уна́зі. S⁴. [Омолібе́н.]

внутри. Дотéрібі. D².

внушать (человѣку). Ку́де сана́ wалла̄ба́бе. D².

внятно. Гетуку́н. D².

внѣ, вонъ. Бе́де. D².

вода. О́со. D². О́зо. D⁴. D⁶. S². Осо́.* S². Озо́. S¹. S². Мӯ. S³. S⁴. S⁵. S⁶. S⁷. S⁹. S¹⁰. S¹¹. Мо. S⁸.

водка. Аракі́. S¹⁰. S¹¹. Арабі́. S⁴. Аркі́ муре́н. S⁵. Арігі́. D⁴. [Арбі́.]

воевать. Аларці́ці ці́рлiде іці́цзі алалці́бе. D².

вожакъ. Теребу́ле јаре́бу. D².

вождь. Біге шуа́i. D².

возвращаться. Базірбе́. D². Базіребе́. D³. Бедеребе́i. D³. Морківе́i. D³. Мочоура́н. S⁹.

возвращать. Таодебе́. D².

воздухъ. Ау́ра, ау́ре. D².

возобновлять. Ердезі́ даі̆ дасазі́ бі̄бе. D³.

возрастъ. Насу́н. S⁴.

возъ. Не́ке теры́бе. D².

возьми. На́да аубе́i. D⁶. Барі́. S⁷. Гаха́i. S¹⁰.

войди. Вазіро́. D⁴. Вазіра́. D⁴.

войлокъ. Сісы́ге. D⁴. Сісі̄бі́. S¹¹. Сісі̄бе́. S¹¹.

войско. Чуба́. D². Чоба́. D². S¹⁰. Ме́iза. D⁵.

волосы. Ху́зу. D⁴. Нірукта̄. S¹⁰. Нурукто́. S⁸. Нуру́кте. S⁴.

вонъ. Бе́де. D².

вонъ. Петкуну́р ва́те. D².

вооруженіе. Чооɥе́i а́бура ца́ка. D².

воровать. Холобе́. D².

вороная лошадь. Кара́ мо́рін. S¹⁰.

ворота. А́уда. D⁴. Га́да. D⁶. Га́ды. D⁶. Ха́лаба (-га). D². Ха́лга. S⁴. Ка́лга. S¹⁰. [Балага.]

ворочаться. Мочоура́н. S⁹.

воръ. Хуала́ба. D².

восемь. На́ima.* D¹. D². D⁴. Цабку́н. S⁸. Забку́н. S¹¹. Цабху́й. S⁷. Цабке́н. S⁶. Цабко́. S⁴.

восемьдесятъ. Наiе́. D¹. На́ije. D⁴. Наi. D². Цабкунгі́. S⁸. Забхунгі́. S¹¹. Цабкорі́нгі. S⁴. Цабху́ббу. S⁷. Цаканбу́й. S⁶. [Наiа́.]

воскурить ѳиміамъ. Ку́зі сітабе. D².

воспитанникъ. Сábі. D². Ташкуі ку-
кýру: D².

востокъ. Нáра гараӡóкуӗ. D². Нáра
гархóін боі́. D³. Дѣӗечá ӱрéн. S⁸.
Суӗіӗá. S⁹. Ці̆ӡуӊд̣ӗ. S⁵.

восторжествовать. Шенцáн тар-
кыбé. D².

вострубить. Ӗáба хýӗубе. D².

вошь. Кумкá. S¹¹.

вощикъ. Теры̆ӡе геӗýӡу кутулý. D².

впервые. Етé мудáн. D². Етéнек мудáн. D².

впереди. Емы̆не бейéде áбе (áбе находиться). D².

вполнѣ. Харбóбо. D². Дýрку. D².

враждебный. Кíмынтéі. D².

враждовать. Кíмынбé. D¹.

врачевать. Аýре дасабé. D².

временно. Такáі. D².

4 времени года. Дурбы̆н форӡóн. D².

въ то время. Неӗерӗáн. D².

вселенная. Тенгéр дуарíӡі. D².

вскипѣла вода. О́со баціӗдéн. D².
Чахý уӗӏчóне. S⁵.

вскорѣ. Гýӊфу ӡíге уӡéі. D².

вслушиваться. Санá тáӗӡі сóн(о)су
(сопсéн). D².

встать. Іӗӗáн. S¹⁰.

— отъ сна. Журéне. S⁵.

вступить въ должность. Тушáн аӗі-
бé. D².

всходить (на гору). (А́ула) ӡарбé. D².
(Урé-де) туктірéн. S⁹.

всякій. Намарӡí. D³.

втащить. Туатірдá (Тотірдá) шоробé.
D².

второе число. Іркекíн ӊур S⁹.

второстепенный. Цаі зíрӡе. D².

входить. Ваӗӗаӡáбе. D².

не входить ни во что. Э̣́ці ýӗе гуáн-
ӗа. D².

вѣтеръ. Адíне. S⁴.

вязать (вещи). Тумкэ̣ӗ¹). S¹⁰.

вы. Та. D². D³. Таӊде. D¹. Сӯ. S⁹.

———

1) Почти Тумкуэ̣́ӗ.

выбаллотировать. Јаӗаӡáзі ӡарӡáбе. D².

выбирать. Саіп цакá јаӗегéзі гар-
ӡáбе. D².

вывозить. Цаксуӗé ӡарӡáбе. D².

выговоръ. Аі́ӗӡа. D².

выгораживать. Заӊці̆зі ӡарӡáбе. D².

выгружать. (Цакá) боаӗӡáбе. D².

выдавать провіантъ. Цаӗáӊ таӗе-
бé. D².

выдержать экзаменъ на доктора.
Зíн-ші оӗобé (оӗосáн). D².

выключать со службы. Тушáн ва-
кыӗабé. D².

высокій, высотою. Ӡундýр. D². Гугдá. S⁹.

высокосный годъ. Анаӡáн сартé
выходить. Ӡарбé. D². [хон. D².

Гарнизонъ. Карóса саоӡáӡу чуӡá. D².

гвоздь. Тебкосýп. S⁵.

гдѣ. Хáна. D².

глаза. Нíде. D². D⁴. S⁶. Нідé.* S². S⁷.
Нідӗ̣. S¹. Нýду. D⁶. Јéса. S¹¹. Éпа.
S¹⁰. Јéпе. S⁸. Јáсыӗе. S³. Јасы̆ӗе
S⁵. Ісáӗ. S⁴.

глядѣть. Узібé. D². Узí (Узé). D¹.

глотка. Сап. D¹.

глупый. Хоудý. D². У́бутуру. D¹.
Ментухýӥ. S⁹.

гнѣваться. Кубурí. D¹.

гнѣвливый. Саіп кубурí. D¹.

говори. Усуӗзí. D². Керí (кеӗí). D¹.

говорить. Усуӗзíбé. D². Усугу усуӗ-
цібéі. D⁴. Узгуӗці-бéі. D⁶. Узгуӗці.
D⁸. Уӗгучáнен. S⁹. Уӗгучáнан. S¹⁰.
Уӗгучéнерé. S⁴. [Уӡеӗчінé.]
я буду говорить. Бі усуӗзіјá. D².

годъ. Зíрі. D¹. Хуáн D³. Хóн. D². D³.
Анá. S⁹. Аӊгáн. S¹¹. Ангáні. S⁴.
[Зíӗе.]

голова. Торӡó. D¹. О́кі. D². D⁴. S⁶.
Окí. D⁴. Хекí. D⁶. Дӯ́ӗі. S⁹. Дӯ́ӗ. S¹⁰.

голодать. Бадá угéіӗо. D¹.

голубой. Цíнкерí. D¹.

голый. Дéре угéӗі. D¹.

гора. А́ула. D². D⁴. D⁶. Сай. D¹. Уре (-дукі съ горы). S⁹. Біраха́н (sic!). S¹⁰.

камен. гора. А́оре. D¹.

большая гора. Ха́да. D².

малая гора. А́ула. D². S⁶.

гордый. Бі́іхе. D¹.

городъ. Хото́н. D². Хуту́ц. D¹. Кото́н. S¹⁰.

горохъ. Бо́рціхе (Бо́рціх). D¹.

горшокъ. Ло́нко́. S¹¹.

горькій. Хелу́н. D². Ва́іла. D¹.

горячая вода. Хало́н о́зо. D⁴.

господинъ. Ноі́н ку. D¹. Нойо́н. S⁴.

госпожа. Аі́іці́н (Аі́ці́н). D¹.

въ гости ходить. Німауре́н. S¹⁰.

гостинница. Дан-гері́. D¹. D².

государство. Гуру́н. D².

грабитель. Мао ку́. D¹.

гребенка. Сункса́нда. D⁶.

греча. Ха́оле. D². S⁶. Нерыга́. S¹¹. Нербга́. S¹¹.

грибъ. Мо́гу. S¹¹.

гроза. Чаохерха́. D¹.

громъ. Уре́. S¹⁰.

— гремитъ. Таліре́. S⁴.

грубый. Буду́н. D². D⁴. Дера́м. S⁹.

грудь. Ерчу́н. D². D⁶. S⁶. Ерчу́. D⁴. Кенгы́ре. S⁴. (Ме́ван. S¹⁰.). [Ебшу́.]

грязь. Шаб(у)ра́. D¹. Ша́ура. D⁶. Аку́. S¹⁰.

губы. Аму́. S⁴. Ему́н. S¹¹. Буі́ле. S⁵.

гусь. Галу́. D⁶. Кару́ (Кара́у). D¹.

Давній (см. старый). Хуці́н. D¹. Каоці́н. D².

да́жень (генералъ). Амба́н. D⁴.

дай (см. возьми). На́да аубе́і. D⁶.

далекій, далекое мѣсто. Газіре іру́. D¹. Горо́ бобо́. S⁹.

далеко, -ій. Хо́ло. D². Горо́. S⁹.

два. Хоjу́р. D². Хоіро́. D⁴. Коіро́. D³. Хоіра́. D¹. Цуо. S⁸. Цо. S⁷. Цур. S⁴. Дур. S¹¹. Цу́ру. S⁴. S⁶. [Хоjре.]

двадцать. Хорі́. D². Хо́рін. D⁴. Хэ́рі. D¹. Орі́н. S⁶. S⁷. S⁹. S¹¹. ́Орі́н. S⁸. Урі́н. S⁴. [Хо́рі.]

двери, дверь. А́уде́ (на улицу). D². S⁸. Ауды́. D¹. Ге́шан. D². S⁶. Ге́шей (внутр.). S⁸. Геса́н. D⁴. Урке́. S¹⁰. S¹¹. Укке́. S⁴. [У́де.]

двѣнадцать. Цан цур. S⁴.

двѣсти. Зур (Цур) jама́зі. S¹¹.

девяносто. Jі́ре. D¹. D³. Jі́ре. D⁴. Іре́н. S⁸. Jіро́п. S⁴. Jіра́н. S¹¹. Уіцу́. S⁷. Уіццу́н. S⁶. [Іре́.]

девять. Jісу́. D². D⁴. Jісу́. D¹. Jебгі́н. S⁸. Jеі́н. S⁷. Jе́ын. S¹¹. Jабгі́н. S⁴. Уі́н. S⁶. [Jісе.]

день. Уду́р. D². Уду́р. D⁶. Гненгі. S¹⁰. Гнеці́. S¹⁰. Іпенбгі́. S⁴. [Удере́.]

деревня. А́іле. D². Аі́л. S¹⁰.

дерево. Мо́до. *D². D⁴. S⁶. Мо. S⁴. S¹⁰.

десять. Ха́рба. D². D⁴. Бга́рба. D¹. Цан. S⁴. S⁸. S⁹. Зан (Дан). S¹¹. Цай, Цуа́й. S⁶. Цуй. S⁷. Ца. S⁴. [А́рба.]

десять тысячъ. Не́ге цан. D¹. Ту́мо. D². D⁴. Тумо́.* S⁸. Туме́. S⁴. Туме́н (Ему туме́н). S¹¹. S⁷. Ту́мен. S⁶.

десятый годъ. Цуанці́ ана́. S⁹.

десять разъ. Цан зірбе́і. S⁹.

десятое число. Цан. S⁹.

длинный. О́рто. D². D³. Гоно́м. S⁹.

для, ради. Толде́. D³.

добросердечный. Саі́н сапа́теі. D².

дождь идетъ. Хуа́ра варбе́і. D⁴. Одона́. S⁴. Уды́н уденен. S⁹. Тегдере́н. S¹⁰.

въ долгъ давать. Акшука́н. S¹⁰.

долото. Чу́ці. D⁶.

домой идти. Jабуга́н. S¹⁰.

домъ. Гері́. D¹. D². D⁶. Ге́рі.* D⁴. Зу (Цу). S¹⁰. S¹¹. Цу (цӯ). S³. S⁴. S⁷.

докторъ. Енубу́ дасара́ даіпу́. S⁴.

дорога. Тыргу́л. D⁶. Терегу́л (терегу́ле). D².

доска. Картаза́. D⁴. Карты́с. D². Каптабго́н. S¹¹. Каптусу́п. S⁸. (Чечубга́. S¹⁰).

дочь. Уні́н. D². Уі́н ко́уке. D⁴. Уі́н. D². S⁷. Уі́н. S¹. Убгі́н. S². Уна́зі. S⁶. Уна́-

зі утэ̄. S^9. Катуӊа́н. S^{10}. Нечіху́н уна́зі. S^4. [Бішіӊа́ іӊе́.]
дрова. Мо́ду. D^6.
дрофа. Т'уа́да. D^6.
другой человѣкъ. Бісін-ку. D^3.
другъ. Сан-гучу́. D^6. D^8. Іꙗга ма-чёс. S^{10}.
дуло (у ружья). Нуӊу́. D^6.
думать, -ю (я — о тебѣ). (Бі шама́і) санабе́. D^2.
дуракъ (см. глупый). Ада́зу, Адо́зу. D^6.
духъ (см. богъ). Ендурі́. S^9.
дымъ. Санйа́н. S^{11}.
дыня. Даӊу́р кёнке. D^4.
дюймъ. Цуӊ. D^2.
дѣвица, дѣвушка. Угі́, Уӊі́н. D^6. Уна́зі. S^{11}.
дѣдъ. Ута́ці. D^2. S^6. Ота́чі. D^4.
дѣлать. Кібеі. D^3.
ты что дѣлаешь? Сі joxі ӡабе́. D^2.
дѣло казенное (частное). Сіде́н (Чосу́і) ба́іта. D^2.
дѣти. Кекуре́. D^3. Куку́ру. D^2.
дядя. Ашік. D^2. Ама́. S^7.
Его. Теры́ӊе. D^3. Ноӊаргі́н. S^9. Іні́. S^7.
ежедневно. Уду́р туала́н. D^3.
если понимаешь. Гурурекі́. S^9.
есть. Беі[1]. D^2. S^6. А'бе. D^2.
есть ли? (-живы ли?). Бісіӊгі́, Бішіӊгі́. S^8.
еще. Басе́. D^3.
еще не. А'ӊгарен. S^{10}.
Желать понять. Гуруӊе́р унён. S^9.
желтый. Ша́ра. D^6. S^2. Ҫа́ра. S^8. Шаре́. S^2. Сіӊгарі́н. S^{11}. Сіӊарі́н. S^4.
желудокъ. Кélі. D^2. D^4.
желѣзо. Касо́. D^2. D^4. Ҫéле. S^{11}. Шело́. S^{10}. Ерселе́. S^4. [Хасу́.]
жена. Емы́ге. D^2. Емыге́. S^1. S^2. Асі́. S^4. S^{10}. S^{11}. Асі́н. S^6. Атырка́н. S^{11}. Хéхе. S^7.
жениться. Асі гада́. S^4.

женщина. Емéге[1]. D^4. Амун-ку́. D^6.
жерди (у крыши). Чоꙮчоху́. S^5.
жеребецъ. Адырга́ морі́н. S^4. [Азі́рӊа́.]
жилетъ. Херегéчі. D^4. Декылé. S^8. Чібкéза. S^1.
жить. Анда́бе. D^2.
журналъ. Да́ӊза. D^2.
Заболѣлъ. Аурта̄. D^2.
заборъ. Ка́лга. S^{10}.
завтра. Бендуру́. D^2. Бундуру́. D^6.
задній. Амаргу́ бэіjé. S^9.
вода закипѣла. О'со баціꙮдéн. D^2.
замерзать. Хуꙮдубé (-дусéн). D^2.
замокъ. Joш(у)ху́. S^{11}.
замужъ выдти. Ojóн генерé. S^4.
(велѣлъ)заниматься дѣлами. Ба́іта ісікі цаабé[2]. D^2.
западъ. На́ран ванаӊо́куꙮ. D^2. На́ра уанобéі боѓ. D^3. Цулілé. S^8. Езілé. S^9. Баранда́. S^5.
запрегъ телегу. Терга́н тухуча́. S^{10}.
звать. Куˉі оріб́é. D^2.
звѣзда. Тукшу́. S^{10}. Вусіха́. S^7. О'сікта. S^4. Ошікто́. S^5.
созв. «Три звѣзды» (созв. Орла). Горібіде. D^3. Jаꙮо ошікте. S^5.
здравствуй. Абӊара́. S^{10}. Аjа́. S^8.
я здѣсь. Бі енда́беі. D^2.
здѣсь. Енде́. D^2. Éне газі́р. D^2. Еꙮе́. S^9.
зеленый. Чуӊурі́н. S^4. Наху́н. S^8. Іма́гін. S^{10}. Сіꙮа́н. S^{11}.
земля. Гаӊір. D^6. Газі́р. D^2. [Газіре́]. Ко́онді (планета). S^{10}. Туӊа́ла. S^4. Ба́лӊа (въ фанзе, полъ). D^4. Токола́ (полъ). S^{10}. Іꙮӡа́н (полъ). S^{11}. Інӊа́ (на улицѣ). S^{10}. Туꙮа́ (тоже). S^{11}.
зеркало. Бу́ꙮке. S^5.
— мѣдное на одеждѣ шамана. Толі́. D^3. То́ло (большое). S^5. Неыкерé. S^5.
зима. Уӊуꙮе (Уӊéле). D^2.
8 знаменъ. Цакóн гóса. D^2.
знаменный. Чуаӊé-ху. D^2.

---

1) Почти Бі.

1) Почти Емых.

1) Паабé сказать.

знать, — ю. Медене́. D⁶. (Бі) метте́. Таӊіре́н. S⁹.

зола. Ху́нзу. D². S⁶.

золото. А́лта. D². D⁴. Алта́.* S⁴. Алта́н. S¹⁰. S¹¹.

золотые прииски. Алта ’уілоу (веіло́у) газі́р. D².

зубы. Ікте́. S³. S⁵. S¹⁰. S¹¹. Ґкте. S⁴. Сіде́.* S².

Иголка. Цу. D⁶.

иди сюда. Енды́іре. D⁶.

идти. Jабо́. S¹⁰.

— пѣшкомъ. Jооӊа́ уліре́н. S⁴. Jаӊу́н улуре́. S³.

извощикъ. Те́ріӊе гелеку́. D⁴. Терега́ нелбуру́н. S¹¹. Теріге́ ілбере́ беіjе́. S⁴. [Теріге́ гелӊе́ хуй.]

или нѣтъ? Ача́ӊо́. S⁴.

Императоръ. Еце́н. D².

имя. Геріб́е́. S⁴. Ге́рбу. S⁸. S¹⁰.

испражня́гься. Іка́пан. S¹⁰. Амуна́н. S¹¹.

ихъ. Тезе́. D³. Тарі́н. S⁹.

Казенная бумага Сіде́н ба́іта. D².

казенное (присутственное) мѣсто. Албе́ газі́р. D².

казенный домъ. Албе́ гері́. D².

казенная теле́га. Алабе́і теры́ӊе (теры́х). D².

казначейство. Муӊгу́ін намы́н. D².

какимъ образомъ. Херзі́. D³. Кере́ D³.

какой. Jама́р. D⁶. Jамуре́. D⁶. Jе́му. S¹¹.

кальянъ. Му́-дамга. S¹⁰. Суі-jай-да́і. S⁴.

камень. Чоло́.* D⁶. Цоло́. S⁸. S¹⁰. Цо́ло. S⁴. ӡоло́. S¹¹.

капъ. Хуа́ла. D². D⁴. S². Хуалы́н. S⁵. Хуа́р. S¹. Куала́н. S⁸. Кула́н (Кула́н.) S¹¹. На́ӊан. S¹⁰. Наӊа́н. S³. Іте́. S⁴.

капуста. Ціӊа́ ноӊа́. D⁴. Нунӊа́. S¹⁰. Нунга́. S¹¹. Сірӊе́кте. S⁴. [Ціӊа́ нуӊа́.]

караулъ. Каро́. D².

картофель. Ту́ду. D⁴. D⁶. S¹¹. Карто́шка. S¹⁰.

каша (буда, см. ѣсть). ӡа́кта. S¹⁰.

кашлять. Сімкіре́н. S⁹.

кипятить воду. Му́jу уjуре́н. S⁹.

кирпичъ. Уа́са онці́. S⁵.

кисетъ. Тартыга́. D⁴. Каптурӊа́. S⁸. Хаптурӊа. S⁴. Хабтерге́. S¹¹. [Хабтаӊа́.]

кислый. Ту́суп. D².

кисть (писчая). Пі. D⁴. S⁶. S¹⁰. Фі. D².

клаияться. Муруӊубе́і. D².

книга. Бітеӊе́ (Біты́х).* D². Бітехе. S⁸. Бітхе́. S⁴. Біті́ӊе. D⁴. Біты́ӊе. S¹¹. Бітке́. D⁵. Дентеле́. D⁶. [Бітӊе́.]

кнутъ. Чечіӊу́ (Чочоӊу́). S⁴.

кобыла. Го́у морі́н. S⁴. [Ку мо́рі.]

кожа. Арса. D³. Нана́. S¹⁰.

козелъ. Іма́. D². S². S⁶.

козуля. Цу́ру. D².

колесо. (Терга́н) курду́. S⁵.

кольцо на большомъ пальцѣ. Ур(у)гуптун. S¹¹. Урӊу-ӊебте́н. S⁸.

колѣно. Толці́х. D³. Туарчіга. D⁴. ’Енге́. S⁴.

конница. Морі́н чуӊа́. D².

конопля. О́лозо. D⁶.

копье. Гіда́. S⁹.

корзинка (плетеная, круглая). Алдама́. S⁵.

коробка. Ке́ӡа. S¹¹.

корова. Уні́н. D⁶. Уку́ру. D⁴. Уку́р. S¹⁰. S¹¹.

коровье молоко. Уне́-су́. D⁶. Уні́су́. D⁴. Укку́н. S⁸.

короткій. Вака́р. D². Урункун. S⁹.

коса (волосъ). Гедіге. D⁴. Гедыӊе́н. S¹¹. Гетӊун. S⁵. Гекте́. S³. Гыці́га. D⁶. Геці́ге. S². S⁸. Нурікте́. S⁴. Нуректе́. S¹¹. Не́рукте. S¹⁰. [Кезіге́.]

кошка. Кеке́. D². S⁶. Ке́ке D⁶. Кэкэ́. D⁴. Хе́хе. S⁴. Кака́. S¹⁰.

красный. Хула́. D⁶. S². Хула́н. S⁸. Уларі́н. S⁴. S¹⁰. Уларі́н. S¹¹. Каjе́р. S¹⁰. [Ула́.]

кровь. Чосе́. D³.

крыло (для пыли). Дебтеле́. S⁵.

крыша. Нембузу́. D⁶. Денді́н (-зі́н). S¹⁰.

крышка. Да́іба. S⁵. Да́іву. S⁸.

куайцзы (палочки для ѣды). Са́рпо. D⁴. Сарпо́. S⁵. S⁸. Ҫарпо́. S¹¹. Чарпу́. S¹⁰.

куда. Хаіда́. D².

кулакъ. Нуруга́. S¹¹. Норва́. S⁴.

кумирня. Ма́о. S¹⁰. S¹¹.

кунжутное масло. Балаі-тазу́. D⁶.

купецъ. Цангуіде́. D⁴. Пу́шеле. S¹⁰.

купить. Гада́н. S¹⁰.

курительныя свѣчи. Кузі́. S¹¹.

курить табакъ. Да́нва уобéи (уобé). D⁴. Данва імере́. S⁴. Дамга́ омпа́н. S¹⁰. Дамува́ емука́л. S¹¹.

курица. Какара́ (вообще). D⁶. S⁶. S¹⁰. S¹¹. Кавара́. D⁴. Еміне́ какара́. D⁶. Куро́ ненéн. D².

курма. Олоńде́. S⁴.

курокъ (у ружья). Зі́зы. D⁶.

курьеръ (кит. сунъ-вэнь-шу-ды). Веńшу́ куцıу́-ху́. D².

Лавка. Пусы́ле. D². Пу́зыл. D⁶. Пу́веле. S¹⁰.

лагерь. Коара́н ге́рі. D².

ладонь. Гаре́ хуру́. D⁶. Алва́. S³. Аранга́. S⁸.

лапша. Ма́іса гулі(н). S¹¹.

левъ. Арсала́. S⁴.

легкій. Ху́нген. D².

легкія. О́ркі. D².

лежать (см. лечь). Кулере́не. S⁵.

лепешки. Бін. D². Харсы́н уту́мо (кит. го-ку́й). D².

лечить. Ау́ре дасабе́. D².

лечь. Угıа́ран. S¹⁰.

лицо. На́дыма. D⁴. D⁶. Дере́. S⁴. Дере́. S¹⁰.

лобъ. Мангі́л. D⁶. Мангі́л. S⁴. Ма́нгіле. S³.

лодка. Ці́ві. D⁶. Зе́бе. D⁴. Зе́бі. D⁵. Де́ві. S⁷. Манго́. S⁹. Монго́. S¹⁰.

локоть. Іча́ (Іча́). S⁴.

лошадь. Мо́рі. D². D⁶. S⁶. Мо́рін. D². Мо́рін. D⁴. Морі́. S¹. S². S⁷. Мо́рін. S⁴. S¹⁰. S¹¹.

лошакъ. Ло́за. S⁴.

лукъ (для стрѣльбы sic!). Со́му. D⁶.

луна. Са́ра. D¹. D⁴. Саро́ро. D⁴. Бе́ва. S⁴. S⁹. S¹⁰. Бе́га. S¹⁰. Ба́ва. S⁵. Бі́ва. S⁴.

луна взошла. Саро́ро гаці́рзан. D⁴. Бе́ган декдеча́. S¹⁰.

луна зашла. Бе́ган манауча́. S¹⁰.

1-ая луна. А́на са́ра. D⁴. Ане́ бе. S¹¹. Ане́ бі. S⁴.

2-ая луна. Зу́о бе. D⁴. Цу́о бе. S⁴. S¹¹.

3-ья луна. Ҙалы́й бе. D⁴. Ґлан бе S¹¹. Іла́н бе. S⁴.

4-ая луна. Ду́ін бе. D⁴. S⁴. Ду́ін бе. S¹¹.

5-ая луна. Та́нгун бе. D⁴. Сунца́ бі. S¹¹. Сунва́ бе. S⁴.

6-ая луна. Ні́нгу́й бе. D⁴. S⁴. Ну́вун бе (бі). S¹¹.

7-ая луна. На́дан бе. D⁴. S¹¹. Нада́н бе. S⁴. S¹¹.

8-ая луна. Ца́ху́й бе. D⁴. Цаву́й бе. S⁴. За́хуй бе. S¹¹.

9-ая луна. Уімбе́. D⁴. Уıу́н бе. S¹¹. Уıу́н бе. S⁴.

10-ая луна. Цуа́й бе. D⁴. S⁴. S¹¹.

11-ая луна. Уı́нсі́й бе. D⁴. У́ішун бе. S¹¹. Умшо́й бе. S⁴.

12-ая луна. Ане́ са́ра. D⁴. Зурву́н бе. S¹¹. Цуруву́н бе. S⁴.

люби Госіка́р. S⁹.

любить. Госіре́н. S⁹.

любящій человѣкъ. Госіре бэіе́. S⁹.

лѣвый. Соло̌во́і. D². Зевінгіде́. S⁹.

лѣнивый. Цалко́. D².

лѣсъ. Тун. D⁶.

лѣто. Назі́р. D⁹.

Мальчикъ. Но. D².

малый. Учі́кен. D⁶. Ушхы́н. D⁶. Іші́кен, іці́кен. D².

масло. Уры́м. D⁴. Токсо́. D⁴. То́со. D². Іму́рту. S⁶.

мать. Эуэ́. D⁶. Еуо́. D². S². Аб. D⁴.
Уо́. S¹. Емо́. S⁶. Анíн. S³. S¹⁰. S¹¹.
Опе́н. S⁶. Ане́. S⁸. Эне́. S⁷. S⁸. Эне́.
S⁴. Ережíн. S⁸. [Ме́мо.]
махалка (отъ мухъ). Арпуку́. S¹⁰.
машина швейная. Цӯ уорí оῑрдебе́.
D².
медве̌дь. Каруку́. D⁶.
Большая Медве̌дица¹). Доло́ хото́.
D³. Надо ошíкте. S⁵.
мельница паровая. Гали́-íн̨. D². Га́-
лí-мо́со. D².
меринъ. Акта́ морíн. S⁴. [А́кта мӧрí.]
мести. Есу́ру. D⁴.
метелка. Есу́ро. S⁸.
мои вещи. Минí цака́. S⁷.
молиться (богу). Цалбара́н. S⁹. Мур-
гуре́н. S¹⁰.
молнія. Адíнен. S¹⁰.
молодецъ. Саін е́ре. D².
молоко. Уне́-су́. D⁶. Унí-су́. D⁴. Ук-
ку́н. S⁸.
молотокъ. Ланту́. S⁴. S⁵.
молчи. Сíнгада́. S¹¹.
морковь. Уларíн лобо. S¹¹.
мочиться. Цíженéн S¹¹. Чíгéн-муре́н.
мочь (могу). Шадбéи. D³.   [S¹⁰.
мужъ, хозяинъ. Данжа́да-е́ре. D⁴.
мука. Хулíн. S⁸. Ма́іза железо. S⁴.
мусульманинъ. Хуíза. D².
мухогонка. Абкí. D². S⁶. Арпуку́. S¹⁰.
мущина. Ержу́н. D². Ергу́н-ку. D⁶.
Н̨ара́ви-бэjé. S⁹.
мы. Ба́жа. D². Бе́да. D³. Míту́. S⁹.
мыло. І́за. D². S⁶.
мысль. Сана́. D². Жалí. S⁹.
мыть лицо. Чубула́кта. S¹⁰.
мыться.- Омпа́баi. D⁴.
мышь. Ачíжа́н. D⁶.
мясо. Ма́жа. D². Маха́. S¹. Jа́лі. S⁷.
У'ле. S¹¹. Уле́ (Уло́). S¹⁰. Уллí. S⁶.
Уλдо́. S⁴. [Ма́жа.]
ме̌дь. Га́оли. D². D⁴. S¹¹. Го́лі. S⁴.
[Жо́iле.]

ме̌дный чохъ. Га́оли зіжа́. S¹¹.
ме̌нять (деньги). Алзíбе́. D². (Цажа́)
цугутта́н. S¹⁰.
ме̌шокъ. Теребте́i пу́за. D⁴. Фолого́.
D⁹. Коуде́.* S⁴. Ку́де. S⁸. Ку́ды. S¹¹.
— для табаку. Улуку́ (Олоку́). S¹⁰.
Набрюшникъ. Уребту́н. S¹⁰.
назадъ. Хуаiжанда́. D³. Амасха́кі. S⁹.
наемная теле̌га. Туружу́н терыже.
D².
нанимать теле̌гу. Терíже туругун-
деоба́i. D⁴.
нанимать. Турмíбе́. D².
напередъ. Ордо́. D².
написапо. Балчíра́н. S⁸.
напиться пьянымъ. Сортосо́н (напился). D³. Соктоора́н. S⁹.
народъ. Іреже́н. D².
наштанники¹) Араму́ш. S¹⁰.
не, не̌тъ. У'ле. D².
я не пойду. Бí уле-цімбí. D².
не говори. Бу усужí. D⁴.
не знаю. Медеку́ угéи. D⁷.
не понимать. Аженíн гуруре́. S¹¹.
не понимаешь-ли? Асíн гуру́рен.
S⁹.
небо. Тенгерí (-гéри). D². Ба́га. S⁶.
Бо́жа. S⁹. Угíле́ божа́. S⁴. (О'жікта.
S¹⁰). [Тенгере́.]
неве̌жа. Буду́н-ху. D².
ниже. Дуа́ра. D³. [До́ро.]
пизкíй (нижнíй). Бо́бони. D². Ам̂ла́.
S⁴. Некте́. S⁹.
низъ. Дуа́ра. D². Ержíле́. S⁹.
нитка. Сíра́с. D¹. Шíла́зу. D⁶.
новый. Сíнке́н. D².
нога. Ку́лі. D². D⁶. S⁶. Беждíр. S⁴.
Былке́. S⁷. Алжа́н. S⁹. Алга́н. S¹⁰.
S¹¹.
нога до коле̌нъ(голень). Куруме́лто.
D⁴.
ногти. Ужíкта́н. S¹⁰.
ножъ. О'нцí. D⁴. О'нцы. D². О'нчí. D⁶.
Унчí. S¹. Учко́. S⁵. Учíке́. S⁴. Уцí-
кап. S⁶. Кото́. S¹⁰. S¹¹. [Жотожо́.]

---

¹) Буквально «7 звѣздъ».

¹) Отъ сапогъ до колѣнъ.

—дорожный (кит. ху-чжао-дао). Нéригу óнці. D⁴.
ноздря. Ілекчá. S¹⁰.
носъ. Хамáр.* D². Хамы́р. D². S¹. S⁶.
  Хамырá. S². Хамурý (Хамарý). D⁴.
  Хамурí. S⁷. Онуктó. S⁸. ’оноктó.
  S¹⁰. ’Анѕоктó. S¹¹. Нíнза.S⁴. Нáнсе¹).
  S³. S⁵.
ночь. Сунí. D⁶. Долбó. S⁴. Інéн. (?) S¹⁰.
  [Сун.]
нѣжный. Нарíн. D¹.
нѣтъ. Угéи. D². D⁶. Уѕéи. D². Уѕéи.
  D². D³. Уwéи. D². D³.
Облако. Туксé. S⁴. Тукшí. S⁹.
обмануть. Улогетéн. S¹⁰.
овесъ. Арбá. D⁹. Хуалíмбо. D⁶. Куалíмпо. D². S⁶. Кулíмпа. S¹¹.
овладѣть. Еѕелебéи. D³.
огниво. Гандý. S¹¹.
огонь. Гáлі. D². Тоѕó. S⁴. S⁵. Т’оó.
  S⁶. Туá. S⁷. Таó, Тавó. S¹¹. [Ѕáла.]
огородъ. Керѕé. D⁴.
огурецъ. Кéнке. D⁴. Кынкé. D⁵. Кем-
  кé. S¹⁰. S¹¹.
одиннадцать. Харýн негé. D¹. Хар-
  бы́н нéке. D². Хáрбан некé. D⁴.
  Цан амó. S⁴. Цан емýн. S⁸. Ѕан
  емýн. S¹¹. Цуѝ емý. S⁷. Цуáн, цаѝ
  емы́н. S⁶. [Арбáн негé.]
одинъ. Нéге. D¹. D². Нéке. D². D⁴.
  Амó. S⁴. Емýн. S⁶. Эмýн. S⁸. Емкé.
  S⁷. Умýн. S¹¹. [Негé.]
одѣвать (платье). Теттéн. S⁹. Татгéл.
  S¹⁰.
  » шапку. Аулахáл. S¹⁰. (повел.
  накл.).
одѣяло. Тансы́. S⁵. Улá. S¹⁰. Улá (Уллá). S¹¹. Улдá. S⁴.
озеро. Нáура. D⁶.
(я) ожидаю, буду ожидать. (Бі) ен-
  куѕéбе. D².
окончиться. Бардабéи. D³.
окно. Чóнху. D⁴. Чонкý. D⁶. Чанкó.
  S¹⁰. Чонкó. S¹¹. Чонѕó. S⁵. Чуáнху.
  S⁴. [Чонѕó.]

1) S³. произносилъ въ носъ все слово.

онъ. Терé. D¹. D².
онъ ушелъ. Тéре іцісéн. D².
опіумъ. Ектé дамуѕá. S¹¹.
опять. Басé. D³.
осень. Намýру. D².
осина. Чагáн jамá. D¹.
оспаривать, спорить. Темшелце-
  бéи. D³.
отецъ. Ецы́ге. D⁴. Ачá. D². D⁴. D⁶.
  S². Ачá. S¹. Ечíге. S⁸. Абá. S⁴. Амá.
  S³. S⁶. S⁷. А’ма. S⁸. Амíн. S⁹. Утэ̣.
  S¹⁰. Утé. S¹¹. [Аѕé.]
откуда. Хáна. D².
отослать. Укуцíбе. D².
отправляться въ городъ. Хотон-дé
  ценегéр. S⁹.
отпрягать телѣгу. Тергé тáса. D¹.
отрава. Мáо óмо. D¹.
отрядъ. Нéге цýру (цýру). D¹.
офицеръ. Хавé хафáн. D². Хавáн. D⁶.
охранять. Саíбé. D².
охраняющій. Саѕіѕý. D³.
очагъ. Кообы́ц. S³. Кóбуц. S¹⁰.
Палецъ на ногѣ. Шарбагáн. S¹⁰.
палецъ (5 пальцевъ). (Тáун) хорó. D².
  D⁴. S⁶. Хурý. D⁶. Унаѕáн. S¹⁰.[Ѕорó.]
  большой палецъ. Ѕеры́ге. D².
  Хéріге. D⁴. Уруѕýн. S³. S¹¹. Ур-
  ѕýн. S⁸. Орогýн. S⁴. [Ерѕí ѕорó.]
  указательный палецъ. Хорó. D⁴.
  Оі¹) хорó. D². Онѕá. S³. Унаѕá.
  S⁴. Унаѕáн. S⁸. S¹¹.
  3-ій (средній) палецъ. Дуандíѕе
  хорó. D². Дуáнде хорó. D⁴. Делгý (Дулгý). S¹¹. Долѕó унаѕá. S⁴.
  Долѕó унíѕáн. S⁸. Дóло онѕá. S³.
  4-ый (безъимянный) палецъ.
  Нерé уѕéи хорó. D². Ілáці хорó.
  D⁴. Герíбé áці онѕá. S³. Унíѕáн.
  S⁸. Цáраткі. S¹¹.
  мизинецъ. Ушхíн хорó. D⁴. Суітко́.
  D². Суіткí. S⁸. Цімíткі. S¹¹. Чи-
  меркí. S⁸. Чоідогó. S⁴.

1) Отъ Оібé шить — палецъ, кото-
торымъ шьютъ.

палка (трость). Су́су мо́до. S⁸. Мо̄.
S³. S¹¹.

палка для вѣшанья¹) Сіібо́. S⁵.

пальто. Кайта́за. S¹⁰.

паспортъ. Терегу́л jау̯ду̯ па́о. D².

пахать. Тарра́н. S⁹.

пашня. Тарга́н (-дан). S¹⁰.

Пекинъ. Бо́зін. D⁴.

пепелъ. У́лепте́н. S¹⁰.

первое число. Іркекі́н. S⁹.

первостепенный. У'зі саі́н. D².

переводчикъ. Хао мутубе́і. D¹. Тун-
ші гуруко́. D⁴.

перевозъ. Зе́бе еделге́баі. D⁴.

передній. Емь́не. D³. Зулуд̯у̯ бэіjе́.
S⁹.

переночевать. Не́к-суні лантаба́і.
D⁴.

переправиться черезъ рѣку. Му́ре
еделбе́. D⁴. Ча́шкі нгееке́л. S¹⁰.

переправлять. Ду. D¹.

перецъ. Чінзо́. S⁴.

песокъ. Сергі́. S¹⁰. Шілута́н. S⁴. Ші-
лукта́н. S⁸. [Сар хомуге́.]

печать. Доро́н. D².

печень. Хельі́х. D³.

писарь. Ваіла́н. D². Аісіла́ра. D².

писать. Біте́де кіібе́. D². Бітехе́ кібеі. D⁶. Бічі́к кіібе́. D⁴. Бітіге́ оора́н.
S⁴. Біте́де. S¹⁰. Балчіра́н. S⁸. [Біте́де
дінé.]

питать. Тед̯ебе́і. D³.

пить (воду, чай). Уб́. D². (Ці̀аі) уобе́.
D⁴. Уобе́і. S¹. (Мӯ) імке́. S³. (Мӯ)
імре́не. S⁵. Імь́ік. S⁶. (Бітеге́. S¹⁰).

плакать (о ребенкѣ). Сопдоро́но. S⁵.

платокъ (кусокъ холста). Ху́нко. D⁴.
Ху́нку. S⁸. Уд̯ку. S¹¹. Умку́. S¹⁰.

платье. Терыгексе́. S⁹.

» шамана. Самасд̯і (Самасд̯і).
D³. S⁵.

плевать. Томона́н. S⁹. S¹⁰. Тумуне́н.
S¹¹.

1) На веревкахъ подвязывается къ балкѣ
подъ крышей.

плеть. Морі́ (Мо́рі) міна́. D⁴. D⁵. Чі-
чу́да. S⁴. Чечуга́. S¹¹. Чечі́д̯у. S⁵.

плечо. Му́ру. D⁴. Мі́рі. S⁴. [Ме́ре.]

плошка. Пьі́нса. S¹¹.

побѣдить. Шенд̯а́н таркыбе́. D².

поварешка. Маша́оза. D⁴.

поводья. Дело́. D⁶.

подбородокъ. Цад̯і́. S⁴.

подмышка. Оонé. S⁴.

подобно, похожій. Адалі́. S⁹.

похожій на меня. Мінгеці́н. S⁹.

подорожная. Теред̯у́л jау̯ду̯ па́о. D².

подражаю. См. слѣдую.

подсвѣчникъ. Лата́і.* D⁴.

подстилка. Дел̯д̯е́. S⁴. Сактууре́н. S¹¹.
[Дебд̯е́.]

подушка. Деріба́. D⁴. Дерыбо́. D².
Деребо́. S⁸. Дербу́. S⁴. Теру́. S¹¹.
Теру́. S¹⁰. [Дере́.]

пойдемъ. Jабо́. S¹⁰.

по́йти (пр. вр. отъ ід̯ібé.). Іді́сен. D¹.

показывать. Уку́ узі́де. D¹.

покупать. Дуру́лдебе́. D².

половина. Ду́ндере. D¹.

полотно. Мо́бурі. D¹.

полъ (см. земля). Шілле́. D⁶.

понимать. Гуруре́н. S⁹. S¹¹.

понялъ. (Бі) гетку́н болодо́. D².
Гуруд̯а́. S⁹.

понимаешь-ли? (Нạд̯у́н усугу́) гу-
ру́ бісіjа́. D⁴.

послѣ, послѣ того какъ (D².). Ху-
а́іна. D². Хуаінасы́. D³.

посмотри. Ічеке́л. S¹⁰.

посылать. Такараба́і. D³.

потолокъ. Пын. D⁶. Jе́ві. D⁶.

по́-три. Jіла́та́р. S⁹.

почта. (?) Долбо́. S¹⁰.

почтовый (человѣкъ). Г̍аму́н-ху. D².

поясница. Да́рма. D². Да́рума. D⁴.

поясъ. Пу́за, Пу́за. D⁴. Бьі́зе. D⁶.
Самасд̯і¹). D³. Омоло́. S⁸. Омо́л. S⁴.
Ому́л. S⁸. S¹⁰. S¹¹.

1) Шаманскій, съ побрякушками.

поѣхать въ телѣгѣ. Тергáн jабучá.
» верхомъ. Каi-дáу. S¹⁰. [S¹⁰.
правый. Барáн. D². Ангiдá. S⁹.
прежде. Ордó. D².
прежнiй. Ордонiӊí. D³.
преступникъ. Уеilé уачá бэijé. S⁹.
(я) прибылъ сюда. (Бi) ангадí куцiрзá. D².
прикладъ (у ружья). Дáлбаӊа. D⁶.
принесъ (?). Емергечá. S¹⁰.
пришелъ. Iртéн омычé. S⁸. Емергечá. S¹⁰.
провожатый. Терегýле укоцíу хаФáн. D².
продавать. Дурубé. D².
произношенiе. Аílӊа. D².
пропитывать. Теӈебéi. D³.
просо (кит. ми-цза). Сiдiмé. S¹¹.
Сабсу и прочiе 3 человѣка. Сабсý тарíн iлáн бэjé. S⁹.
прошенiе. Гýiвеiнi. D³.
прошу. Гóiбеi. D². D³.
прощай. Аjакáнӡi. S¹⁰.
прутья. Mō̃. S⁴.
прѣсный. Болóн. D².
пряжка на поясѣ. Ӊургí. S⁸.
птица летящая. Деӊíл деӊiлiré. S⁴. [Деӊí.]
пуговица. Тóрчi. D⁴. Тóбчi. S⁸. Тобчí. S⁴. S⁸. S¹⁰. S¹¹. [Табшí.]
пушка. Ӊíге пао. D².
пшеница. Мáiза. D². S⁶.
пшено (кит. сло-ми-цза). Нарéм. D².
пьяный. Сортосóн. D³.   [S⁶.
пятнадцать. Харбы́н тáӊу. D². Цан тангýн. S⁶. Цан торонӊá. S⁸.
пять. Тáбу. D¹. Таáӊу. D². Тáван. D⁴. Тунӊá. S⁴. Тунгá. S¹¹. Тунгáн. S⁷. Туангáн. S⁶. Торонӊá. S⁸. [Табá.]
пятьдесятъ. Тáбi. D¹. D². Тáiбi. D⁴. Туанӊí. S⁴. Торонгангí. S⁸. Тананӊí. S¹¹. Сусái. S⁶. S⁷. [Тебé.]
пѣтухъ. Андáне. D². Амiнá какарá. D⁶. Какарá. S⁶.
пѣть пѣсню. Учýн учулерé. S⁹.
пѣсня. Учýн. S⁹.

пѣхота. Jауӊáн чуӊá. D².
пѣшкомъ идти. Jаувáн jауijá. D². S⁶. Jаукáн jабурéн. S¹¹. Jаӊýн улурé. S³. Jооӊá улiрéн. S⁴. [Jабаӊá jабанá.]
Работать. Уарáн. S⁹.
равнина. Гаӈíре пiн. D⁶.
радоваться. Акдырéне. S⁵. Урунéн. S⁹.
разбуди. Селыӊé. D².
разсердить. Кýï Фанчáбе. D².
реестръ. Чéза. D².
ремень. Усí. S⁴. Ушiхáн. S¹⁰. Сiдыӊýн. S¹¹.
рисунокъ. Нiруӊáн.* S⁴.
рогожка. Дéрезу. D⁴. Дерзó. S¹. S². Дерзó. S⁸. Дерсýн. S⁵. Дересýн. S¹¹. Дéрешiýн. S¹⁰.
рожь. Jýме. D⁶.
ротъ. А́ма. D². D⁴. S⁶. Амá.* S¹. Амаӊá. S³. Амӊá. S⁴. Амугáн, Амгáн. S¹¹. Ангái. S⁷. Амýн. S¹⁰. Iнькге. S⁵.
роща. Тун. D⁴. Бургáн. S⁴. Мóса. S¹¹.
рубаха. Вáхала. D⁴. Хантáцiнцi. D⁴. Кантачiнкi (короткая). D⁶. Чамчá. S¹⁰. Чамӊá. S¹¹.
ругать (браниться). Еiдé турáнi. S¹¹.
ружье. Маонáн. D⁴. Мáочáн. D⁶. Маоцíн. D². Jан-пáо. D². Мачáн. S⁴. [Бо.]
рука. Гáрi¹). D². D⁶. S⁶. Гарí. S⁷. Гáде. D⁴. Галé. S¹. 'Гáла. S¹⁰. Ӊáла. S⁴. S¹⁰. Нáла. S³. S⁵. [Ӊарá.]
рыба (рыбу ловить). Алó. S¹⁰.
рукавицы. Бéле. S⁸.
русскiя серебряныя деньги. Луáцi мýнгу зiӊà. D².
рѣдька. Лóбӊ. S¹¹. [Лóбо.]
рѣка. Мýру.* D². D⁴. D⁶. Хурага. D³. Бiрá. S⁴. S¹¹. Амýр. S⁷. Гóлi. S⁶. S⁷. Бiргáн. S¹⁰.
рѣчка. Цун. D⁶. Хуáрага. D⁶. Бiргáн. S⁷. Бiргáн. S¹⁰.

¹) Одна рука Нiндýр гáрi. D²., двѣ руки — цурý гáрi. D².

Садись. Сáу (Сáȯ). D⁴. Таухéӣ. S¹⁰.
Тенынéӣ. S¹¹.
садиться, сидѣть. Текé. S³.
самовольно, самъ собою. Iнí чісуí. S⁹.
самъ (пойду, пошелъ). Уорé (іцібé, іцісéн). D².
сани. П'áра. D⁶.
сапоги. Кочóро. D². D⁴. S¹. Кучýр. D⁶. Гочóро. D⁴. Гочóрі. S⁷. Ҕочóро. S⁸. Хочорó. S². Унтá. S⁴. Унтv́. S¹⁰. Керачýн уктá (кожаные сапоги). S¹¹. Олóці. S⁶. [Турíтé ҕотóл.]
сахаръ (бѣлый). Са-тáц. D⁶. (Гіӣтарíн) шатáц. S⁴. [Ціҕáн шатá.]
свинья. Гáха. D¹. Гáҕа. D². S⁶. Гаіха. D⁴. Гáга. D⁶. S¹. Уӣгéн. S⁴. Уӣгéн. S¹¹. Выцгí. S⁷. Чонкó. S¹⁰. [Ҕахá.]
связка (1000) чоховъ. Мáнҕа ҕаҕá. D⁴.
свѣчка. Ла. S¹¹.
сгорѣть. Тулердебéі. D³.
сегодня. Е'недурý. D³.
семь. Долó.* D¹. D². D⁴. Надá. S⁴. Надáӣ. S⁷. Надáн. S⁸. Ѝадáн. S¹¹. Надéн. S⁶. Надó. S⁵.
семьдесятъ. Дáла. D². D⁴. Дáра. D¹. Надайцý. S⁶. S⁷. Надацҕí. S¹¹. Надарангí. S⁸. Надарíнҕí. S⁴. [Далá.]
сердиться. О'рі сірáн. S⁴. Ауpісчаjáне. S⁵. Панчíбé. S⁸. Тегуӣчáн. S¹⁰. Туҕулáн. S¹¹.
сердце. Цурýҕу. D². Ҙурýҕу. D². Маевáн. S¹¹. Дȯ S⁹.
серебро. Мýнго. D⁴. Мýнгу. D². Мунгý. S⁴. Мецгýн. S¹⁰. Мецгýӣ. S¹¹. [Мунгó.]
сестра. Унáці. S¹⁰.
младшая сестра. Уѝ-дý. D². ¹) D⁴. S¹. Неҕýн. S¹¹. Некýн. S¹¹. Упáзін некý(н. S³), S⁴.
старшая сестра. Экȯ́. D⁴. S². Ехé. S⁴. Е'кці. D². Окці. S¹. Окíн. S³. Акá. S¹¹.

1) У D². и S¹. еще слышалось дóу.

сзади. Хуáіна. D³.
сидѣть. (Jаобáі. D⁴). Тегеттéн. S¹⁰.
сила (способность). Шаделé. D³.
синій. Курí. D⁶. Чуҕутурíн. S¹¹. Сіӣáн. S⁴. [Ціӣáн.]
сказать. Усуӣзібé. D². Цаабé (= приказать). D².
онъ скажетъ. Терé усуӣзібé. D².
я тебѣ скажу. Бі шамáда цájа. D³.
сколько. Кедé. D⁷. Jокíн. D⁴. Jоҕíн. S¹¹. Оҕікчá. S⁴.
сколько тебѣ лѣтъ? Адечí. S⁸.
сколько верстъ. Хедéн ҕазíр. D².
сладкій. Дасýц. D².
слово. Усуҕу (Усýгу). D². Уҕé. D⁶. Уӣгýр. S⁹.
слушай. Доӣзіҕá. S⁹.
слушать. Дуоӣдерéн. S¹¹.
я слышалъ. Бі соноцсáн. D⁴.
слѣдую, подражаю. Ацгірáн. S⁹. Алмарáн. S⁹.
слѣдъ. Алҕá. S⁴. [Аӣó.]
слѣпой. Соҕýр. D².
смотрѣть. Учерéн. S¹⁰.
смѣяться. Iнектерé. S³. Iнтерéне. S⁵. Ѝактырéн. S⁹. Iѝактырéн. S¹¹. Цугуттéн. S¹⁰.
снять (платье, пов. накл.). Локкóӣ. S¹⁰.
» (шапку) Аталкáн. S¹⁰.
снѣгъ. Манá. S¹⁰. Інҕá. S¹⁰.
» идетъ. Іманарá. S⁴. Jіманáран.
собака. Нóҕо. D². D⁴. Нуҕó. D⁸. Інахí. S⁴. Нінакíн. S¹⁰. Гашкáн. S⁶. [Нохóі.]
созвѣздіе. Чолпýн. S⁵.
солдатъ. Укшíӣ. S¹⁰.
солнце. Нáра. *D¹. D². D⁴. Нáрі. S⁷. Делечá (Делечá). S¹⁰. Çігýн. S⁵.
солнце взошло. Нáра гацірзáн. D⁴. Делечá декдеçá. S¹⁰.
солнце зашло. Делечá долбочó. S¹⁰.
соль. Катá. D². D⁴. D⁶. S⁶. Хатаҕáн. S¹⁰. Доосóц. S⁴. [Дабсá.]
сорокъ. Дýці. D¹. D². D⁴. Дéҕі. S⁴.

Дехí. S⁷. Деҕí. S¹¹. Деҕín. S⁶. Де-
кín, S⁸. [Душé.]
сосна. Цакдá. S¹⁰.
  » большая, черная. Рáкта. S¹⁰.
сохатый. Хаiдагá. D⁶.
спасибо. Алецáу. S¹⁰.
спать. Вынсерé. D¹. Вантебéi. D².
Вантыбái. D⁴. Уантабéi. S⁸. Асінá.
S⁴. Асынé. S⁵. А́сімі. S⁶. А́ҕінан.
S¹⁰. Аҕінéн. S¹¹. [’Онтанó.]
хочу спать. А́шінан. S¹⁰.
спина. Аракын. D². Аркáн. D². S⁶.
Чогдонó. S¹⁰.
спички. Цуі déҕ. D². S⁶. S¹¹. Цуі
дыҕ. D⁴. Чуі дыҕ. D⁶.
способность. Шаделé. D³.
спроси. Хасó. D³.
спускаться. Еурín. S⁹.
  » (съ горы). (А́ула доргідá)
буобéi. D². (Уре-дукí) аурéн. S⁹.
средній. Дулімбуҕá. S⁴.
станція. Гáмын. D².
старикъ. Сагды етыркáн. S¹¹.
старый. Каучín. D⁶. Каоцín. D².
стекло. Гу. D⁴.
стемнѣло. Суні болзáн. D⁴.
степень, рядъ. Зірҕе. D². Зірҕé. S⁹.
Цергí. S⁹.
сто. Нéге цао. D¹. Цао. D². D⁴. Німázі. S⁸. Намázі S⁴. Намázі. S¹¹.
Е́му тац-гу́. S⁷. Туангéн. S⁶. [Цó.]
столица. Бодín хутуҕ. D¹. Ызín хотон. D⁴.
столъ. Сірэ. D². S⁶. Бадá сірé. D⁴.
Сірé.* S⁴. Шірé. D⁶. S². Шірé. S⁵.
S⁸. S¹⁰. S¹¹. [Сілé.]
большой столъ. Бандéн сірэ. D².
S⁶.
стоять. Іліáн. S¹⁰.
стулъ. Бандáн. S¹¹.
стýпа (буд.) Собургá. D².
стýпай. Ябукáл. S¹⁰.
ступня. Кýлі. D⁴.
стремя. Дурéлеге. D⁶.
стрѣла. Нéме. D⁶.
стрѣлять. Одáран. S¹⁰.

стряпка, поваръ. Чýза. D⁴. Чýза.
D⁶.
стѣна. Дузé. D⁶. Дузэ. S⁸. Десó. S⁴.
Тохолá. S¹⁰.
сундукъ. Гýсе. S¹¹.
съѣстные припасы. Зібтерé цакá.
S⁹.
сынъ. Кéку. D². D⁶. Кóуке. D⁴. Учіхéн куку́. S⁷. Куахáи. S¹¹. Утé. S⁴.
Утэ¹). S⁹. S¹⁰. У́нту. S⁶. [Бáху
хуукдé.]
сыновья, дѣти. Уріл. S⁹.
сытъ (наѣлся). Кéлі чаттá. D⁴. Ел-
лецáу. S¹¹.
сѣверъ. Хуáін боí. D³. Хуáіна. D².
S⁸. Амеілá. S⁹. Амілé. S⁵.
сѣдлать коня. Токоукáл. S¹⁰. (пов.
накл.).
сѣдло. Эмэлэ. D². D⁴. S⁶. Емéле.* D⁶.
S⁸. Емыре. S¹. Амыҕéле. S⁴. Еме-
ҕéл. S¹⁰. Емыгéл. S⁹.
сѣно. Рókто. S¹⁰.
Табакъ. Дамагá. D⁶. Дамгá. S¹⁰.
Данга. S². Данҕá. S⁴. Дáнҕа. D⁴.
Дáнга. S¹. Дамбагу́. S⁷. [Дамҕá.]
тамъ. Тендé. D². Терé газір. D². Талá. S⁹.
тарелка. Дéза. D⁷. Дéза. S⁸.
твой. Сіхáнінге. D². Сіні. S⁷. Шіні. S⁸.
телѣга (D². почтовая). Терыҕе. D².
Тéріҕе. D⁴. (Гáмын) терыгé. D².
D⁶. S⁴. Тергé. S¹. Тергéн. S¹⁰. Тер-
ҕéл. S¹¹. Сезín. S¹¹. [Терігé.]
терпкій. Гасун. D².
тетка. У́мо. D².
тигръ. Тасхá. S⁴.
тонкій. Нарín. D¹. D². Немкýн. S⁹.
топоръ. Сугу́. D⁶. Сýку. S⁵. Цугé. S⁴.
[Суҕé.]
торговать. Унінмáтаі. S¹⁰.
тотъ. Тéре. D².
трава. Áуза. D⁶. Кáна.* D⁴. S⁵. Орóкто. S⁴. Арооктó. S¹¹. Чýка¹). S¹⁰.

1) Одинъ сынъ Уму утэ. S⁹, зур утэ.
S⁹. — два сына. Много — Уріл. S⁹.
1) Зеленая трава.

трезубецъ (шаманскій, кит. сань-гу-чá). Сырé. D³.

третьестепенный. Кутáра ȝіреꞯéі саін. D².

третье число. Іркекін ілáн. S⁹.

три. Гýрба. D¹. Гуáрба. D². D⁴. Ілáн. S⁶. S⁷. S¹¹. Ілáн. S⁴. Jілáн. S⁹. S¹¹. Jелáн. S⁸. [ꞯорбó.]

тридцать. Гóці. D¹. D². Гýці. D⁴. Гутíн. S¹¹. ꞯотын. S⁸. Кутэ. S⁴. Гусíн. S⁶. Госíн. S⁷. [Гóші.]

трижды. Jелáн ȝіреꞯéі. S⁹.

триста. Ілáн jамáȝі. S¹¹.

тронная. Еꞯéн бáіта ісікéу чаофáꞯ герí. D².

трубка. Дéіра. D⁶. Дáіре. D⁴. S⁸. Даірá. S². Даірí. S¹¹. Дарí. S⁷. Дерí. S¹⁰. Даі. S³. S⁵. Де.* S⁴.

туфли. Сáві. S⁴.

тушь (для письма). Бокé. S¹⁰.

» красная (киноварь). Чонкýꞯ.

ты. Ці. D¹. Сі. D³. S⁹. Ші. S⁸. [D².

тыква. Уогé. S⁵.

тысяча. Нéге міꞯмíꞯ. D¹. Мáнга. D². Мáнꞯа.* D⁴. Мінгá. S⁴. S⁸. S¹¹. Е́му мінгáꞯ. S⁷. Мáнгаꞯ. S⁶.

тяжелый. Хýнду. D².

тяжелой дѣлаться (о болѣзни). Кучуребé. D³.

Убить. Вáран. S¹⁰.

убѣжать. Чачарáꞯ. S⁹.

убѣжавшій человѣкъ. Чачачá бэjé. S⁹.

убѣжалъ. Хорогусáꞯ. D². Jаосáн.

уголь. Іꞯчí. S¹¹. [D².

какъ удобно. Санá іꞯꞯí. D³.

узда. Хадáла. D². D⁶. S⁶. Морíн ꞯадалá. S⁴. Кадáла. S⁸. [Хаȝáр.]

узкій. Нарíн. D². Сіленкýн. S⁹.

указывать (челов.). (Ку) ȝурібé. D².

указъ. Кéсе. S⁹.

у меня есть. Намáнда беі. D⁶.

умереть, умеръ (отецъ, чиновникъ). У́беі. D⁶. (Кавáн) бучá. S¹⁰. (Амíн) бусé. S⁴.

умѣешь или нѣтъ. Атéне ѳсíні. S⁹.

употреблять. Такурáбеі. D².

усиливаться (о болѣзни). Кучуребé. D³.

усы (см. борода). Сáꞯала. D². S⁶. Саꞯалá. D⁴. S³. Гурꞯактá. S¹⁰. S¹¹.

утверждаться. Токторóн. S⁹.

утка. Нáузу. D⁶.

учебная команда. Урубýре меíн. D².

учитель. Сáꞯ-сéн. D⁴.

учиться (языку). (Усýꞯу) соробéі. D². D³. Таттáн. S⁹.

» (о солдатахъ) Урубурéн. S¹⁰.

учить. Ȝáрна. D¹.

ушелъ. Дулꞗсо. D².

уши. Цікі. D². Ціке. D⁴. Ціké. S⁷. Чікі. D⁶. S¹. S². Сан. S⁶. Сеꞯ. S⁸. S¹⁰. S¹¹. Се. S³. S⁴. Сі. S⁵. [Сіхé.]

Флагъ. Ціза.* S⁴.

Халатъ. Цéꞯці. D². S⁶. Цáꞯці. D⁴. Цамꞗі. S⁷. Сун. S¹⁰. Куучí. S¹¹.

хлѣбъ. Утыма. D⁴. Утума. D². S⁶. Утумó. S¹. S². У́туме. D⁶. Оуó. S⁴. Эвȝí. S⁷. Уóꞯ. S¹⁰. S¹¹. Уꞯóн. S¹¹.

ходить. Ічібé. D⁶. Генерéн. S¹⁰.

» пѣшкомъ. Jаꞯýꞯ улурé. S³. Jоꞯꞗ улірéꞯ. S⁴.

хозяинъ. Балтý. S¹⁰.

холодная вода. Гензó озо. D⁴.

холстъ. Бáшу. S¹¹.

хорошая погода. Чекалáу. S¹⁰.

хорошій. Сен. D⁶. Саíн. D². Аjá. S⁸.

хочу пить. О́зо оубáі. D⁴. Бі ѳбáі. D⁶.

» ѣсть. Бі ідебéі. D⁶. Вараꞗóу. S¹⁰.

худой. Му. D⁶.

хэшанъ. Саоwэн. S¹¹.

Царь. Ѣȝíн. D⁴.

цѣпочка¹). Куїргíн. S¹¹.

Чай. Чаі. D². S⁶. S¹⁰. Цаі. D⁴.

чайникъ. Цахý. D⁴. Чахý.* D². S³. S⁸. Чакý. S¹. Чáку. S¹⁰.

чашка (чайная). (Ча) чáчока. D⁴. Чáчуку. D². Чáчуху. D⁶. S⁴. Чáчуꞯу.

---

1) Тонкая, стальная.

S⁵. S⁸. Чáчеку. S¹¹. Чáдінку. S¹⁰.
Туангарá. S⁶.
человѣколюбіе. Буí цуанемéне. S⁵.
человѣкъ. Ку. D². D⁶. Хун. D². Бојé.
S⁸. Бәјé. S⁹. Бәіјé. S⁹.
чемоданъ (кожаный). Утагáн. S¹⁰.
черепъ. Дýлі. S⁴.
черный. Кáра. D⁶. Карá. S⁸. Харá.
S². Хоннорíн. S⁴. S¹¹. Коннорíн. S¹⁰.
Ноӊгорíн. S¹¹. [Хáра.]
черный хлѣбъ. Кáра ýтуме. D⁶.
чесать волосы. Тарабá. S¹⁰.
четыре. Дýрба. D¹. Дурýбо. D². Дур-
бá.* D⁴. Дегíн. S⁶. Дербíн. S¹¹. Дірíн.
S⁸. Дігéн. S⁴. Дыíн. S⁶.
Чиновникъ (D². гражданскій). Дан-
гíн. D⁶. Хавáн. D⁶. Хавóн. D⁴.
(Бітебé) хафáн. D². S⁴. S⁹. Нојóн.*
D⁴. S¹¹.
чиновники. Хафасáр, Хапсáл. S⁹.
чинъ. Зíрбе. D².
читать (книгу). (Бічík) даутбé. D⁴.
чохъ. Цабá, Забá. D⁴. Цагá. S¹⁰. Ці-
бá. S². S⁴. Зібá. D².
чулки. Уáза. D⁴. Вáса.* S². Вáса. S¹¹.
Добтóн. S¹⁰.
чумичка. Чабулбíн. S⁵.
Шаманъ. Самáн. D⁶.
шапка (D². S⁶. съ шарикомъ). (Дóрі)
мábала. D². S⁶. Мáхала. D⁴. D⁶. S¹.
Мабалá. S². Махалá. S⁷. Аʼбун. S³.
S⁸. Аʼун. S³. S¹⁰. S¹¹. Абý(н). S⁴.
  » дахурская, войлочная. Шок-
шохé. S¹⁰.
  » шамана. Серкí. D³.
шарикъ на шапкѣ. Дínза. D². D⁴.
шишка на шапкѣ (мао-га-да). Умбукé. S¹⁰.
шесть. Зурбó. D¹. Зірбó.* D². D⁴. Нін-
бó. S⁴. Нінгíн. S⁶. Нінгун. S⁷. Нунгун. S⁸. Нунбýн. S¹¹.
шестьдесятъ. Зáра. D¹. D². D⁴. Нін-
цý. S⁶. S⁷. Нінбунгí. S⁴. Нунгунгí.
S⁸. Нуунгí. S¹¹. [Зарá.]
шея. Куцý. D². Бýзу. D⁶. Комогá.
S¹⁰. Комоугé. S¹¹. Кóма. S⁴. [Хуцý.]

широкій, въ ширину. Аʼу. D². Авóн.
S¹⁰.
шить. Оібé. D². Улірé. S⁹.
штаны. Акóро. D². Акорó. D⁴. Фохорí. S⁷. Оккí. S⁴. Еркí. S⁸. S¹⁰. S¹¹.
шуба. Дéлі. D⁶. Зібцá. S⁷.
шумѣть (буянить). Тогілцібéі (Чогіл-
цібéі?) D³.
Щеки. Хацíра. S³. Аӊчýн. S⁵. Аӊчá.
S⁴. [Хасíр.]
щипцы для огня. Сарпó. S³.
Ѣсть. Бодá ідебé. D⁴. Будá ідé. S¹.
Зібтéн. S⁹. Цобтéн. S¹⁰. Цактбí зіб-
тé. S⁵. S⁸. Цактбí цібтéн. S⁴. Цактбí
цібкé. S³. Зáктбі біптéн. S¹¹.
ѣлъ. Зібчá. S⁹.
ѣшь. Зібкé. S⁹.
ѣхать верхомъ. Мóрі óнді јаубé. D⁴.
Морітí јабурéн. S¹¹. Морíн октé. S⁸.
  » въ телѣгѣ. Терегýле јаубé.
D². Térіге сáубе јаубé. D⁴. Терыгáн теуксá јабурéн. S¹¹.
Этотъ. Еʼне. D².
Югъ. Ембіне. D². Ембíн боí. D³. Цулʼ-
лé. S⁵. Зулеібá. S⁹. Нáру онохó. S⁸.
Я. Бі. D¹. D². D³. S⁸. S⁹.
явиться къ начальству. Елéге баі-
бé (баісéн). D².
являюсь къ начальству. Бі елéге
бáіні (елегебаіјá). D².
завтра явлюсь. Бендурý бі елéге
баіцібé. D².
языкъ. Іныгé. S⁵. Іӊгé. S¹⁰. Іӊгí. S¹¹.
Ірíӊгí. S⁴.
яйцо, яица. Ендугý. D⁶. Омуктáн. S¹¹.
ямынь. Намáн. D⁴.
ясно. Гетукýн. D².
ясное небо. Гегéн тенгері. D².
Царін богó. S⁹.
ясный день. Гегéн удýр. D². Нáран інеӊбí. S⁹.
ящикъ (коммодъ). Сáра кузí. D⁴.
  » (простой). Кузí. D⁴. Гýсе. S¹¹.
ящичекъ. Нéмо. S⁸.

ПРИЛОЖЕНІЕ.

СПИСОКЪ СЛОВЪ БАРГУ-МОНГОЛЬСКИХЪ.

Аїгé. чайная чашка.
амá. ротъ.
анá (маньчж.) сарá. 1-ая луна.
алó. слѣдъ.
албаӊá хýн. служащій.
алтá. золото.
áрба. десять.
  арбáн негé. одинадцать.
арсалá. левъ.
арӊі. вино (маньчж. аркі).
áкта морí. меринъ.
ахá. старшій братъ.
аӡé. отецъ.
  аӡé уксé. отецъ умеръ.
азірӊá. жеребецъ.
Ебдыгé. колѣно.
міні бейé ебшітé. я боленъ.
ебшý. грудь.
емéле. сѣдло.
éму абунá. жениться.
éмуде. штаны.
емугé. жена.
еіӡігé. лошакъ.
ерý. подбородокъ.
ерӊі ӊорó. большой палецъ.
еӊéн. господинъ.
(бада) іденé. ѣсть, ѣстъ.
ірé. девяносто.
іӊéн болӊoнá. выдти замужъ, выходитъ замужъ.
іхен-дý. младшая сестра.
Омолó. внукъ.
  омол-іӊéн. внучка:
одó. звѣзда.

осó. вода.
  óспе дé. кальянъ (кит. шуй-янь-дай 水 烟 袋).
'онтанó. спать, спитъ.
оролó. губы.
  дéре орлó. верхняя губа.
  доró орлó. нижняя губа.
óро ӊуренé. сердиться.
Убшíн цасакчí сáн-шеӊ. докторъ.
  Послѣднее слово китайское 先生, въ этихъ мѣстахъ произносимое за сянь-сэнъ.
ýде. двери.
удерé. день.
ундýр ӊоró. 3-ій палецъ.
улá. красный.
уӊеічіне. говорить.
уӊýӎ. быкъ.
Jабаӊá jабанá. идти (идетъ) пѣшкомъ.
Jісé. девять.
Пýселе. лавка (маньчж. съ кит.).
Бáра. тигръ.
бáху хуукдé. сынъ.
бéре абунá. жениться (женится) на второй женѣ.
бітӊé. книга (маньчж.).
бішіӊá іӊé. дочь.
бо. ружье.
бóбо. хлѣбъ (кит. 餑 餑).
боró оронó. идетъ дождь.
бурé уӊозібéн. играть на флейтѣ.
бурӊáн. богъ, изображеніе его.

Фа-я́о-за. лихорадка (кит. Фа-яо-цза 發 要 子).

Ва́са. чулки (кит. ва́-цзы, ва́-цза 襪 子).

ву́ле. облако.

Ма́нһа. тысяча.

малаһа́і. шапка.

маһа́. мясо.

ма́һала. шапка.

ме́мо. мать.

ме́ре. плечо.

мо́до. дерево.

мо́рі. лошадь.

мурі́ хе́ші. берегъ рѣки (маньчж. хе-шен).

му́ру. рѣка.

му нго́. серебро.

Таба́. пять.

табші́. пуговица.

тебе́. пятьдесятъ.

темо́. верблюдъ.

те́за. ассигнація (кит. тѣ-цза 帖 子).

теріге́. телѣга.

теріге́ гелһе́ ху н. кучеръ.

тенгере́. небо.

тенгре́р (те нгы́р) шаһалһа́ шо-һоно́. громъ гремитъ.

толоһо́і. голова, черепъ.

тоһо́. локоть.

тумо́. 1000.

туріте́ һото́л. сапоги (кожаные).

Дабса́. соль.

дамһа́. табакъ.

дала́. семьдесятъ.

де. трубка (кит. дай изъ янь-дай 烟 袋).

дебце́. подстилка.

де́со. веревка.

де́ре. верхній.

дере́. подушка.

деһі́. птица, ср. Мк. däxi (М.) птица, маньчж. dejembi летать, dejenge ле-тучій.

ге́рі дото́р. въ комнатѣ.

доло́. семь.

доро́. нижній.

бітеһе́ доһодона́. читать (читаетъ) книгу.

дӯ. младшій братъ.

душе́. сорокъ.

дурубде́р һоро́. 4-ый палецъ.

дурбе́. четыре.

Са́ра. луна.

са́р хомуге́. песокъ (желтый, Монг. шіра хумаги).

саһала́. борода.

се́лһі (салі́һі). вѣтеръ.

сіде́. зубы.

сіре́. столъ.

сіхе́. уши (Монг. чіхін).

со́ро. ремень.

соһо́. подмышка.

сун. ночь.

суһе́. топоръ.

су́ісе. молотокъ (кит. чуй-цзы 椎 子).

Шоро́. земля.

шохо́. лобъ.

Наја́. восемьдесятъ.

на́дыма. лицо,

на́ра. солнце.

неріг̓у́ һоро́. 2-ой палецъ.

неге́. одинъ.

ні́де́. глазъ.

ніруһа́н. рисунокъ (маньчж.).

нојо́н. чиновникъ.

нохо́і. собака.

на́іма. восемь.

Ла (кит.) сара́. 12-ая луна.

лата́і. подсвѣчникъ (кит. 蠟 臺).

ла нто́. большой молотокъ (маньчж. ла нту отъ кит. ла́нъ-тоу 榔 頭).

ла́ха. канъ, родъ лежанки или теп-лыхъ наръ (маньчж. нахан).

ло́бо. рѣдька (кит.).

Ка́о. мостъ, кит. цяо, кяо 橋.

кеды́се. брюхо.

кезіге́. коса (на головѣ).

ку мо́рі. кобыла.

ко́у де́. мѣшокъ, кит. ко́у-дай 口 袋

Газіре́. земля.

ге́рі. домъ.

го́ші. тридцать.

џа́ла. огонь.

џа́лага. ворота.

џара́. рука.

џаха́. свинья.

џеле́. языкъ.

бітџе́ џіне́. писать, пишетъ.

џотоџо́. ножъ.

џорбо́. три.

џорле́. мука́.

џо́іле. мѣдь.

џурене́. см. о́ро џурене́.

џуке́. зеленый.

Ҳаје́. стѣна (въ комнатѣ).

хабтаџа́. кисетъ.

хама́р. носъ.

хада́за. гвоздь.

хасі́р. щеки.

хасу́. желѣзо.

хан. Императоръ.

ха́ꞥта (кит. хань-дао 旱 稻) бада́. рисъ.

хале́са, хале́за. роща.

ха́ра. черный.

хаӡа́р. узда.

мурі́ хе́ші. см. подъ мурі.

хе́хі. кошка.

хоі́ре. два.

хоі́р сара́. 2-ая луна.

хомуге́. см. ꞔар хомуге́.

хо́рі. двадцать.

худо́. средній.

хуꞥӡу́л. одѣяло.

хулуне́ оло́. слѣдъ.

хурумо́. курма (маньчж. куруме, курумо).

хуꞔу́. шея.

хуісе́. сѣрый [кит. хуй-сѣ (шай) 灰 色].

Ча́са. бумага.

ча́са ороно́. идетъ снѣгъ.

чаху́. чайникъ (кит. 茶 壺).

чонџо́. окно (съ кит.).

чоло́. камень.

Ці́за. флагъ, кит. ци-цзы 旗 子.

цінӡо́. перецъ, кит. цинь-цзяо 秦椒.

ціла́н. синій.

ціксі́ џоро́. мизинецъ.

ціџа́н. бѣлый.

ціџа́н ла (кит.) свѣчка.

ціџа́ нуџа́. капуста.

ціџа́н шата́. сахаръ, кит. ша-танъ 沙 糖.

Ꞔо́. сто.

Ꞔо́ (маньчж. џоргоꞥ) сара́. 11-ая луна.

џо́до. чохи, мѣдная китайская монета.

ӡара́. шестьдесятъ.

ӡе́ӡе. старшая сестра, кит. цзѣ́-цзѣ 姐.

ӡі́ле. годъ.

ӡірџо́. шесть.

ВАЖНѢЙШІЯ ПОПРАВКИ И ДОПОЛНЕНІЯ.

Страница:	Строка:	Столбецъ:	Напечатано:	Вмѣсто:
III	30		與	與
1	11		послѣ адечі добавить: Ман. удучі.	
16	1	1	áма. S^3.	áма. S^8.
16	4	1	S^1. S^7.	S^1. S^6.
16	24	1	амо	амó
17	21	1	аранга	арангá
17	32	1	аркí мурéн. S^4.	аркí мурéн. S^5.
18	1	2	еркí	еркí
18	17	2	еӟілé	еӟілé.
18	21	2	эмýн. S^6.	эмýн. S^8
18	39	2	дан	данӈá
19	13	1	інéн. S^{10}.	інéн. S^{10}. (ночь) (?)
19	19	1	выпустить слово інынге. S^5.	
19	45	1	іічí.	іічí.
19	4	2	омычé.	омычé.
19	9	2	іркекін.	іркекін.
20	13	1	оӆоӈде	оӆоӈдé.
20	18	1	олóці. S^7.	олóці. S^6.
20	29	1	орхýн. S^3.	орхýн. S^8.
20	36	1	оккí. S^3.	оккí. S^8.
20	41	1	Уáсе	Уáса
20	14	2	уóн. S^{10}.	уóн. S^{10}. S^{11}.
20	38	2	переставить S^{10} къ S^9.	
21	39	1	ӆéбо	ӆóбо.
21	46	1	урӈýн. S^3.	урӈýн. S^8.
22	13	1	послѣ словъ: быкъ (дх.) прибавить: корова (S^{10}. S^{11}.).	
22	40	1	учікé. S^3.	учікé. S^8.
22	42	1	добавить: учýӈ учулерé. S^9. пѣть пѣсню.	
22	26	2	jáлі. S^8.	jáлі. S^7.
22	41	2	jéму. S^{10}.	jéму. S^{11}.
23	15	1	добавить: jоӈíн. S^{11}. сколько.	
23	26	1	пуӈелé	пуӈеле.
23	44	1	боӈа. S^4.	боӈá. S^4.
23	4	2	бéле. S^3.	бéле. S^8.

Страница:	Строка:	Столбецъ:	Напечатано:	Вмѣсто:
23	5	2	белдéр.	белдíр.
23	23	2	бітыӊé. S[10].	бітыӊé. S[11].
»	»	»	бітхе.	бітхé.
»	35	»	бojé. S[9].	бojé. S[8]. бэjé, бэijé. S[9].
23	26	2	бісіӈгі	бісіӈгі
24	34	1	выпустить S[4].[1]	
24	38	1	мáнгіл̇	мангíл̇
24	14	2	дерево. S[11].	дерево. S[10]. S[11].
25	41	2	то'о	то'ó
25	42	2	тобчí. S[3]., тóбчі. S[4].	тобчí. S[4], тóбчі. S[3].
26	21	1	то'о	то'ó
26	39	1	wickel	wickle
26	34	2	дебтелé. S[3].	дебтелé. S[8].
27	19	2	долӊо	долӊó
28	3	1	дoy. S[8].	дoy. S[1]., S[8].
28	22	1	сарпó. S[8].	сарпó. S[5].
28	38	1	сáӊала. S[7].	сáӊала. S[6].
29	8	1	сірӊектé.	сірӊéкте.
29	41	1	добавить: Ш̇ара. S[8]. желтый.	
29	21	2	надéн. S[7].	надéн. S[6].
30	1	2	5-ая,	6-ая,
31	39	1	каньтáза	кантáза.
31	40	2	куахаṅ	куахáṅ
32	23	1	каі-дáу. S[11].	каі-дáу. S[10].
32	34	2	г̇удег̇é	гудегé
33	10	2	хýнзу. S[8].	хýнзу. S[6].
34	17	1	чіӊáн. S[3].	чіӊáн. S[8].
34	15	2	цікэ̇.	ціке́.
34	34	2	послѣ слова десять добавить: 10-ое число.	
35	12	1	цаӊí.	цаӊí. S[4].
35	39	1	цу̇о. S[3].	цу̇о. S[8].
35	1	2	цуваṅпí	цуаṅпí.
36	32	1	аṅé сáра	аṅé сáра. 12-ая луна.
36	23	2	арігí	арігí.
36	25	2	арба	арбá.
37	6	1	ачіпан	ачіпáн.
37	21	2	баібé	баібé.
38	6	1	ергýнку	ергýн-ку
38	1	2	послѣ слова барабанъ добавить: Ман. імпін (стар. імпі) одноручный бубенъ.	
38	16	2	(бі) óбаі. S[6].	(бі) óбаі. D[6].
39	12	1	уáза. D[8].	уáза. D[4].
39	15	1	передъ у í н добавить: уӊíн,	
39	8	2	послѣ: См. узгулці добавить: и отр. VII на стр. 8—9.	
39	27	2	послѣ слова усýгу добавить: усýӊу	

Страница:	Строка:	Столбецъ:	Напечатано:	Вмѣсто:
40	20	1	уҕéле	уҕéле.
40	44	1	аудьі-дýр	аудьі-дýр
40	46	1	уҕеле	уҕеле
40	15	2	еӯó. D¹.	еӯó. D².
40	24	2	чуҕа	чуҕá
40	46	2	вставить: уіліҥге. D². арестантъ.	
41	7	1	вставить: jéві. D⁶. потолокъ.	
41	11	1	Пáньза	Паньза
41	6	2	вставить: балабéі. D². вкапывать (埋).	
41	15	2	бардаӡі (-беі)	бардаӡі (-беі)
41	21	2	вставить: баціл̣дéн. см. óсо —	
42	39	1	будýн. D¹.	будýн. D⁴.
42	22	2	вставить: валлаҕáбе. D². входить	
43	4	2	мурҕубéі.	муруҕубéі.
45	1	2	jауҕу.	jауҕу́.
45	27	2	вставить: тушáн алібé. D³. вступить въ должность.	
46	18	1	д̣аӥ-герí. D¹. D⁵	д̣аӥ-герí. D¹. D².
46	31	1	дарума	дáрума.
47	4	1	переправляться	переправлять.
47	2	2	вставить: с̇áбі. D². воспитанникъ.	
47	17	2	саӥгучý	саӥ-гучý
47	45	2	серкí. D².	серкí. D³.
48	23	1	сíнкéн.	сíнкéн.
48	42	1	сононсан	сононсáн.
48	10	2	сунодá	суӥдэ.
50	39	2	вставить: ташкуі (Ман. тацікуі) кукýру. D². воспитанникъ (-и?).	
51	21	1	кыӥкé. D⁴.	кыӥкé. D⁵.
51	28	1	гочóро. D⁵.	гочóро. D⁴.
52	42	1	боí	боí.
53	12	1	гу́івеіні	гу́івеіні.
53	35	2	едуро	едýро.
54	13	1	хоірá, хоірó	хоірá, хоірó.
55	1	2	у́ле	у́ле
56	16	2	дань-цзы-ды	дань-цзы-да